Praise for

The People in the Room

"A great book about interreligious relations, Jim's life, and his unique contributions to advancing—substantially and significantly—Jewish ties to other faiths, deepening their understanding of Jews and Judaism."

—**Kenneth Bandler**
American Jewish Committee Director of Media Relations

"This beautifully written and insightful volume takes its readers behind the scenes in detailing the most important Jewish-Christian events of the past 30-plus years. Through his many books, essays, and speeches, Rudin has kept his eye on the ball in terms of what unites and what threatens Jewish-Christian relations. . . . He soberly assesses the challenges imposed by the future . . . and a decrease in European and American religious commitment. But Rudin is ever the optimist. He, along with the prophet Zechariah, is a 'prisoner of hope.' *The People in the Room* **is a treasure.**"

—**Alan L. Berger**
*Raddock Family Eminent Scholar Chair of Holocaust Studies,
Florida Atlantic University*

"This wonderful book provides an invaluable eyewitness account of ventures that have built understanding among Jews, Catholics, African American churches, mainline and Evangelical Protestants, and others. Rabbi Rudin speaks of interreligious legislative efforts on behalf of those in need, and concludes with practical and concrete guidance, built on a lifetime of experience, for promoting interreligious dialogue and amity. Readers will quickly find that this book is filled with **insight, compassion, wit, and true wisdom** and will not be able to put it down."

—**Philip Cunningham**
*Director, Institute for Jewish-Catholic Relations and
Professor of Theology and Religious Studies, Saint Joseph's University*

"This book by Rabbi Rudin is **a must-read for anyone interested in Jewish-Christian relations**. The author has been deeply involved in dialogues and joint projects with Christians since before the Second Vatican Council. He narrates, explains, and indicates the lasting significance of key moments and developments in this ongoing and ever-deepening relationship through the lens of his own life and his interactions with others, both Jews and Christians. I highly recommended this book for Catholics, Protestants, and Jews. Muslims may also find it of deep interest."

—**Eugene J. Fisher**
Distinguished Professor of Theology, Saint Leo University

"I recommend this memoir for many reasons. It tells the story of [Rabbi Rudin's] activism in Soviet Jewry advocacy. More, it covers his pioneering leadership in interfaith dialogue and cooperation. Finally, in writing about his life, he takes notice of recent changes in America following the election of President Trump in 2016. While at one time viewing the post-World War II era as a golden age for American Jewry, he is now more cautious in his analysis of the present and future standing of Jews in America."

—**Fred A. Lazin**
Professor Emeritus, Ben Gurion University, Beer Sheva, Israel
Honorary Outgoing Chair, RC05 Comparative Studies of
Local Govt. & Politics, IPSA

"Rabbi Rudin has come to understand the meaning and challenge of authentic interreligious dialogue through active participation. His reflections on key moments over the past half century offer an enriching learning experience for those who have followed the path he helped to construct. This volume **exemplifies what interreligious encounter has been—and what it may yet become.**"

—**John T. Pawlikowski, OSM**
Professor Emeritus, Catholic Theological Union, Chicago

"In this always interesting and insightful book, Jim blends the personal and the historical. He tells the story of his own life, along with giving an insider's account of some of the pivotal interfaith events that have marked this time. In addition, he offers insightful accounts of various religious movements he has encountered and the dynamics of the dialogue. He offers sage advice about how to sustain the progress that is so obviously precious to him. This book is **essential reading for anyone interested in interfaith dialogue.**"

—**Rabbi Daniel Polish**
Congregation Shir Chadash of Hudson Valley, LaGrange New York
Author of "Talking About God: What We Can Learn from Kierkegaard,
Buber, Tillich, and Heschel"

The PEOPLE in the ROOM

Rabbis, Nuns, Pastors, Popes, and Presidents

Rabbi James Rudin

IPUB CLOUD INTERNATIONAL
POUGHKEEPSIE, NEW YORK

Published in the United States by
iPub Cloud International
Poughkeepsie, New York 12603
www.iPubCloud.org

All rights reserved. No part of this book may be reproduced, stored in a retrieval system, or transmitted, in any form or by any means, electronic, mechanical, photocopying, recording, or otherwise, without the express written permission of the publisher.

Copyright © 2021, 2025 by James Rudin
Second Edition
ISBN: 978-1-948575-56-0
eBook ISBN: 978-1-948575-57-7
Library of Congress Control Number: 2021925060

Several pieces contained in this book were originally published with permission from Religion News Service. See more at https://religionnews.com.

Cover and interior design by: Luis F. Ramos

Acknowledgements

I could not have written this book without the guidance, support, cooperation, and inspiration of many people and institutions.

My dear friend and longtime interreligious colleague, Dr. Leonard Swidler of Temple University, first suggested I write a description of my life and career.

The gifted people at iPub Cloud International put this book together. Special thanks to my brilliant editors at Religion News Service and Reform Judaism.org: Joan Connell, Kevin Eckstrom, Aron Hirt-Manheimer, Paul O'Donnell, and Jerome Socolovsky.

While this book is the work of a single author, my numerous Jewish and Christian friends taught me more than they will ever know, and I am grateful to all of them.

I especially appreciate the suggestions and comments of Dr. Mary C. Boys of Union Theological Seminary, Rabbi David Rosen, the American Jewish Committee's (AJC) International Interreligious Director, and Dr. Marvin R. Wilson of Gordon College.

The AJC has been my professional home for more than fifty years, a precious gift I never take for granted. Since 1991, Religion News Service (RNS) has distributed my commentaries, and Reform Judaism.org (RJ.ORG) has also circulated my book reviews and commentaries. It is an honor to have been one of the founders in 1998 of the Center for Catholic-Jewish Studies (CCJS) at Saint Leo University (SLU) where I serve as a Visiting Professor of Religion and Judaica. I am grateful to the staff of the AJC Archives in New York City and the American Jewish Archives in Cincinnati for their excellent research facilities.

I am indebted to Rabbi Marc H. Tanenbaum, my mentor in Christian-Jewish relations, and that debt of gratitude extends to my fellow AJC staff members, both past and present. Shulamith Bahat, Donald Feldstein, Bert Gold, David Gordis, David Harris, Ira Silverman, and William Trosten, my AJC bosses over the years, provided strong positive leadership especially when global interreligious relations became stormy and turbulent.

The views and opinions expressed in this book are my own, however, and do not necessarily reflect those of the AJC, RNS, RJ.org, SLU, or CCJS.

Finally, the best for last. My love goes out to my wife Marcia, whose excellent taste in clothing not only greatly improved my wardrobe, but she changed my life as well. And three other women bring me constant joy: our daughters Rabbi Eve and Jennifer, and our granddaughter Emma Mollie.

This book is lovingly dedicated to Marcia who forever changed my life by driving her car around the block a second time …

Table of Contents

Foreword I	*xi*
Foreword II	*xiii*
Introduction	*xxi*
CHAPTER 1: *Why is This Autobiography Different from the One I Would Have Written Four Years Ago?*	1
CHAPTER 2: *Birth in the "Steel City" and Growing Up in Robert E. Lee's Hometown*	4
CHAPTER 3: *Choosing the Rabbinate Thanks to a Pair of Mentors*	10
CHAPTER 4: *I Led Two Lives as a Seminary Student*	15
CHAPTER 5: *Wearing Air Force Blue in Japan and Korea*	19
CHAPTER 6: *Being a Rabbi in America's Midwest*	26
CHAPTER 7: *How a One-Year Job Became a Thirty-Two Year Career*	32
CHAPTER 8: *A Romantic Miracle on East 56th Street*	36
CHAPTER 9: *Roman Catholics and Jews: Fellow Revolutionaries*	38
CHAPTER 10: *Bitter Memories: Auschwitz Convent Crisis*	61
CHAPTER 11: *Two Earnest Attempts to Confront the Holocaust: One Catholic, the Other Jewish … Did They Succeed?*	67
CHAPTER 12: *"Mainline" Protestants and Jews! It's Complicated!*	74
CHAPTER 13: *Black Churches*	85
CHAPTER 14: *Evangelicals and Jews: The Last Frontier in Christian-Jewish Relations*	99

Chapter 15: The Battle of Camp David: A Victory in 1991, But Could It Be Won Today?	114
Chapter 16: Two Passion Plays Convinced Me the Play's (Not) the Thing!	124
Chapter 17: Special Assignments: Things I Never Learned in Rabbinical School	135
Chapter 18: The Interreligious Struggle to Free Soviet Jewry	155
Chapter 19: The Future of Christian-Jewish Relations	169
Chapter 20: Ten Personal Interreligious Commandments	176
Chapter 21: Some Basic Questions that Will Never Appear on "Jeopardy!"	182
Chapter 22: The Unfinished Journey: To Infinity and Beyond	186
Afterword I	190
Afterword II	194
Suggestions for Further Reading	198
Index	203
About iPub Cloud International	211

Foreword I

Among the far-reaching changes of our modern world, the Jewish experience has been dramatic. For more than half a century, Rabbi James Rudin has not just been a part of momentous developments in this regard but has been a leading actor in the amazing transformation of the condition of the Jewish People, of American society, and of the place of the Jewish community within the US and the world.

His childhood recollections reflect a world in which anti-Jewish prejudice was still the norm, but one which was beginning to undergo significant shifts influenced both by internal dynamics in American society as well as, in no small part, by global geopolitical developments.

His commitment to his religious heritage, which led to his choice of vocation, together with the profound loyalty to the land of his birth that was instilled in him from the earliest age, led to his service as a US Air Force Chaplain in Japan and Korea, before serving American Jewish communities as a congregational rabbi.

Surely his background and experience made him remarkably suited for the subsequent direction of his professional career, participating in, and leading the groundbreaking work in the field of interreligious relations—in particular, Jewish-Christian relations—under the auspices of the American Jewish Committee (AJC) where he became and served for many years as the organization's Director of Interreligious Affairs.

Long before I was honored to succeed him in this position, he served as a model and inspiration for me in my own interfaith work.

These chapters recount some of the most impressive highlights of his rich life, ranging from his involvement in the civil rights movement, his efforts in the struggle for freedom for Soviet Jewry, to his representation of Jewry through his chairmanship of the International Jewish Committee for Interreligious Consultations to the highest levels in Christendom, and some of his notable achievements in these regards. His leadership and collegiality have made him one of the most admired Jewish figures of our time, across faith communities and denominations.

His writings serve as a veritable archive of information on the most historic period of the transformation of the relationship between Jewry and the Christian world—in particular, the Catholic Church. These are greatly enhanced by his articles as a commentator that have offered greater nuance to the events and personalities involved. His ongoing reflections, carried in the media, continue to provide invaluable insight into the issues that preoccupy those interested in interreligious affairs and the relationship between religion and society in general.

Beyond his remarkable role in these fields and numerous awards and recognition that he has received accordingly, this book reflects his personal qualities that make his impressive achievements stand out to an even greater extent. I refer to his personal integrity and goodness which are enriched by a lovely natural modesty and great humor. Modesty is not something one associates with those who have traversed the corridors of history and who have wined and dined with national and global religious, civic, and political leaders. But Jim is far too levelheaded to allow any of this to lead to any self-intoxication. However, his well-developed critical capacities have not in any way weakened his passion for the causes in which he believes, and which are dear to his heart. This commitment, and these qualities of modesty and humor, have enhanced the universal respect and affection in which he is held.

Above all they have made him one of the most delightful and insightful colleagues to work with and a blessing for all who have enjoyed his wisdom and guidance, which this publication will continue to provide for generations to come.

Rabbi David Rosen
American Jewish Committee Jerusalem-based Director of
International Interreligious Affairs
2022

Foreword II

What a personal privilege and delight to commend this engaging volume and its accomplished author. The life story of Rabbi A. James Rudin is at once highly readable, deeply engaging, and remarkably informative. Jim Rudin's lively prose is fast moving, down-to-earth, and richly insightful. Here is an intriguing account of a scholar-teacher and prominent religious leader which models a balanced career that brilliantly weds theory and practice. Below, it is my plan to place the significance of Jim's professional life in a broad historical context. In doing so, I will add my personal perspective on how Jim has positively contributed to the shaping of interreligious relations nationally and internationally throughout his very active career.

Since the early 1970s, it has been my good fortune and great joy to know Jim and work closely with him. On many occasions, we served as interfaith partners engaged in orchestrating, contributing to, and bringing to completion a variety of interfaith conferences, dialogues, writing projects, and special events. Over the years, I especially came to appreciate Jim as a delightful friend and professional colleague. Now in retirement, as I look back and reflect on this *mensch* of a man, I realize I often looked to Jim as a trusted, personal mentor regarding the varieties of Judaism and the nuances of Jewish life and community. But I also came to value Jim as an experienced, highly respected leader of interfaith dialogue as I saw him in action at our many joint engagements throughout America aimed at promoting positive Christian-Jewish understanding and relations.

I celebrate this autobiography for in it, Jim thinks deeply about the diverse experiences of his illustrious career. Especially meaningful are some of the personal highlights and most satisfying moments he enjoyed within this never-dull-but-always-challenging world of interfaith relations. All who read this lucid autobiography will be wiser and more thoroughly informed of the potential successes and disappointments, the ups and downs, the steppingstones and pitfalls found in interfaith encounters. In addition, there are many striking surprises and subtle nuances that await when one tries to navigate successfully and make sense of the modern American interreligious landscape.

In Jim Rudin's lifetime, the world witnessed several landmark events and interfaith developments that have affected and continue to impact Christian-Jewish relations in remarkable ways. This is one of the reasons Jim's autobiography is so thoroughly fascinating, fast-paced, and filled with many stimulating challenges and defining opportunities. Each new situation requires considerable patience and insight for reflection, reform, resolution, and remembrance in order to make progress and advance the good. To be sure, as this work shows, Jim's very active life has been anything other than "plain vanilla."

Each of the significant events and developments I mention below has affected Jim on a personal, professional, and Jewish communal level. Throughout his career, these "game-changing" situations typically called for Jim's focus, study, response, and bridge-building skills. Accordingly, Jim was a multitalented man capable of wearing many hats, including that of thinker, writer, strategist, and activist. My aim is to comment briefly on some of the major developments that have provided the religious background and setting for so much of the creative energy Jim expended throughout his professional career.

At the outset, it is important to note Jim was born during the infamous Holocaust years of 1933–45, the period when Hitler and his minions were in power. Who would have thought that Hitler's "willing executioners," combined with the general malaise and indifference of European nations and the guilty silence of the church would have led to such an ignominious snuffing out of six million precious Jewish lives? The catastrophe of the *Shoah* rocked Jews and Christians around the world. Many American Jewish families lost relatives or loved ones in the Holocaust. Not all victims were Jews, but all Jews were victims.

This indescribable tragedy provoked numerous unanswered questions: How would the world respond to Hitler's attempted "Final Solution" to the so-called Jewish problem? Why did so few Christians speak up? Where was God in all this suffering? Would systemic antisemitism and the ongoing hatred and hostility toward Jews ever end? After World War II, would Jewish survivors and Jews of the diaspora ever again be able to befriend and trust self-identifying Christians?

Having to engage such a dilemma, one of Jim's earliest and most difficult interfaith challenges was in dealing with the still very palpable wounds of the Holocaust. How would this horrendous event impact the viability and future of Christian-Jewish relations? In short, if Nazism could exist among Christians of Europe, what likely would be the prospects for Jews living in post-Holocaust America?

Three years after the War, in 1948, the State of Israel was remarkably established by courageous Jews and a vote of the United Nations. Despite arguments to the contrary, this incredible event has never been casually viewed by Jews as some appropriate act of atonement or appeasement meant to help salve the conscience of the Western world for allowing the Holocaust to happen in "Christian" and cultured Europe. Indeed, already in the late 1800s, the early wave of Zionist pioneers had started to settle back into their ancestral homeland. The newly established State of Israel, however, provided a place of refuge and self-determination for Holocaust survivors and for others among world Jewry seeking the freedom to practice their religion, language, and culture within their ancient historic home. The State also became an important destination for Christian pilgrims, tourists, and students from around the world, many seeing the need to affirm and support this fledgling State on judicial, historical, moral, and even prophetic grounds.

For decades, Jim Rudin spent considerable time lecturing and speaking on why a strong Israel is important to Jewish survival. He did this in churches, synagogues, at conferences, and on radio and TV, in addition to his writing in the press. Further, he rightly emphasized why the call by certain Christian denominations for boycott, divestment, and sanctions against Israel is a discriminatory act and an affront to the Jewish people. In seeking to understand the complexities of modern Israel, I often turned to Jim Rudin's book, *Israel for Christians*. During the 1980s and '90s, when I led many tours to Israel, I strongly recommended Jim's book on Israel for pre-departure reading.

For most in world Jewry, if Auschwitz stood for death, Israel represented resurrection, life, and hope. Accordingly, no matter how bleak things in Israel or the interfaith scene may have appeared, Jim Rudin was at heart an optimist; he typically shunned despair and defeat. Rather, he insisted Jews and Christians remain "prisoners of hope" (*asire ha-tikvah*) [Zech 9:12]. The word ha-tikvah, "The Hope," is the word universally recognized as the name of Israel's national anthem. Over the years, I came to be a believer in Jim's realistic optimism about interfaith relations.

As Jim often put it, "It is better to be content with modest successes than experience colossal failures." Or, as Jim often described the unpredictable and often volatile interreligious world, "We often move three steps forward, then two backwards." Any way one wishes to define the wording, this spells progress, for success is usually incremental and requires much patience and resolve.

Another major post-war development was the Second Vatican Council (1962–65). This groundbreaking event would radically alter Catholic-Jewish relations. The Council issued *Nostra Aetate* ["In Our Time"], a document dealing with the relation of the Church with non-Christian religions, by Pope Paul VI. This declaration called for a reexamination, reform, and reversal of a two-millennia long adversarial history with the Jewish people. Among its landmark reforms were an affirmation that the covenant between God and the Jewish people continues, a call to pursue positive dialogue, a renewed appreciation for the Jewish Scriptures (the Christian Old Testament) and the removal of the teaching of contempt, including the charge of deicide.

The interreligious relations department of the American Jewish Committee, the place Jim Rudin served most of his career, had some major input into the shaping of *Nostra Aetate*. Jim would later reflect on the significance of this event in his book, *Cushing, Spellman, O'Connor*, a surprising story of how three American cardinals transformed Catholic-Jewish relations through their input into the Second Vatican Council.

Over the years, Jim has had a significant interest in following and supporting the ongoing implementation of the reforms initiated by *Nostra Aetate* at the Council. Toward this end, in recognition of Jim's many valuable local, national, and international interfaith contributions, in 2002, Saint Leo University of Florida appointed James Rudin the Distinguished Visiting Professor of Religions and Judaica. As a public speaker and internationally recognized religious leader, Jim garnered many invitations to speak at various interfaith venues.

But one of Jim's major concerns in his interfaith work with Catholics was to see that the transformative framework established at the Vatican Council was being effectively communicated to laypeople within parishes to effect positive change in attitudes and actions. For Jim, this type of pragmatic inquiry has always been the bottom line for measuring success in his interfaith bridge-building philosophy.

The American Jewish Committee has been a longtime advocate for human rights and cutting-edge interreligious relations. The AJC was one of the first para-synagogue organizations to take an active role in building relations with mainstream Protestant Christian denominations. During his tenure as national interreligious affairs director at the AJC, Jim Rudin had an important part in continuing to cultivate these relationships. Especially considering the overall failure of the church to intervene during the Holocaust years and because of the ongoing scourge of antisemitism around the world, the ecumenical Protestant community became more and more pricked in conscience; it began to call for a collective need for repentance and self-correction regarding its relation to the Jewish community.

While Jim Rudin was working in interreligious relations at the AJC in the final decades of the twentieth century, many of the mainstream Protestant denominations, following *Nostra Aetate*, issued their own formal statements concerning the Jewish people. Most called for a condemnation of antisemitism, Christian supersessionism, and institutionally supported programs to missionize Jews. Further, many denominational statements affirmed the need for a stronger emphasis on the Jewish roots of Christianity and on the Jewish context of the life and teachings of Jesus.

In addition, various statements cautioned Israel not to demonize or delegitimize the rights of the Palestinian people. For the reader, Jim Rudin's informative volume, *Christians & Jews, Faith to Faith: Tragic History, Promising Present, Fragile Future* continues to provide a useful resource for understanding many of the issues that led to the need for a revision of the position of various mainstream Protestant denominations. These church bodies had largely emerged during the five-hundred-year period since the start of the Protestant Reformation and needed to re-examine and reform certain negative teachings held concerning Jews and Judaism.

The final significant development I will comment on regards the leadership of Jim Rudin and the American Jewish Committee in being at the forefront of building meaningful interfaith relations with the Evangelical Christian community. Prior to the 1970s, Jews and Evangelicals had very little formal contact. Professional and lay leadership of both communities knew little about the other and had—only on rare occasions—mainly exchanged salvos. At the time, there were few local or national attempts to organize meetings or conferences with the aim to befriend and learn from the other and to explore the prospects of fruitful and respectful dialogue. It was primarily by working together in this context that I came to greatly appreciate Jim Rudin as a cherished friend and valued professional leader and colleague through his advocacy, support, and participation in Evangelical-Jewish dialogue.

Between 1973 and 1995, Jim and I had the challenging and rewarding experience of co-planning and co-directing four different three-day national conferences of Evangelical and Jewish scholars and religious leaders. Through these events, we worked together to co-edit and publish four volumes of essays compiled from these conferences at which Jews and Evangelicals were able to exchange their perspectives on various themes from Scripture, theology, ethics, and history.

Jim contributed important chapters to each of these publications and, in this connection, also spoke at numerous press conferences and on radio and TV about this relatively new and growing phenomenon of Evangelical-Jewish relations. As an interfaith partner, I had the privilege over the course of three decades of sharing the platform with Jim at a variety of interfaith events around the country. This included speaking in synagogues, churches, colleges, conferences, and at clergy gatherings and media events. We also participated in various Evangelical-Jewish dialogues and in several trialogues with Muslim scholars joining in the conversation.

One of the events I personally enjoyed the most was the occasion we invited Jim to speak a special, four-part lecture series at Gordon College, an Evangelical Christian liberal arts institution where I served on the faculty for over fifty years. This event was part of a required convocation series for students titled, *Exploring Psalms with the Rabbis.* In the presence of more than a thousand students and faculty, Jim gave a masterful exposition of Psalm 8 and a very informative Q and A afterwards. This was one of several important visits Jim made to lecture at Gordon College in classes and at conferences.

I am very thankful Jim has authored this autobiography, sharing much of his personal life story. I am sure in some of my numerous interactions with Jim, my recollections may have a slightly different slant than Jim's. However, putting everything together within this autobiography, the reader will have many striking snippets, vignettes, and sometimes longer glimpses into the rich life of this extraordinary leader, a rabbinic mind graced with intelligence, compassion, humor, and a passion for justice.

I hasten to point out that Jim's modesty, humility, and characteristic reserve doubtless have kept him from revealing other facts about himself. In my earthly journey as an octogenarian, I consider Rabbi A. James Rudin one of very few close, Jewish scholar-teachers who have consistently proven to be a great source of blessing and inspiration. As a newly minted professor decades ago, Jim encouraged me to pursue areas of research, writing, and professional relationships that moved me the most: love of the Jewish Scriptures, exploration of the Jewish roots of the Christian faith, pursuit and cultivation of an accurate understanding of Jews and Judaism, and the quest for developing positive and productive Christian-Jewish relationships. Jim was a catalyst for the above and so much more that has enriched my life and made my long teaching career so personally meaningful.

We are all indebted to Jim for sharing this inspiring story of a life well lived. Jim's extraordinary giftedness and his capability of bringing Jews and Christians of different stripes together to forge new and constructive relationships is a legacy to be esteemed and honored.

I conclude with the sincere wish Jim and Marcia experience good health, happiness, and strength along the road ahead. And for my friend, Rabbi A. James Rudin, may the light of your life and the fruit of your interfaith work continue to shine and increase for the blessing of humanity for countless generations to come.

Marvin R. Wilson, PhD
Professor Emeritus, Department of Biblical Studies Gordon College,
Author of *Our Father Abraham: Jewish Roots of the Christian Faith*
2022

Introduction

I sat in an ornately decorated reception room at the Vatican waiting for a private audience with Pope John Paul II. Because I was a frequent visitor to the Vatican, the colorfully uniformed Swiss Guards whisked my group of American Jewish Committee leaders and me through the security metal detector and as a result, I arrived earlier than expected for the papal meeting. I actually had time to examine my surroundings.

It was an enormous room of high ceilings and polished marble floors, with oil paintings of angels and decorated damask drapes. Because the waiting room was in a recessed part of the Vatican City complex, the usual loud street noises of Rome, especially blaring taxi horns, were not heard; the only sound was the crisp click of shoes on the marble floor as Vatican staff members walked past the nearby open doorway.

While I was climbing the massive staircases leading from the street-level St. Peter's Square to reach the waiting room, I noticed large mosaic maps of the world's continents and oceans mounted on the walls. It was just one of many signs that the Roman Catholic Church perceived itself as a global religious institution.

A Vatican aide, a layman dressed in an elegant tuxedo complete with tails, vest, and a freshly starched white shirt, quietly entered the room to inform me the scheduled meeting with the Holy Father would be slightly delayed. I thanked him, and the extra time I now had set me thinking about the events and personalities that brought me to this unique place.

In June 1968, I joined the American Jewish Committee (AJC)'s Interreligious Affairs Department as a staff member where I remained for thirty-two years. Today, I am AJC's Senior Interreligious Advisor after having served as the Department's Director between 1983 and 2000.

The AJC, founded in 1906, is our country's oldest human rights organization. I was the AJC's representative at hundreds of interreligious meetings, academic conferences, Church gatherings, religious services, and conventions throughout the world.

My itinerary included the Vatican, Beirut, Amman, Geneva, Warsaw, Vienna, London, Seoul, Athens, Salonika, Prague, Hamburg, Trier, Belgrade, Budapest, Kiev, Paris, Madrid, Krakow, Berlin, Munich, Oberammergau, Aarhus, and, of course, Jerusalem.

The worst of my professional travel destinations was Auschwitz, a place my wife accurately described on a visit with me as "The Vortex of Evil." I actually felt inner trembling vibrations within my body during my trips to that mass murder Nazi German death camp.

During my three-plus decades of active duty service with the AJC, I made forty-two round-trip trans-Atlantic flights, and I became an expert about various aircraft, airline seat selection, baggage check-in, passport control, and duty-free shopping. But I never mastered the art of sleeping through a long night flight in a cramped coach seat.

As the AJC's National Interreligious Director, I appeared on radio and television programs in many countries and was the subject of numerous newspaper and magazine stories—all focused on building positive interreligious relations. I wrote articles and books and delivered more than a thousand speeches in churches, synagogues, and classrooms in the United States and abroad that ranged from nursery schools and kindergartens to universities, colleges, and seminaries.

As part of my work, I met Pope John Paul II eleven times, Pope Benedict XVI twice, as well as Presidents Jimmy Carter, Ronald Reagan, George H.W. Bush, Bill Clinton, and Vice President Al Gore. While a congregational rabbi in Kansas City, I participated in an unforgettable luncheon conversation with Harry S. Truman.

I always joke that I had numerous meetings and conversations with enough Roman Catholic Cardinals to form a St. Louis baseball team. They included Archbishop William Keeler of Baltimore, Archbishops James McIntyre and Roger Mahony of Los Angeles, Archbishops James Hickey and Wilton Gregory of Washington, DC, and New York Archbishops John O'Connor, Edward Egan, and Timothy Dolan.

I remember with appreciation Archbishop Joseph Bernardin of Chicago, four Vatican Cardinals who directed global Catholic-Jewish relations: Johannes Willebrands, Edward Cassidy, Walter Kasper, and Kurt Koch. Included in my "red hat" list are Polish Primate Joseph Glemp, my New York City television show colleague Edwin O'Brien, and theologian Avery Dulles, the son of Secretary of State John Foster Dulles.

I often encountered prominent evangelists Billy Graham, Jerry Falwell, Pat Robertson, and National Council of Churches and World Council of Churches leaders Claire Randall, and the Reverends Arie Brower, Joan Brown Campbell, Philip Potter, and Konrad Raiser. And finally, there was Greek Orthodox Archbishop Iakovos and Bartholomew I, the Eastern Orthodox Ecumenical Patriarch.

During my years with the AJC, I was always in a hurry, constantly in a rush to reverse twenty centuries of negative attitudes towards Jews and Judaism. To accomplish this difficult task, there was always one more bishop to meet, one more Christian seminary to visit, one more sermon to deliver in a church, basilica, or cathedral, one more Christian educator asking my advice on a proposed book about Judaism, one more international conference to attend in order to rally interreligious support for Soviet Jewry, one more radio or TV talk show to discuss the inextricable connections and significant differences between Passover and Easter, one more journalist working on deadline who wanted my views on the anti-Jewish elements in the world-famous Oberammergau Passion Play in Germany, one more public criticism on Christian attempts to convert Jews, one more media comment on the Vatican statement on the Holocaust, one more attendance at a Good Friday service as an unannounced visitor to hear how the clergyperson described the death of Jesus vis-à-vis "the Jews," and so many other encounters, gatherings, meetings, colloquia, news conferences, panel discussions, classroom lectures, and media appearances.

Rapidly moving from place to place, from one meeting to another, I spent almost no time wondering how a Jewish boy from Virginia chose to become an "Ambassador to Christians" as his life's work. My private slogan was "So Many Christians, So Much to Change, So Little Time."

While waiting to meet the Pope, my thoughts carried me back to a vivid memory of my rabbinical school years. One of the teachers at the Hebrew Union College—Jewish Institute of Religion in New York City told me that all authentic theology is autobiographical. He meant the revered theologians of the past or the present do not shape our core beliefs. Instead, personally lived experiences and encounters in everyday life do more to create our religious values and views.

That was certainly true for me, and it explains why those personal relationships afforded me with an insider's "front row seat" of some extraordinary events and provided a unique insight into how positive history is made. It happens when leaders develop trusted relationships with one another. Personal relationships, I discovered, frequently count for more than differences in ideology, theology, or politics. This was certainly true in the post-World War II revolution that has dramatically improved Christian-Jewish relations.

The decades since 1945 and the end of the Holocaust have been momentous ones as Jews and Christians, two ancient religious communities, reached out to one another to reverse centuries of suspicion, hatred, and mistrust. And I was lucky enough to play a major role in that extraordinary effort.

I met many skeptics, including members of my family, who perceived interreligious relations as a worthwhile pleasant distraction, a "nice thing to do." But I always believed it was much more than that because throughout history and continuing to this day, religion has often been a demonic force that provided divine justification for the slaughter of millions of innocent people. In addition, religion has frequently shaped politics, culture, science, medicine, and economics in negative ways. I call my career "a brush with history."

Deeply held religious beliefs are like radioactive material. If handled carefully, they can be of great positive value. But if mishandled, they can be a source of human destruction and pain. I saw my task on the stage I occupied to make sure religious leaders, and hopefully their followers, would handle the radioactive material in beneficial ways.

It wasn't always easy, and there were many off-the-record heated meetings, closed-door angry encounters, and stormy confrontations that had to be overcome. But progress, albeit hardly enough, has been made, and I strongly believe these advances in mutual understanding and respect between Jews and Christian are irreversible.

While there have been great advances, I have no illusions that the task is complete. I see myself as a religious explorer, a pioneer who helped set in motion an irrevocable process of ending once and for all time to come the alienation among followers of the world's religions.

This book is my story of that effort.

My private musings and reveries in the vast Vatican waiting room ended abruptly when the papal aide returned and said: "Rabbi Rudin, the Holy Father would be delighted to see you and your group now."

CHAPTER 1

Why is This Autobiography Different from the One I Would Have Written Four Years Ago?

I HAVE ALWAYS described Christian-Jewish relations in positive terms combined with great hope for the future. And there were many reasons for my optimism.

In October 1965, at the conclusion of the Second Vatican Council in Rome, the world's Roman Catholic bishops overwhelmingly adopted by a vote of 2,221 to 88 the now historic *Nostra Aetate* ["In Our Time"] Declaration. The English translation from the original Latin text was only 624 words, but it set in motion a revolution of the human spirit and sparked a serious and systematic effort by the Catholic Church as well as other Christian bodies throughout the world to improve their past bitter and negative relationships with Jews and Judaism.

Similar statements repudiating antisemitism have been issued by other Christian bodies, including the World Council of Churches, the Lutheran World Federation, the Southern Baptist Convention, the United Church of Christ, the United Presbyterian Church (USA), the United Methodist Church, and the Anglican Communion.

In 1987, the General Synod of the United Church of Christ adopted a statement affirming that "Judaism has not been superseded by Christianity," and that "God has not rejected the Jewish people." In fact, since 1965, there have been more positive encounters between Christians and Jews than there were in the first 1900 years of the Church.

The key provisions of the Vatican Council Declaration read:

> "What happened in his (Jesus's) passion cannot be charged against all the Jews, without distinction, then alive, nor against the Jews of today. The Jews should

not be represented as rejected by God or accursed, as if this followed from Holy Scripture. All should see to it, then, that in catechetical work, and in preaching of the Word of God they teach nothing save what conforms to the truth of the Gospel and the spirit of Christ."

The declaration also stated:

"(In) her rejection of every persecution against any man, the Church, mindful of the patrimony she shares with the Jews and moved not by political reasons but by the Gospel's spiritual love, decries hatred, persecutions (and) displays of antisemitism directed against Jews at any time and by anyone."

Beginning in 1968, when I joined the American Jewish Committee's Interreligious Affairs Department, I worked with Christian and Jewish colleagues in constructing a seemingly sturdy interreligious edifice that is now shaky and under direct assault. A major foundation of that structure was the Vatican Council's call to reject all forms of *antisemitism directed against Jews at any time and by anyone.*

But recent disturbing events have unexpectedly challenged my previous hopeful assumptions. Virulent lethal antisemitic acts, once small in number since the end of the Holocaust in 1945, have reemerged, especially in Europe and the United States. It is an epidemic with the potential to become a pandemic of hate.

In October 2018, an armed assailant entered Pittsburgh's Tree of Life synagogue building and murdered eleven Jews at prayer, including my cousins Cecil and David Rosenthal. It was the worst antisemitic act in American history. There have been recent attacks in Kansas City, Missouri; Monsey, New York; Poway, California; Jersey City, New Jersey; Sarasota, Florida; Halle, Germany; Paris and Toulouse, France; Colleyville, Texas, and other cities.

In the United States, especially since the end of World War II, American Jews believed they were living in a new "Golden Age" of security and freedom from the ugly scourge of antisemitism.

Of course, there were always random antisemitic acts of vandalism, usually committed by disaffected young men who frequently painted the swastika, the dreaded symbol of Nazism, upon Jewish gravestones or synagogue exteriors.

But during the past few years, American Jews have been jolted out of their complacent feelings of security. Those previous sporadic defacements of Jewish sites have been boosted by antisemites who publicly spew ugly anti-Jewish conspiracy theories; they were clearly visible in the 2017 Charlottesville, Virginia hate marches where they carried both Nazi and Confederate flags as they chanted expressions of hatred.

For many Jews in the United States, there is now a growing sense of anxiety that antisemitism, emerging from both the political left and right, has moved from the shadows of society and the fringes of social media into the American political, social, cultural, and religious mainstream.

Neo-Nazis, white supremacists, and white populist nationalists are now joined by so-called anti-imperialists, anti-Zionists, and anti-colonialists. Frequently included in this openly antisemitic ferment are Islamic extremists and some Black individuals who link "white privilege" with the conspiratorial myth about Jewish "control" of the print and electronic media, government, and Hollywood.

In addition, many observers claim the Boycott, Divestment, Sanctions (BDS) movement, now active on numerous university and college campuses, targeting the State of Israel represents a not-so-subtle form of classic antisemitism.

Some university and college Jewish faculty members and students have been victims of overt antisemitism on campuses. Their alleged "crimes" are supporting the State of Israel, purportedly participating in the victimhood of people of color and indigenous peoples, and promoting colonialism and latter-day apartheid.

The public emergence of antisemitism in America has compelled many Jews to echo Jeffrey Myers, the Tree of Life congregational rabbi, who laments that despite his previous long-held belief that Jews were safely living in a "Golden Age" in the United States, he now believes Jews will always remain "other," never fully welcomed here in America.

And I wonder about the lasting beneficial impact of my work of thirty-two years at the American Jewish Committee as a global interreligious leader who was deeply involved in a myriad of programs and projects whose goal was to combat antisemitism and construct sturdy enduring human bridges of mutual respect and reconciliation.

This book tells why that goal became the lodestar of my life and how I labored with like-minded Christian and Jewish colleagues to make it a permanent reality.

CHAPTER 2

Birth in the "Steel City" and Growing Up in Robert E. Lee's Hometown

MY FATHER, PHILIP Rudin, was the son of Samuel, a bootmaker, and his wife, Rose. They immigrated to Pittsburgh from Belarus at the turn of the twentieth century. But, because handmade boots were not in fashion for most Americans of that era, my grandfather was forced to open a grocery store in Pittsburgh's Hill District. Young Philip lived behind the store with seven other family members.

After attending Schenley High School, my father graduated from the University of Pittsburgh Dental School in 1925. A year later, he married my librarian mother Beatrice Rosenbloom, an Allegheny High School alumna.

The daughter of Louis Rosenbloom, Beatrice and six other family members lived above her father's clothing store on Pittsburgh's "Nor Side"—the area north of the Allegheny River. Louis, and Beatrice's stepmother, Jenny, were both born in Lithuania.

Despite the Great Depression, my father had a thriving dental practice until 1941. During that time, my brother Bert and I were both born at Allegheny General Hospital. Like our father, Bert also graduated from Pitt Dental School.

In 1932, Philip joined the Army Reserves as a cavalry officer. Years later, he told me he joined the Army in response to Hitler's antisemitism. Perhaps. But I think my father liked his officer's uniform with its Sam Browne belt and saber. I treasure a photo of him sitting atop a large steed.

In August 1941, Philip was called up for one year of active duty at Fort Belvoir, just south of Alexandria, Virginia, but once America entered World War II, he remained on active duty until 1947. Nearly every male in my extended family above the age of 18 was in the Army serving in Iwo Jima, Tunisia, Iceland, France, Belgium, Germany, and Czechoslovakia.

My parents permanently put down family roots in Alexandria, Virginia, and today the fourth Rudin generation still lives in Northern Virginia. Philip retired from the military in 1957 with the rank of Lieutenant Colonel, and both of my parents are buried in Arlington National Cemetery, a few miles from Alexandria.

But I still have cousins who live in Pittsburgh, and I made many visits to the city as part of my AJC interreligious work. The most memorable of those Western Pennsylvania visits actually took place in Greensburg, about thirty-five miles east of Pittsburgh.

It was a highly publicized interreligious meeting in a local movie theater that featured the Dalai Lama, the famed internationally known Tibetan Buddhist leader. A young local imam and I were also speakers, but merely the "supporting cast" for the event.

It's often forgotten that "Mr. Rogers" was an ordained Presbyterian minister and his PBS-TV show originated in Pittsburgh.

The Muslim religious leader and I were the first to take our seats on the stage. The theater was packed with excited folks and some of the overflow crowd was forced to stand in the back of the old movie palace. An organizer of the event approached the imam and me and whispered: "When the Dalai Lama comes onto the stage, it is customary to bow as he enters."

He quickly moved away before I could explain to him that as a Jew, I bow only to God during a special designated part of our religious services. The imam looked a bit worried, even frightened, as he told me Muslims bow only to Allah, not to any human being. I reassured him that I would, of course, join him in not bowing before the Dalai Lama.

It all worked out well as Mr. Rogers, the imam and I simply shook hands with the Tibetan spiritual leader. My Muslim colleague thanked me again and again that afternoon for my emotional support and assistance. And, of course, the two of us were simply the "religious wallpaper." The real star of the entire program was not even the Dalai Lama. It was the wonderful Mr. Rogers the crowd really came to see. I cherish the photo of the event. After all, it's not often one can see a living legend: in this case the great Fred Rogers.

When I grew up in Alexandria during the 1940s it was a small town dominated by a distinct Southern ethos. Its thirty thousand residents were incredibly conscious of their community's long history. It was founded in 1749, nearly a half century before the establishment of America's nearby capital city named for Alexandria's most famous neighbor, George Washington, who resided at nearby Mount Vernon. Another well-known resident was Robert E. Lee, who, as a youngster, lived with his family in Alexandria.

For most Virginians, Charlottesville represents the historic home area of Thomas Jefferson and the city itself is the location of the University of Virginia, a school founded by our third president.

But in August 2017, Charlottesville was the scene of a hate rally that focused on antisemitism, and the rioting resulted in the murder of an innocent bystander.

The deadly violence in Charlottesville, Virginia, and the images of white nationalists, the Ku Klux Klan, and neo-Nazis carrying Confederate and swastika flags shouting, "Jews will not replace us!" and "You will not replace us!" stunned millions of people throughout the world.

But I was not surprised. As a Jewish youngster growing up just a couple hours' drive away in Alexandria, these sentiments were plain to see.

I first encountered them in the early 1950s at an outdoor revival meeting in a huge tent erected about ten miles south of Alexandria on US Route 1. While it was my first revival meeting, it was old stuff to my three high school friends—all Evangelical Christians—who had invited me to join them on a hot Saturday night in May.

The all-white congregation of about 500 people (I was told the "colored" conducted separate revivals with their own preachers) sat on hard metal folding chairs. The huge number of light bulbs strung across the top of the tent created a fire hazard and raised an already high temperature. The lighting and the natural heat produced hundreds of sweating people.

The meeting itself consisted of an emotional mix of well-known Christian hymns and a fiery sermon describing the many sins humans regularly commit. The highlight came when the white-haired preacher issued the call for people to come forward, kneel in front of the makeshift altar, and "accept Jesus into their hearts."

Strangely, the sermon didn't resonate too well that night. I was later told that most of the audience, many of them habitués of such outdoor religious meetings, had come forward at previous revivals. My three classmates remained in their seats and did not respond to the preacher's call.

However, the atmosphere inside the tent rapidly changed when the preacher began speaking about the "the plagues sweeping our beloved America."

I mistakenly thought he would tick off the litany of the ten woes that descended upon ancient Egypt listed in the biblical book of Exodus. Perhaps the speaker would release some frogs (one of the plagues) to illustrate his sermon.

But instead of the biblical catastrophes that are a part of the Passover Seder narration, the animated preacher cited the modern ills ostensibly polluting America.

They included the organized labor movement, the subversive Communists working in Washington (it was the McCarthy era, after all), the Federal Reserve System, sexual promiscuity, the excess numbers of foreigners in America, the demeaning of the Confederacy, and one "plague" that really surprised me: the Federal government's trampling of "states' rights." It was a concept taught in some of my high school history classes as the basic reason—not slavery—for the Civil War.

Finishing up, the preacher shouted: "Let's take back America! They have stolen America. It's our country, our America!"

Unlike the congregation's tepid response to the preacher's earlier call to accept Jesus, this time the crowd arose from their chairs, began cheering, and then spontaneously started singing an emotional rendition of "Dixie," the song most linked to the Confederacy.

I was only 16 years old that night, but the "tent people's" sense of fury has remained with me.

The preacher's heated cry that America had been stolen was no run-of-the-mill conversion sermon, nor was it the recitation of the traditional biblical plagues I had anticipated. Instead, it was a white Christian nationalist outburst that stunned me with its anger and rage and its call for the violent "restoration" of a "Christian America," an America that had no place for me as a Jew.

The crowd that night believed something precious had been "stolen" from them as Christians which had to be "reclaimed."

That long-ago bitter sermon provides a warning as Americans ponder this question: Was the lethal violence in Charlottesville a one-time event or does it represent the future of an America religiously and politically at war with itself? In such a war, constructive Christian-Jewish relations would be among the first casualties.

A few weeks after my rabbinical ordination in 1960, I entered the United States Air Force as a chaplain assigned to Japan and Korea. I recited the oath to support and defend the Constitution said by all American military personnel and elected officials. In a ceremony administered by an Alexandria attorney friend of my father, I noticed a large Confederate battle flag hanging on his wall. I sarcastically wondered aloud whether I was entering the US or the Confederate Air Force. My father laughed, but the lawyer was not amused.

In the second grade, our teacher insisted on reading a selection from the New Testament every morning. Concepts and principles such as church-state separation and the First Amendment were not her "first principles." My parents sharply protested the New Testament readings, but the teacher's response was to make me and the two Catholics in our class leave the room while she read to the remaining Protestant students, who were mainly Southern Baptists. It seemed she did not consider Catholics fully "Christian." We three exiles comprised ten percent of the class and felt humiliated at being singled out for special treatment.

Each morning we were forced to stand together outside the classroom door while the New Testament verses were read to the 27 other members of our grade. The school principal, also a Southern Baptist, quickly intervened when she learned of my parents' displeasure and similar complaints from the Catholic parents.

In a meeting with the upset parents, she reprimanded the teacher: "You mustn't separate children based on religion. Everyone's equal here, and besides, Bible reading is for church and home. You know we Southern Baptists don't believe it belongs in the schoolroom. Mr. Jefferson taught us about the wall of separation between church and state."

In the Virginia of that era, invoking the name of Thomas Jefferson was almost equal in sanctity and power to quoting something written by George Washington. The exile quickly ended, and the New Testament readings ceased.

My fifth-grade teacher at the same elementary school was from Georgia, and she was either unable or unwilling to pronounce the name "Abraham Lincoln." When we studied the "War Between the States," aka "The Civil War," she always called Lincoln "The sixteenth Federal President." However, she had no trouble mentioning the Confederate President, Jefferson Davis, by name.

She once asked us to interview older family members in order to learn how they or their ancestors had survived the Yankee aggression in the South that took place eight decades earlier. I was spellbound as my 10-year-old classmates proudly recounted how members of their families, usually great-grandparents, had outwitted the fiendish Northerners in Virginia and other Southern states.

Especially gripping was my teacher's own tale of how her Georgia relatives had escaped the destruction and killing carried out by General William Tecumseh Sherman's Federal troops during the bloody march from Atlanta to Savannah in 1864.

When I reported on my own historical research (limited to interviews of my parents), I quietly said my ancestors in the 1860s were living somewhere in Poland or Russia. But in a louder voice I added that they spent a lot of time avoiding the Tsar's cruel secret police. I also noted that many young Jewish boys were drafted into the Russian army for a twenty-five-year tour of duty. Finally, in an even louder voice, I said my US Army father told me Adolf Hitler is much worse than General Sherman.

It was the autumn of 1944; a time I later learned was the deadliest year of the Holocaust. My teacher nodded her head in approval, but then she scowled a bit and in her thick Georgia drawl gently said, "Jimma, that was a good report, but where exactly are your parents from?" I mumbled, "Pennsylvania." "Oh, that explains everything," she said with a smile.

Each December our neighborhood association sponsored a Christmas home lighting contest that awarded prizes for the best outdoor holiday decorations. These usually included reindeer, Santa Claus, elves, toy soldiers, sleighs, model trains, and a dazzling assortment of colored lights that covered the entire front of many houses. It was always a highly competitive contest with a committee of participants judging the creativity of other participants, a recipe for controversy.

Tempers flared one year when a hotly disputed winners' list was announced. There was a severe pushback by the losers and the association announced an elimination of all future contests. In desperation, our squabbling neighbors asked my parents—we were the only Jewish family in the neighborhood—to judge the lighting contest the following year. Their reasoning was quite simple: the Rudins, who only lit candles in their Hanukkah menorah, would be impartial judges.

And so, for several years, each December my father, brother, and I trudged around our Alexandria neighborhood, sometimes in the snow, evaluating a myriad of Christmas lights. And our decisions were never questioned.

It was an unforgettable introduction to the concept of religious pluralism and Christian-Jewish relations.

CHAPTER 3

Choosing the Rabbinate Thanks to a Pair of Mentors

My rabbinic journey began when I was a six-year-old student at Temple Rodef Sholom in Pittsburgh during Sukkot, 1940. While standing on the building's front steps, Rabbi Solomon B. Freehof, the congregation's senior rabbi, handed me a bright red apple to commemorate the fall harvest holiday.

I proudly took the rabbi's gift home, where it was treated as a sacred object, sitting on our mantelpiece as long as nature would allow.

The following year, when my father was called to active Army duty and stationed at Fort Belvoir near Alexandria, Virginia, we joined Temple Beth-El, the local Reform congregation. But Rabbi Freehof's influence remained strong in our home, because Rodef Sholom regularly sent us printed texts of his sermons and book reviews.

Even as a youngster, I appreciated his beautifully crafted phrasing, his command of Jewish sources, and how his love of Shakespeare was woven into many of his writings—and during the darkest days of World War II, Rodef Sholom's rabbi always ended his sermons with realistic hope. His public book reviews attracted audiences of both Jews and Christians, numbering between 1,500 and 2,000.

Many years later, I visited Rabbi Freehof in his study and reminded him of the gift apple, and he gave me another gift: several old prayer books he had personally restored and re-bound, and a Passover *Haggadah* published in Nazi Germany in the fateful year 1938.

Rabbi Freehof was a superb interpreter of Jewish responsa, offering rabbinic answers to questions that provided guidance about Jewish customs, liturgy, ceremonies, and the adaption of traditional values in the modern world. His mastery of the traditional texts allowed him to shape Reform Judaism to meet changing modern conditions, and he did so by asserting his teachings were "not governance, but guidance."

His illustrious career included serving as a Hebrew Union College professor and as president of both the Central Conference of American Rabbis and the World Union for Progressive Judaism. He died in 1990 at age 98.

Here is the rabbinical legacy that Rabbi Freehof bequeathed to me: Always be meticulous in your preparations for public presentations whether written or oral. Take your audience seriously and never attempt to "wing it." Offer authentic realistic hope to the Jewish people. And never underestimate the memory of young children.

Rabbi Hugo Schiff was spiritual leader of Beth El Hebrew Congregation in Alexandria, a congregation founded in 1859 primarily by German Jews who had come to the United States following the unsuccessful 1848 revolution in Europe. Before 1938, Dr. Schiff had been the rabbi of a thousand-member synagogue in Karlsruhe.

In 1938, Rabbi Schiff and his wife Hannah were rescued from Nazi Germany; he had been interned in the Dachau concentration camp near Munich following the *Kristallnacht* pogrom. "Dr. Schiff," as he insisted on being called, had a PhD from Erlangen University in Germany; surprisingly, his doctoral thesis focused on the American philosopher, essayist, and poet, Ralph Waldo Emerson. During his time in Alexandria, he augmented his meager rabbinic salary by teaching religion courses at Howard University in Washington, DC.

Dr. Schiff was always impeccably dressed, ultra-serious, and often humorless. He had a laser-like intellect and revered academic study, especially philosophy and biblical texts. Like Rabbi Freehof, he had been a military chaplain in World War I, but on the opposite side of the barricade.

Although he officiated at my *bar mitzvah*, I did not fully appreciate Rabbi Schiff until much later during my first year at Wesleyan University, and it was there I first thought of becoming a rabbi.

I was selected for a Great Books honors class taught by Dr. Victor Butterfield, Wesleyan's President, and among our readings were selections from Emerson and what most Christians call "The Old Testament." Because my family attended hundreds of Sabbath services conducted by Dr. Schiff, I heard him deliver many brilliant sermons about the Hebrew Bible and, of course, his beloved Emerson.

Although Dr. Butterfield was an excellent teacher, I quickly recognized that Dr. Schiff's extraordinary biblical and philosophical teachings were superior to what I was learning in college. When I told him I was thinking about the rabbinate, he was pleased. Indeed, he played a key role in my choosing to go to Hebrew Union College - Jewish Institute of Religion (HUC-JIR), the Reform Jewish seminary.

Rabbi Dr. Hugo Schiff was the personification of the dynamic and intellectually rich Jewish community that was brutally destroyed during the Holocaust. He died in 1986 at the age of 93.

Both of my mentors were immigrants. Solomon Freehof was born in London and came to Baltimore in 1903 at the age of eleven. He elevated his rich English vocabulary with an eloquent speaking voice; Hugo Schiff personified the proud German Jewish scholarly tradition, but as a displaced refugee with a heavy foreign accent, he had a harder time finding acceptance and appreciation in his new land.

The other thing my two brilliant mentors had in common was their scholarly mastery of Jewish texts and tradition, combined with a deep appreciation of classic literature, attributes that have informed my 60-plus years as a rabbi.

The Alexandria school system of my childhood was so strapped for funds that it did not offer an eighth grade. As a result, I "jumped" to the ninth grade at the age of twelve. As I neared high school graduation, I was accepted at Wesleyan University in Middletown, Connecticut, and was a month shy of my seventeenth birthday when I first arrived on campus. My three dormitory suite mates—Harry, Michael, and Bob—were Christians, and as first-year college students have done for generations, we had countless discussions—"bull sessions"—about our personal religious beliefs.

The trio had limited knowledge about Jews and Judaism. I soon found myself answering their many questions even as I learned about their spiritual beliefs and/or their professed atheism and agnosticism. To my surprise, I enjoyed the back-and-forth interchange of ideas and soon became sure-footed in my comments about my Jewish identity.

Adding to the dormitory interreligious scene was the fact there were no Jewish fraternities at Wesleyan. I joined the Beta Theta Pi fraternity and one of my closest "Beta brothers" was John Gorsuch from Colorado who later became a prominent Episcopal priest. He was an uncle of US Supreme Court Justice Neil Gorsuch.

I became a member of the freshman wrestling team weighing in at 127 pounds! I was also a classical music disc jockey on the college radio station, WESU, and a columnist for the school newspaper.

The academic year 1951–1952 was the last time Wesleyan, founded as a Methodist institution in 1831, required students to attend weekly religious services. Looking back across the decades, it was ironic I chose to become a rabbi during a campus debate about a centuries-old weekly chapel attendance requirement.

A long academic trail lay ahead of me: three more undergraduate years and then five years as a rabbinical student at HUC-JIR which had branches in Cincinnati and New York City. One of the major entrance requirements was Hebrew language "fluency in the narrative portions" of the Bible. I lacked that skill because my Alexandria synagogue only taught me the ability to read basic Hebrew phrases and prayers. I required intensive preparation to gain rabbinical school admission.

In the early 1950s, there were few American colleges and universities that offered a Jewish studies program of any kind. However, today many institutions of higher learning have strong Judaic Studies departments that include Hebrew, Bible, history, and a host of other related subjects. Among that group is Wesleyan University. But that was not the case as I neared the end of my first year of college. I needed private tutoring to gain the language proficiency necessary to gain admission to HUC-JIR and spending three more years in Middletown could not meet my urgent needs.

After meeting an excellent Israeli tutor living in Washington, DC, I transferred to George Washington University—which today also has a superb Jewish Studies program—where I completed my undergraduate studies.

The twice-weekly tutorial fee was five dollars an hour, which my parents were happy to pay. At the end of my junior year at GWU, I attended a summer HUC-JIR "language school" located on a country estate in Towanda, Pennsylvania. It was a full immersion experience with biblical Hebrew instruction combined with religious services, sports activities, and the opportunity to meet fellow college students who were also preparing for seminary admission. Several of the Towanda bunch became lifelong colleagues.

At GWU, I was a history major, an elected student government officer, a sportswriter for the university paper, a track team participant—I competed in the mile and two-mile events—and a member of several honorary societies including "Who's Who" among US college students.

During the summer following my college graduation I worked as an assistant to Bob Wolff who was the TV and radio announcer of the Washington Senators baseball team. It was great working with Bob even though our hapless team lost 101 games in 1955. One of my major tasks was keeping a series of detailed baseball statistics long before the advent of computers. In addition, I met many famous diamond stars of that long-ago era including Ted Williams, Mickey Mantle, Bob Feller, and Al Rosen.

Clark Griffith, the Senators' owner, was an early major league player and team manager. Nicknamed "The Old Fox," I remember meeting him a few months before his death in October 1955 at age 86. He asked me whether I intended to make sportscasting my career. When I replied I would soon be entering rabbinical school, Griffith was at first silent, then shot me a quizzical look and finally said, "I guess they don't keep batting averages for sermons. Good luck!"

CHAPTER 4

I Led Two Lives as a Seminary Student

I BEGAN MY rabbinical studies at the New York branch of HUC-JIR seven years after the two institutions merged in 1948. The Cincinnati school, located on Clifton Avenue near the University of Cincinnati, was founded in 1875 by Rabbi Isaac Mayer Wise, considered the "Father of American Reform Judaism." The JIR, then located on Manhattan's West 68th Street, was established in 1922 by Rabbi Stephen S. Wise. The two famous rabbis with the same last name were not related.

For twenty-five years the seminaries were rivals. Stephen Wise, America's most prominent rabbi during the first half of the twentieth century, had two major reasons for establishing a second Reform Jewish seminary: population and ideology. "Cincinnati was no longer an intellectual, religious, demographical or cultural center of the American Jewish community … [and] the Cincinnati Seminary … had shown a deep-seated intolerance of Zionist advocacy … New York … With its great Jewish population, was made up of representatives of virtually every Jewish community on earth." Wise was a strong advocate of Zionism—a rarity among the Reform rabbis of that era, many of whom opposed the Jewish national movement.

When I entered HUC-JIR in New York City in the fall of 1955, Stephen Wise had been dead for six years, the independent Jewish State of Israel was seven years old, Reform Judaism's positive commitment to Zionism had been settled, but the Jewish population demographics favoring New York City remained. I much preferred studying in dynamic Manhattan for five years with its exciting cultural life instead of Cincinnati located in the more staid Midwest.

In 1955, the Reform movement experienced explosive congregational growth in the decade following the end of World War II. A huge number of American Jews, many of them military veterans, moved with their families from their former urban homes to the suburbs and established new synagogues. To meet the need for spiritual leaders, seminarians were rushed into service as weekend student rabbis.

So, after just a year of studies, my classmates and I were assigned to small, newly created congregations. My "student pulpit" was Temple Zion located in lower Bucks County, Pennsylvania, north of Philadelphia.

The founding families of Temple Zion had arranged to hold Friday evening Sabbath services in an historic Friends (Quaker) meeting house in the area. The Sunday morning classes for youngsters met in a local community center.

Like other student rabbis, I soon settled into a hectic double life. I attended classes Monday through Friday noon. Then I would rush to Manhattan's Penn Station and catch a train to Trenton, New Jersey, where I would switch to a local train that traveled to a lower Bucks County railroad stop. The autumn through spring Friday evening routine was always the same: *Shabbat* dinner with a congregant's family, then a short drive to the meeting house for the service followed by an *Oneg Shabbat* [Joy of the Sabbath] reception with coffee, tea, and baked sweets. I would then catch a late evening local train to "Center City" Philadelphia where I had a permanent two-night reservation at a large downtown hotel owned by a Temple Zion member.

The "Sunday School" concluded at noon and after conducting afternoon training sessions for our volunteer teachers, I would make the reverse trip back to New York City, usually arriving in Manhattan early Sunday evening.

Other student rabbis had shorter, less complicated trips to Long Island, northern Jersey, or southern Connecticut, all areas of growing Jewish communities; however, one of my classmates flew every weekend to and from Florence, South Carolina.

Forty years later, my daughter Eve was a rabbinic student at HUC-JIR in Los Angeles (the school also now has a fourth branch in Jerusalem). Her student weekend congregation was in faraway Ogden, Utah. Some things never change.

The heavy weekly travel schedule meant it was necessary to use the Monday-through-Friday period for study, research, and writing. I made certain to live on the Upper West Side near the rabbinical school so I could walk to classes.

My four years at Temple Zion witnessed constant growth in membership and in time the congregation purchased a large mansion that allowed us to combine religious services and classrooms in one building.

I spent some Sunday afternoons with the leadership of our shared Quaker meeting house and learned a great deal about William Penn, George Fox, and other leaders of the "Society of Friends." Knowing that history and my contact with some of its local leaders was most helpful when it became necessary decades later to confront the American Friends Service Committee, a group whose policies and actions were frequently hostile to modern Israel.

I also interacted, as time permitted, with several Protestant pastors and Catholic priests of the area. It was the first time I participated in clergy inter-religious activities that included joint community Thanksgiving services.

During my last two years as a student rabbi, I was asked to conduct weekly Saturday morning "in town" *Shabbat* services for Congregation Keneseth Israel, known in Philadelphia as simply "KI." The congregation rented space in a Unitarian church near Rittenhouse Square, an easy walk from my hotel.

Solomon Foster, a retired Reform rabbi, attended my Saturday morning services on a regular basis. I was honored by his regular presence, and everything went well at first. He complimented me on my sermons and Torah interpretations. That is, until May of 1959, when I delivered a sermon to mark modern Israel's eleventh anniversary as an independent Jewish state. I chose "Ha-Tikvah," Israel's national anthem, to conclude the celebratory service.

It was my custom to shake hands with congregants as they left the sanctuary. The elderly rabbi approached me as usual, but he did not hold out his hand. Instead, he verbally assailed me for commemorating Israel's national birthday and for adding Ha-Tikvah to the service. He inquired whether I was a student at Cincinnati where he had been ordained nearly sixty years earlier. When I replied I was a fourth-year student in New York, he interrupted and said that Stephen Wise was a loud-mouthed troublemaker and then added: "Young man, it's too bad you are studying in New York at a Zionist school." He concluded by saying he was a lifelong foe of Zionism, but before I could utter a response, he quickly left the church building.

Despite his angry outburst, the rabbi continued to attend the services, but he never again spoke to me or shook my hand. Rabbi Foster would sit in a pew every Saturday morning and glare at me. When I wrote a biography of Rabbi Stephen Wise many years later, I discovered that he and Wise had a fierce, long-running dispute about Zionism. Sometimes, old memories run very deep.

Back then, HUC-JIR in New York had no classes that focused on interreligious relations, the origins of Christianity, or Jewish perspectives on the New Testament. But Cincinnati had Dr. Samuel Sandmel and later Dr. Michael Cook offering such courses, and I regret not having them as my teachers.

But I did have Dr. Harry M. Orlinsky, one of the world's foremost biblical scholars, as my rabbinic thesis adviser. My topic was a textual study of the Book of Isaiah that was among the Dead Sea Scrolls discovered in the Judean wilderness cave in 1947. Orlinsky was and will always remain my mentor in all things biblical.

During my last year of rabbinic school, I was elected HUC-JIR student president, and the night I was ordained in June 1960 at Manhattan's majestic Temple Emanu-El on New York City's Fifth Avenue, I was awarded the annual best sermon award prize.

I did not know then that my next sermon would be delivered four months later in Japan, nearly 7,000 miles from New York City.

CHAPTER 5

Wearing Air Force Blue in Japan and Korea

For nearly twenty years, from 1950 until 1969, the major rabbinical schools representing Reform, Conservative, and Orthodox Judaism had a unique "selective service" policy for their rabbinic graduates. It is a policy rapidly becoming enveloped by the mists of historical forgetfulness.

During these years, newly ordained rabbis were systematically "drafted" into the United States armed forces to serve as military chaplains. Unlike the US government's Selective Service draft, these were self-imposed policies developed within the various religious communities. Because of church-state separation, legislation could not be used to draft clergy into military service; in fact, a 1917 federal law specifically provided for clergy exemptions. As a result, many religious communities, including the Protestant denominations, the American Roman Catholic bishops, and the three major rabbinical schools were compelled to develop policies and strategies to ensure that enough clergy served in the military.

Beginning in 1950 with the onset of the Korean War and ending in 1969 during the Vietnam War, the three major streams of Judaism in the United States "drafted" nearly 400 newly ordained rabbis to serve in the US armed forces.

The chaplaincy tour of duty lasted either two or three years, and some rabbis, eager to start their civilian careers, resented the "draft." Many others, including me, quickly discovered the chaplaincy provided an invaluable insight into and an understanding of a major American institution: the United States military. In addition, there was a clear mandate to meet the unique religious needs of Jewish personnel and their families, many of them stationed overseas.

Two years of duty in Asia heightened my already strong interest in interreligious relations and allowed me to learn in an "up close and personal" manner much more about Christians and Christianity.

My chaplaincy began with a six-week instruction period with seven other rabbis and sixteen Christian clergy at Lackland Air Force Base in San Antonio, Texas. Joining me were HUC-JIR classmates Ralph Kingsley and Philip Schechter.

Once the training period ended, we were assigned to various airbases in the United States, Europe, and Asia. I felt lucky to be sent to Itazuke Air Base on Kyushu Island located about 570 miles southwest of Tokyo. As part of my duties, I also covered several other bases in Japan and Korea along with monthly visits to the US Public Health Service Atomic Bomb Casualty Commissions in Hiroshima and Nagasaki that were staffed by American medical personnel.

My Itazuke boss was Base Chaplain Thomas E. Hepner, an Evangelical and Reformed Church minister from Pennsylvania and a career Air Force officer. Hepner served with distinction during World War II and the Korean and Vietnam wars.

He was a superb commander and exemplified the best in a military chaplain. He embraced a respect and knowledge of other religious traditions and a strict policy of not permitting any form of proselytizing or conversionary tactics to take place on our base.

Hepner maintained an equitable schedule for the clergy under his command, who were required—much like physicians, nurses, lawyers, crash and fire crews, and other first responders—to serve on a rotating schedule as the base chaplain of the day. Like many other rabbis in the military, I regularly volunteered for emergency duty on Sundays, allowing me to observe *Shabbat*.

Hepner was a strong buffer who shielded us from any outside pressure, and he encouraged my Christian colleagues and me to perform our duties without worrying about obsessive oversight, interference, or control by the base commander, the hospital commanding officer, or anyone else.

He demanded hard work from his chaplains, including detailed monthly reports that charted the number of people attending religious services and other programs. In addition, I prepared a weekly bulletin that was given out at *Shabbat* services and edited a monthly newsletter that was distributed to all the other bases I visited on my regular monthly itinerary.

Another remarkable career Air Force chaplain colleague was a member of the Southern Baptist Convention (SBC): Earl Minor, who was stationed at Osan Air Base about thirty-five miles south of Seoul.

Minor and I immediately hit it off during my first visit to bleak, cold, war-torn Korea. Because my hometown of Alexandria, Virginia, was dominated by a Southern Baptist religious ethos, I was eager to learn more about the SBC, the largest Protestant denomination in the United States.

I discovered that Minor was equally eager to learn more about Jews and contemporary Judaism. He had long ago jettisoned the wildly erroneous belief held by some Christians that the Jewish religion "had not changed since the days of the Old Testament"—a phrase I heard from another Southern Baptist chaplain stationed at Itazuke. Minor wanted to learn about Judaism, and I quickly discovered he had no hidden conversionary agenda. He was especially impressed that I grew up in a city with a pervasive Southern Baptist presence and atmosphere.

Until I met him, I had not given much thought to a rabbinic career in interreligious relations, but Minor's obvious interest in exploring what Jews believe compelled me to describe in detail many aspects of Judaism, including how we perceive Jesus and the New Testament. I vividly remember several long discussions—never debates—specifically about Paul's views of Judaism, *kashrut* dietary regulations, and circumcision.

I also spent time describing Jewish holiday observances, the meaning of modern Israel, the horrors of the Holocaust, the root causes of Christian anti-Judaism, the importance of religious pluralism, and a host of other questions. Minor was intrigued by the teachings of Martin Buber, who was a popular religious philosopher in the 1960s.

My Southern Baptist colleague was surprised when I described the various religious streams of Judaism and the centrality of the State of Israel in Jewish life and thought. He was also struck by the similarities in both the Jewish and SBC congregational structures—that is, the independence in ritual and liturgy that each congregation is able to maintain while being part of a large national convention or union.

In return, my dialogue partner explained basic Southern Baptist theology to me, including the central belief that each person, clergy and lay, is capable of interpreting the Bible. Minor also stressed the historic Baptist commitment to the separation of church and state. Minor's genuine interest in Judaism provided hours of serious conversation and good-natured banter. He was a welcome intellectual partner during my monthly visits to dreary Korea.

Our in-depth conversations often took place during shared dinners at the Osan Officers Club during some bitterly cold Korean winter nights. In retrospect, I recognize that my encounters with a sincere inquiring Christian chaplain in a place where we were both strangers in a strange land sparked my initial interest in interreligious relations.

Years later, I was not surprised to learn that Minor had achieved the rank of full colonel and served with distinction as command chaplain for the United States Air Forces in Europe (USAFE).

At Itazuke my closest colleague was a Catholic chaplain with an appropriate first name: Fedelis. Fedelis Connolly was a warm, funny Irishman from Massachusetts (and it didn't hurt that he was a fellow Democrat, since most of the officers I worked with, aside from members of my Itazuke congregation, were Republicans who strongly supported Richard Nixon in the 1960 presidential election). Connolly's infectious good humor and Boston accent added to his charm. He served as an Air Force chaplain between 1957 and 1963 before returning to civilian life.

The three-year-long Second Vatican Council that culminated with the *Nostra Aetate* Declaration on Jews and Judaism began in 1962. But Connolly did not need *Nostra Aetate* to validate his own strong commitment to work for improved relations between Catholics and Jews. In effect, he was already a "Vatican II priest." His personal friendship and his obvious respect for Jews and Judaism left an indelible mark on me.

In years to come, when I served as the American Jewish Committee's interreligious affairs director, I encountered hundreds of Christian clergy throughout the world, including prominent Vatican and World Council of Churches leaders. But I trace the beginnings of my interreligious work to my years in Japan and Korea when I was a freshly minted rabbi and experienced such positive interfaith relationships. Hepner, a "mainline" Protestant; Minor, a Southern Baptist; and Connolly, a Roman Catholic, represented some of the significant differences that exist within the general American Christian community, especially in the areas of biblical study, theology, religious authority, and church polity. Because I worked closely with each of them, I learned the nuances, beliefs, vocabulary, history, and traditions that both unite and separate Christians from one another. But more than that, there was a bond that formed between us.

Perhaps it's because American Jews and Christians were small minorities in that part of the world, or because Air Force chaplains all wore the same uniform and worked in close cooperation with one another—whatever the reasons, I still count Thomas Hepner, Earl Minor, and Fidelis Connolly as important influences on my rabbinic career.

The recent rise of verbal and physical assaults against Asians in the United States sadly reminded me of the anti-Asian prejudice, contempt, and condescension I often encountered from many USAF personnel.

Three such moments are permanently "deposited" in my personal memory bank:

The first incident occurred two weeks after I arrived in Japan. While having a drink at the Itazuke Officers Club, a major introduced himself and quickly told me the Japanese manufactured "crappy products." To "prove" his point, he asked me to look out a nearby window where I spotted a car that resembled a small Checker Cab.

My drinking companion said the car was a "piece of junk" that was rightly named. I took the bait and asked what the name was, and the major gleefully spelled out the letters T O Y O T A. He concluded: "Believe me, that Jap car is junk, just a toy." The rest, as they say, is history.

A few weeks later, again at the "O Club" bar, another officer sat next to me as we both nursed our Jack Daniels bourbon drinks. "Chaplain, the Japanese really need good translators. They make lots of mistakes in English." I innocently replied: "Why do you say that? The Japanese folks I work with at the Base Chapel know English quite well."

My drinking "pal" then pulled from his pocket what appeared to be a cigarette pack covered in black vinyl plastic. He told me it was a "transistor radio," something I had never seen before. He then said: "They stupidly misspelled the lettering on the radio." I looked at the handheld device and saw for the first time in my life the four letters S O N Y. My new "buddy" sneered and said: "Chaplain Rudin, the correct spelling should, of course, be S O N N Y." He then uttered six unforgettable words: "What the hell is this 'SONY?'"

And then there was the contempt American car manufacturers exhibited towards the Japanese. In the early 1960s, Detroit auto companies exported large gas-guzzling vehicles with huge tail fin rear fenders—cars much too big for crowded, tightly packed Japanese streets. Worst of all, the US autos had the steering wheel on the left side, and Japan is a right-hand-drive country.

I had occasion to meet a sales representative of one of the Detroit auto companies. I asked why their cars had the steering column on the wrong side. His arrogant answer said it all: "Oh, the slant-eyed jerks are so dumb;

they don't care where the steering wheel is. They just want to buy our American cars." Sure.

I thought to myself: "If and when the Japanese ever export their cars to America, I bet they will know precisely where to place the steering wheel for Main Street America."

Sadly, the anti-Asian contempt and prejudice I experienced back then has intensified, and today it includes physical attacks and murders.

As in so much of life, context is important. And that is true regarding the coarse anti-Japanese remarks noted above. They were uttered by two officers, both of whom had served in World War II.

In the early 1960s, memories of America's titanic armed struggle against the Axis powers were still raw and bitter. Many of us at Itazuke learned that fifteen American POWs imprisoned at the nearby city of Fukuoka were beheaded even as the war came to an end.

And just fifteen years after their surrender in September 1945, Japanese feelings, though usually submerged psychologically, also ran deep. The American military presence in Japan was the first time in history the "Land of the Rising Sun" was physically occupied by an enemy; a fact that created both anger and a sense of humiliation among many Japanese.

But there is still no way to "dry clean" the bigotry and anti-Japanese stereotypes I encountered among some American Air Force officers during my Asian tour of duty.

However, one important exception was Itazuke's base commander, Colonel Daniel Riva. Born in Hartford, Connecticut, Riva was one of the famous "Boy Colonels" of World War II. Based in Great Britain, he was a youthful command pilot of many B-17 bombing missions over Germany and he emerged from the conflict with a host of military medals and awards.

Itazuke, located on Kyushu Island, was considered a "politically sensitive" air base for several reasons. It was geographically close to Nagasaki, the site of the second atomic explosion in August 1945. There was considerable Japanese anger and questioning about the need for America to drop a second A-bomb on helpless civilians.

In addition, our base was on the front line in the not so "Cold War" because of its proximity to both mainland China and North Korea. We were constantly made aware that any future armed conflict in the region would directly involve the US fighter pilots stationed at Itazuke, and that Kyushu Island would likely be attacked by either "Red China" and/or North Korea.

Riva understood the full implications of our precarious existential situation and he showed great leadership skills in balancing the Air Force's military mission with a pitch perfect understanding of Japanese history, culture, tradition, and national sensitivities. His diplomatic skills constituted a major part of his warm, friendly personality.

When his decades-long Air Force career concluded, he became an academic dean at Rollins College in Orlando, Florida. Daniel Riva had earned a PhD from the University of Missouri, and he served with distinction at Rollins until his death in 2008 at age ninety.

Whenever I recall the anti-Japanese prejudice among some Air Force officers, I always remember the gifted Colonel Daniel Riva. He represented the finest in our nation's military tradition.

CHAPTER 6

Being a Rabbi in America's Midwest

A FEW WEEKS after I completed my USAF tour of duty and returned to civilian life, I became the Assistant Rabbi at Temple B'nai Jehudah in Kansas City, Missouri. Being an Assistant Rabbi at a large congregation is the well-trod career path chosen by numerous recently ordained rabbis.

The goal was to work closely with a senior rabbi—in my case, William B. Silverman—for two years and hone one's professional skills before moving on to a solo pulpit. My duties included supervising the congregation's teenage youth group, leading adult education classes, visiting the ill in hospitals and nursing homes, conducting classes for prospective "Jews by Choice" (a more accurate term than "converts"), teaching in the Temple's religious school, officiating at weddings and funerals, attending many nighttime committee meetings, and, of course, joining the senior rabbi on the pulpit for Shabbat and holiday services.

Besides the usual rabbinic duties, I was the host when local church groups, composed of both adults and youngsters, regularly visited the Temple in large numbers.

I answered their questions about the beliefs and practices of Judaism as well as queries about antisemitism, the Holocaust, and the modern State of Israel. I became proficient in this task and interacting with inquiring Christians—especially curious teenagers—increased my interest in Christian-Jewish relations.

An unexpected highlight of my two-year Kansas City sojourn was a 1963 civic luncheon at the city's iconic Union Station building. I agreed to deliver the invocation at the event even though I dreaded such community functions because many of them were boring.

But to my great surprise I was seated at the head table next to President Harry Truman and former Kansas Governor Alfred Landon, the GOP's unsuccessful presidential candidate in 1936.

Both men were most gracious to me and the three of us had a wide-ranging two-hour conversation. Truman and Landon were interested to learn I had served as an Air Force chaplain in Japan and Korea, and they asked me about my impressions of Asia. Truman grew very grave and said, "Of course, Japan is one country Mrs. Truman and I can never visit."

He didn't have to elaborate. Both Landon and I knew why the land of Hiroshima and Nagasaki was off limits to the former president. The man who ordered two atomic bomb attacks on those cities was not welcome.

The world has little noted nor long remembered that luncheon. But, for me, I will always remember it, and the photograph of a young rabbi talking with two American political giants occupies a prominent place in my study.

I made many personal friendships in Kansas City, especially among congregational members who had fled Nazi Germany and found haven in the United States. When I asked them whether there had been positive relations between rabbis and Christian leaders in Germany during the 1930s, the answer was always a negative one.

Indeed, Rabbi Joachim Prinz, a leading rabbi in pre-World War II Berlin, frequently noted the lack of communication, let alone collegiality and personal friendships, with Christian clergy.

Prinz spoke at the giant August 1963 civil rights rally in Washington, DC, the event where Dr. Martin Luther King Jr. delivered his famous "I Have a Dream" speech.

Speaking just before Dr. King, Prinz told the 250,000 people gathered in front of the Lincoln Memorial: "When I was the rabbi of the Jewish community in Berlin under the Hitler regime, I learned many things … The most important thing that I learned in my life is that bigotry and hatred are not the most urgent problem. The most urgent, the most disgraceful, the most shameful, and the most tragic problem is silence … A great people, which had created a great civilization, had become a nation of silent onlookers. They remained silent in the face of hate, in the face of brutality, and in the face of mass murder. America must not become a nation of onlookers. America must not remain silent."

Like millions of others, I was deeply moved by the huge rally. And six months later, I traveled to Hattiesburg, Mississippi, where I spent seven days participating in a drive for voting rights to support the town's African Americans who were systematically and cynically deprived of the right to vote.

In February 1964, the Rabbinical Association of Greater Kansas City sent me as their official representative to participate in the Ministers' Project. My trip was also sponsored by a group of Kansas City civic and religious organizations. The Hattiesburg Project included rabbis, Presbyterian pastors, and Episcopal priests.

The voting rights drive, based upon nonviolent direct action, included marching each morning with other clergy in front of the Forrest County courthouse, in the afternoon canvassing African American homes for potential voters, and in the evening making speeches at mass meetings in Black churches or doing liaison work with the white religious community in Hattiesburg.

When the drive began in January, only twelve out of 7,000 eligible Black voters were registered. By early April, the number had climbed to nearly 800.

Hattiesburg was a life-changing experience and strengthened my commitment to both interreligious efforts and civil and human rights. When I returned to Kansas City, I wrote an article about my experience that appeared in *The Jewish Frontier*, a national magazine.

I concluded the article with two predictions: there would be violence in Mississippi during the summer of 1964 and total integration would come to the United States within ten years. I was unfortunately correct about the potential for violence. Three young civil rights workers—James Chaney, Andrew Goodman, and Michael Schwerner—were murdered that summer in Mississippi. But I was much too optimistic about the end of racism in the United States. I wrote:

> "The summer of 1964 will be a test for Mississippi because hundreds of Negro and white students will be coming to Mississippi to teach the local Black community the art of registering to vote and being a free citizen ... there are many who believe that integration and an 'open society' will not come in our lifetime ... My trip to Hattiesburg has only re-enforced my opposition to such thinking. When the barriers of segregation, intolerance, and harassment fall, then total integration will take place quickly in most parts of our country—perhaps in the next ten years."

After completing two years at B'nai Jehudah, I became the rabbi of Sinai Temple located in Champaign, Illinois, the home of the University of Illinois. The history of central Illinois was far different from the "Lost Cause"

Southern ethos I had grown up with in Virginia. Illinois was proudly the Land of Lincoln.

In fact, one of the Abraham Lincoln—Stephen Douglas United States Senatorial campaign debates took place in Charleston, Illinois near Urbana in 1858. An elderly Sinai Temple member told me his father was at that debate and years later reminded his young son that Lincoln had a high-pitched, almost shrill voice; a fact confirmed by Lincoln scholars.

Sinai Temple was the only synagogue in the Twin Cities of Champaign-Urbana. There was a student Hillel Foundation with its own rabbi located on the campus of the giant University of Illinois. In fact, the Hillel college movement was founded at the U of I in 1923.

During my tenure, Sinai Temple, founded in 1904, experienced sustained growth, much of it coming from university faculty families who began to assume leadership positions in the congregation.

As soon as I settled in Champaign, I initiated a series of personal relationships with some of the local Christian clergy, and together we participated in interreligious programs, including joint Thanksgiving services. I soon became the "Jewish Ambassador" to the local Christian community.

My four years in C-U (1964–1968) was a tumultuous time for the United States. The civil rights movement was at full tide in the mid-1960s, juxtaposed to the unpopular Vietnam War.

In the 1960s, Champaign's housing was highly segregated with most African Americans living in the city's North End. I supported a proposed integrated housing initiative that became a flashpoint within the general community and among some Sinai Temple members.

In addition, I delivered a sermon supporting President Lyndon Johnson in his 1964 presidential campaign against Senator Barry Goldwater, an act that was both praised and criticized by my congregation's members. While I did not speak against America's involvement in the Vietnam War from the pulpit, I did express my opposition to the conflict in other venues.

Some congregants criticized me because they believed that their rabbi, even a military veteran, should not be an outspoken critic of the war or a public supporter of local fair housing legislation and civil rights, while others supported my right to link the Jewish passion for social justice to the moral issues of the day.

The Israel-Arab Six-Day War in June 1967 was a strong solidifying force for Jews everywhere, including members of Sinai Temple. On the first night of the war, June 5, I convened a community-wide emergency meeting at the Temple that attracted an extraordinary turnout of people and provided emergency financial support for the Jewish state.

In the month prior to that date, Jews everywhere experienced a palpable sense of dread that another Holocaust was about to unfold and a belief that Israel's then population of 2.5 million people was in imminent danger of physical annihilation. Israel's swift military victory overcame that fear and the strong unified public support at the synagogue rally was one of the most gratifying moments of my four years in Champaign-Urbana.

Even before the outbreak of the war, I had made plans for my first visit to Israel. I expected to go in June 1967, but naturally the trip was delayed until the following month. I was among the first group of American rabbis who arrived in Israel after its military triumph.

That exciting month-long trip, and especially my attendance at a rabbinical meeting at Jerusalem's King David Hotel, was literally and figuratively a game changer for me. At the hotel, I heard some of America's leading rabbis focus on the meaning of Zionism and the Six-Day War for Jews and Judaism. As I listened to the speeches of my older colleagues, a figurative light brightened inside my brain.

I believed my successful efforts in rallying my congregation, my well-received sermons, and other public speeches delivered during the war, my local radio and TV interviews were as thoughtful, as inspirational, as powerful, and as learned as anything I heard a month later in Jerusalem. Sitting in the ornate world-famous King David Hotel, I realized I was no longer a young rabbi gaining experience or constantly looking to my elders for guidance and direction.

Seven years after my ordination, including a tour of duty in the Air Force, I had become professionally restless and was ready to move on. After my visit to Israel, I realized I did not want to lead a larger congregation. My work at B'nai Jehudah in Kansas City and Sinai Temple in Champaign-Urbana had revealed both my professional strengths and weaknesses. But one thing was clear: my experience in the interreligious arena was a strong part of my rabbinic identity. While I derived satisfaction from being an intimate part of a congregation and a teacher of adults and youngsters, I recognized that I wanted to play on a much bigger stage.

I had to make a choice: remain in Champaign and complete my PhD thesis in History at the U of I or move on. By 1968, I had completed the required classes and seminars as well as "showing proficiency" in Hebrew and French. All that remained was finishing the thesis I had already begun. It dealt with the 1917 Balfour Declaration, the 1919 Versailles peace treaty, and the personal relationship between President Woodrow Wilson and the prominent American rabbi, Stephen S. Wise.

Nearly fifty years later, I went back to that thesis subject which is included in my 2015 biography of Wise published by Texas Tech University Press. My book, *Pillar of Fire*, was nominated for the 2016 Pulitzer Prize in History.

But despite the nearly successful quest for a PhD degree, there was the relentless march of time that influenced my decision to progress to new experiences. In 1968, I was in my mid-thirties, and during my years in Champaign as a single person, my social life was centered on Chicago, one-hundred thirty-five miles to the north. I often drove to the "Windy City" on Sunday afternoons and returned home early Tuesday mornings. I always stayed at a good friend's apartment in Chicago, but after a while, I knew he had grown tired of my frequent visits.

As I began my fourth year at Sinai Temple, I began inquiring about interreligious jobs in New York City. Happily, such a position existed at the Manhattan headquarters of the American Jewish Committee, a major community relations agency founded in 1906.

During the winter of 1968, I was interviewed in Madison, Wisconsin, by Rabbi Marc Tanenbaum, the Committee's Interreligious Director. He was delivering a speech there about the tepid, sometimes hostile response of many American church leaders to Israel's recent military victory.

I made the 250-mile drive from Champaign and had a lengthy conversation with Marc. As a follow up, the AJC flew me from Champaign to New York City three times over a period of a few months for a series of further interviews with the Committee's Executive Director, the Human Resources Director, and other senior AJC staff members.

After a few weeks of suspense, I received a letter offering me the position as an Assistant Interreligious Affairs Director starting in early June 1968. As a new employee, I would be on probation for one year. If things worked out well after twelve months, I would then become a permanent staff member.

Following a series of lovely farewell parties in Champaign, I moved to Manhattan where my HUC-JIR classmate and former US Navy Chaplain, Rabbi Cyrus Arfa, graciously made his Greenwich Village apartment my temporary residence until I moved into my own apartment in the same building.

At last, I was in the global interreligious arena where I wanted to be, playing on the larger stage I had long sought. I had enjoyed my years in Champaign-Urbana, but what I did not know when I moved to Manhattan was that Champaign would soon appear again in a very personal way.

CHAPTER 7

How a One-Year Job Became a Thirty-Two Year Career

THE AMERICAN JEWISH Committee was the appropriate organization and venue for my long-cherished goal of working full time in interreligious relations. It was founded in 1906 by a group of influential American Jews, most of whom had family roots in Germany, and was a direct reaction to the murderous state-sponsored anti-Jewish *Pogrom* in Kishinev, a city in Tsarist Russia.

To achieve its goals, the AJC, from its inception, has always worked closely with political and religious leaders of the United States and other nations. In addition to protecting Jewish rights and lives around the world, and after 1948, building strong support for the security and survival of the State of Israel, one of its primary mandates has been combating religious antisemitism and building positive relations with all branches of Christianity, Islam, and other religious communities.

In 1968, the Committee had thirty-two regional offices in the US as well as overseas representatives in Jerusalem and Paris. In addition to interreligious relations, the AJC's broad-based agenda included church-state issues, domestic civil rights, combating antisemitism and all forms of racism, global human rights, Jewish communal programs, international affairs, publications, and public relations.

Its professional staff included lawyers, rabbis, social workers, community organizers, authors, editors, archivists, communication experts, and fund-raising specialists plus an excellent support staff.

After four years of being a "solo" congregational rabbi, it was an extraordinary change to have a full-time secretary as well as a fairly predictable nine-to-five, five-day work schedule. It was a joy to work with talented and congenial professional colleagues and exciting to focus solely on interreligious relations.

AJC's senior staff met together every Monday morning and it often felt as if I were sitting in a university faculty meeting because our robust discussions and debates were high level and vigorous. The year 1968 was especially difficult. It saw the assassinations of Martin Luther King Jr. and Robert F. Kennedy, the widespread campus student protests in the United States and western Europe, the Tet offensive in Vietnam, the riots during the Democratic National Convention, the razor-close presidential election result, Israel's fruitless quest for peace following its military victory a year earlier, and the Soviet invasion of Czechoslovakia. A major bright spot during an otherwise *annus horribilis* was the steady positive advance in Catholic-Jewish relations that had begun three years earlier with the conclusion of the Second Vatican Council.

AJC's interreligious leader, Marc Tanenbaum, received his *smi'cha* (rabbinical ordination) from the Jewish Theological Seminary in New York City in 1950. Marc came to his AJC position in 1961 and soon established himself as a talented global interreligious leader. He worked tirelessly in both the run up to and during the Second Vatican Council that began in 1962 and concluded in 1965 when the world's Roman Catholic bishops adopted the *Nostra Aetate* Declaration that has transformed Christian-Jewish relations throughout the world.

Soon after arriving at the AJC, Tanenbaum immediately grasped the potential historical moment as the Catholic Church's leaders, led by Popes John XXIII and Paul VI, moved forward, sometimes haltingly, to reverse its long record of theological and intellectual contempt and prejudice towards Jews and Judaism. One of the highlights of Marc's brilliant career was the key role he played during the Second Vatican Council.

He was a charismatic speaker, a gifted writer, and an indefatigable champion of improving relations between Christians and Jews throughout the world. Marc was a pioneer in understanding the importance of positive interreligious affairs, and I gained a fuller grasp of the Christian-Jewish bailiwick by working with him on many projects and programs.

It was an honor in 1983 to succeed him as AJC's Interreligious Director when he became the Committee's International Relations Director. Alas, Marc Tanenbaum died much too young at age 66 in 1992.

Judith Hershcopf Banki, a graduate of the University of Wisconsin, was also my AJC colleague for many years. She, too, was an Assistant Interreligious Affairs Director and had been hired by Marc's predecessor, Rabbi Morris Kertzer, in 1959.

Judy was a wonderful colleague and an outstanding writer and researcher. She was the author of a detailed history-making memorandum that specifically cited the long sad negative record of Catholic teaching, preaching, and writing about Jews and Judaism. Historians agree that her well-documented study played a key role in the long and arduous four-year effort that finally bore historic positive results in 1965.

That struggle during the Council in Rome has been widely documented in many languages, including my 2012 book, *Cushing, Spellman, O'Connor: The Surprising Story of How Three American Cardinals Transformed Catholic-Jewish Relations*.

Even after only a brief time in my new job, I recognized five major issues and themes that demanded my constant attention and continuing efforts: antisemitism, the State of Israel/Zionism, Jerusalem, the *Shoah* (Holocaust), and religious mission and witness. It was then, and still remains today, a full menu that demands serious and systematic efforts by Jews, Christians, and Muslims to reverse centuries of mutual suspicion, distrust, and in many cases, violence, including deaths.

Numerous volumes have been written about each of the five themes, but a little background will illustrate why interreligious relations is so vital to world peace and stability.

The elimination of all forms of antisemitism has been a fundamental issue for Jews. Although there are many kinds of antisemitism, including economic, political, and racial, most scholars agree that theological antisemitism still remains a pervasive pathology in many societies of the world, and, ominously, it has sharply increased in recent years. As a result, addressing the religious sources of antisemitism occupies a principal place in Christian-Jewish relations.

Many Christian scholars and church leaders have worked hard to eradicate all vestiges of anti-Judaism from church life, particularly in teaching, education, music, preaching, and liturgy. Special attention in this regard needs to be given to the interpretation of the Easter story, particularly the Gospel of John. Another essential requirement is a fuller Christian understanding of the rabbinic background of Jesus and the deep Jewish taproots of Christianity, including the historical fact that the only scripture Jesus knew, of course, was the Hebrew Bible.

But as I soon discovered, many Christians believe that Jews and Judaism should have disappeared from history. One of the first Christian leaders

I met described Judaism as a "booster rocket" that was jettisoned once the "main rocket," Christianity, was launched.

A hallmark of my interreligious efforts was to make certain Christians understand that this (mis)understanding of Jews and Judaism has, sadly, provided theological support for a host of destructive images, negative teachings, and obscene comparisons. Judaism was regularly described as a dry, static religion of strict law while Christianity was portrayed as a merciful faith of compassionate love.

And sometimes, depending upon the time and place, the Christian attitude went much further than mere theological contempt and hostility; enter the monstrous "deicide" charge. Deicide, literally the killing of God, proclaimed that the Jews had willfully murdered Jesus of Nazareth. And because of this infamous act, the Jewish people, then, now, and forever are guilty of the great crime of murdering Divinity.

In 1985, Pope John Paul II declared: "Antisemitism ... has been repeatedly condemned by Catholic teaching as incompatible with Christ's teachings ... Where there was ignorance and prejudice ... there is now growing mutual knowledge, appreciation, and respect." He also taught that antisemitism is a "sin against God."

CHAPTER 8

A Romantic Miracle on East 56th Street

THREE MONTHS AFTER beginning my AJC job, I traveled to Alexandria to join my family for the Jewish High Holydays of *Rosh Hashanah* and *Yom Kippur*. It marked the first time in twelve years that I was not leading those annual services. It was a joy to be simply a "Jew in the Pew" sitting in the synagogue with no concerns about the logistics and concerns of mounting a set of special services that mark the Jewish New Year and the Day of Atonement. The High Holydays have been aptly described as the combined "Super Bowl" and "World Series" for rabbis, cantors, choir members, and synagogue support staff.

While in Virginia, a cousin who was teaching in an Alexandria elementary school gave me the name and telephone number of a friend from her Boston University days. She suggested I might "enjoy" meeting Marcia Kaplan. That turned out be a great understatement.

Once back in New York City, I made the required phone call to set up a "blind date." The very pleasant voice on the other end accepted my invitation, and a mutually convenient time and place was arranged.

A complex plan—always a necessity for a Manhattan rendezvous, especially in the years before the advent of mobile phones—was set in motion. Marcia owned a car because she taught Philosophy of Education and History of Religion at William Paterson College in New Jersey and lived not far from the campus. At the appointed time after work—rush hour—I was to "lean against the outside pillar" of the AJC building on East 56th Street as she drove by. Upon recognition, she would stop; I would hop into her small Toyota, and then travel to a nearby restaurant for dinner.

But the carefully constructed plan nearly failed. As Marcia swung by the building, she immediately noticed I was wearing a baggy suit that was a couple of sizes too big for me. I had purchased it at a Champaign low budget clothing store from a clerk who knew even less about men's fashions than I did. Besides being the incorrect size, the garment's color pattern was a horrific muddy brown combined with a series of uncoordinated wandering white stripes.

Marcia took one look at me from her car, shuddered at my lack of taste in clothing, and sped away. But as she still loves to recount: "I thought … wait a minute … I can fix that sartorial disaster … Let's give it a try." The second time around the block forever changed both our lives.

During that evening's dinner I remarked that Marcia did not have a New York City accent. "No" she replied. "I was raised in a small town in Illinois you probably never heard of—Champaign." I almost choked on my food when I heard this incredible coincidence and said: "Never heard of Champaign? I just left that town three months ago after living there for four years!"

Marcia's father, Dr. Max Kaplan, had been a longtime Sociology Professor at the U of I. A few years before my arrival in C-U, he accepted a teaching position at Boston University and the family moved to Newton, Massachusetts. As a faculty daughter, she had free tuition at BU and graduated with high academic honors including membership in Phi Beta Kappa, the prestigious academic honor society.

Following her BU graduation, Marcia earned a joint master's degree in Philosophy of Religion from Columbia University and Union Theological Seminary, neighboring institutions on Manhattan's Morningside Heights.

Adding to our family's folklore was the fact I, a rabbi, proposed marriage in an unusual setting: a Catholic medical center in Paterson, New Jersey, where Marcia was recovering from a bleeding ulcer. We were later married in the synagogue located at 838 Fifth Avenue, then the headquarters of the Reform Jewish movement in the United States. Cyrus Arfa officiated, and the date was July 27, 1969, a week after Neil Armstrong walked on the moon.

But I had romantically beaten Armstrong to the lunar surface. I was living "over the moon" as soon as I stepped away from the pillar on East 56th Street and sat down next to Marcia in her car. Meeting her, a woman both brilliant and beautiful, did two wonderful things for me. They are not necessarily listed in order of importance: she immediately and permanently improved my taste in men's fashion, and she married me. In time, she became the mother of our two also brilliant and beautiful daughters, Eve, a rabbi, and Jennifer, an entertainment talent agent, and we are blessed with our granddaughter Emma.

CHAPTER 9

Roman Catholics and Jews: Fellow Revolutionaries

BECAUSE THE ROMAN Catholic Church is the largest single body of Christians in the United States, numbering some 51 million members, much of my professional work was involved with many Catholic clergy, including two Popes (John Paul II and Benedict XVI), and many Cardinals as well as Church laypeople. And because of history, geography, and demography, the Jewish people have interacted most often and for the longest periods of time with Catholic Christians throughout the world.

Before we can fully comprehend the recent revolutionary changes that have taken place between these two ancient communities, a bit of history is required.

The worldwide Catholic population exceeds one billion. Brazil has more Catholics than any other country in the world, followed by Mexico, the Philippines, and the United States. The term "catholic" means "universal," and the Church is under the spiritual leadership of the bishop of Rome, who by virtue of his position is the supreme pontiff or Pope of the entire Church. The Pope resides in Vatican City, a small independent enclave in Rome—only 109 acres—about one-eighth the size of New York City's Central Park.

There are 196 Catholic dioceses and archdioceses in the United States, each headed by a bishop, and about 17,000 congregations or parishes. The National Conference of Catholic Bishops (NCCB) is headquartered in Washington, DC, along with the US Catholic Conference (USCC). The latter organization deals with the Church's public, educational, and social issues throughout the country and internationally. The former deals with such Church concerns as priestly education and training, liturgy, family life, and ecumenical and interreligious relations.

There are about 265 active Catholic bishops in the United States and approximately 37,000 priests and 31,000 sisters. The latter two numbers are steadily declining.

John F. Kennedy and Joseph R. Biden Jr. are the only Roman Catholics elected to serve as president of the United States. There are many Catholic-related colleges and universities as well as theological seminaries in the US. In addition, there are many Catholic parochial schools that offer instruction from kindergarten through senior high school.

The first immigration of Catholics and Jews to the colonies in America began in the 1600s. Jews arrived in Dutch New Amsterdam (today's New York City) in 1654 from Portuguese Brazil as refugees from the Inquisition which had reached across the Atlantic Ocean from the Iberian Peninsula. The oldest continuous Catholic settlement in the colonies began at St. Mary's, Maryland, in 1634. Maryland became a haven for Catholics who were not welcome in the other British colonies that were dominated by intolerant Protestant Christians.

But it was not until the nineteenth and twentieth centuries that millions of Jews and Catholics came to the United States. In some ways, both communities share recent immigrant experiences. Catholics, mainly from Ireland, Italy, and Poland, began to encounter Jews, often in the same schools, urban neighborhoods, and workplaces. The immigration experience changed some long-held perceptions and stereotypes, but it did not fundamentally alter the basic outlook and teachings about each other that were carried by the new arrivals from Europe.

Mutual suspicion and theological bias kept Jews and Catholics separated and distrustful of one other. At the same time, Catholics and Jews were themselves often victims of prejudice and discrimination in the United States. Recent Roman Catholic immigration to the United States has come from Latin America and the Caribbean, while Jewish newcomers to America are increasingly from the former Soviet Union, Iran, and Israel.

The revolutionary change in Catholic-Jewish relations began in 1965 at the conclusion of the Second Vatican Council in Rome. The world's Catholic bishops issued the landmark *Nostra Aetate* Declaration, an authoritative Catholic teaching that repudiated the false belief that Jews are guilty of deicide. *Nostra Aetate* also specifically condemned antisemitism, and it called for "mutual understanding and respect which is the fruit, above all, of biblical and theological studies as well as fraternal dialogues."

In 1966, the NCCB established a Secretariat for Catholic-Jewish Relations whose first director was the Rev. Edward H. Flannery, and he was succeeded by Dr. Eugene J. Fisher. Both men were my cherished and highly capable colleagues for many years.

There is also a Pontifical Commission for Religious Relations with the Jews based in Vatican City. Since the Second Vatican Council concluded, there have been many important follow-up Roman Catholic statements and declarations.

Chief among them are three official Vatican documents on Catholic-Jewish relations: the 1975 "Guidelines" and the 1985 "Notes" that augmented *Nostra Aetate* by presenting specific guidelines and goals for Catholic teachings. In 1998, the Vatican issued "We Remember: A Reflection on the *Shoah*," a document that focused on the Holocaust. The "Catechism of the Catholic Church," published in English in 1994, also contains significant material on Catholic-Jewish relations.

As a result of the breakthrough achieved with *Nostra Aetate*, there have been more positive encounters between Catholics and Jews than there were in the first 1900 years of the Church, a fact dramatically symbolized by Pope John Paul II's visit to the Great Synagogue in Rome in 1986 and his 2000 visit to Israel. Both the synagogue visit and the journey to the Jewish state were positive "game changers" for the Catholic Church and its often-hostile relationship with Jews and Judaism.

One of the notable positive achievements of improved Catholic-Jewish relations was the establishment of full and formal Vatican-Israel diplomatic relations in June 1994. This action normalized relations between the Roman Catholic Church and the Jewish people throughout the world, and it closed the chapter on an important unresolved issue of the dialogue.

But flashpoints continue to occur between Catholics and Jews, as well as among other Christian groups and the Jewish community. When the Auschwitz convent controversy first erupted in the mid-1980s, a group of European Jewish and Catholic leaders jointly agreed that the Carmelite convent established in 1984 inside the death camp's theater where Nazis stored the poison gas used to murder more than 1.5 million Jewish victims of the Holocaust—should be moved to new quarters away from the original death camp structure. Although the crisis escalated and strained Catholic-Jewish bonds throughout the world, the controversy was satisfactorily resolved in 1993 thanks to Pope John Paul II's direct intervention and the strength and effectiveness of Catholic-Jewish relations that had been carefully nurtured for over twenty years.

The Carmelite convent was ultimately moved to a new building—an interreligious center—just outside the death camp. I had the honor of speaking there several times during my career.

In January 1991, the Polish Catholic bishops issued a pastoral letter that was read in every Catholic church in Poland. Among other notable things, the statement strongly condemned antisemitism and asked forgiveness from the Jewish community for anti-Jewish acts that were carried out by Polish Catholics during World War II. My friend and colleague Archbishop Henryk Muszynski, the Primate Emeritus of Poland, was the driving force and principal author of that important constructive statement.

In a twist of history, I was his house guest when he was the bishop of Wloclawek, a city forty miles west of Warsaw on the Vistula River. During the Nazi occupation of Poland, the Germans converted the bishop's residence in that city into the Gestapo headquarters for the region. During my visits to Wloclawek, Archbishop Muszynski made certain I slept in the bedroom that had been the Gestapo chief's private quarters: it was a bittersweet historical moment for a rabbi.

In 1990 at a meeting of the International Jewish-Catholic Liaison Committee (ILC) in Prague, Cardinal Edward Cassidy, the then Vatican leader in charge of global Catholic-Jewish relations, expressed the need for *teshuva*, or repentance, toward Jews on the part of the Roman Catholic Church. In 2004, the Vatican reaffirmed its commitment to the State of Israel, calling on Catholics to repudiate all forms and expressions of anti-Zionism which it termed a form of antisemitism.

Since the Second Vatican Council, thousands of lay Catholics and Jews have participated in intensive "living room dialogues" throughout the United States. Many of those have been cosponsored by the American Jewish Committee in cooperation with appropriate Catholic partners. Such dialogues need to be intensified and broadened.

However, I am concerned that the historic advances in Catholic-Jewish relations achieved since 1965 may be minimized or even marginalized as both communities turn inward to address their unique problems and issues. Indeed, for many young Catholics and Jews, both clergy and lay, there is a sense that all the work in interreligious relations has been completed.

In addition, there is also a sense that there has been limited, even negligible, implementation of *Nostra Aetate* and subsequent positive Church teachings on Jews and Judaism at the local level within the Catholic community. A common perception is that despite the extraordinary statements, declarations, and preaching and teaching guidelines, too little is known inside Catholic seminaries and churches about the recent advances in Catholic-Jewish relations.

The American Jewish Committee, the Archdiocese of Los Angeles, and the Southern California Board of Rabbis have done significant work in Catholic-Jewish relations. They have published excellent joint statements on such themes as abortion, caring for the dying person, the single-parent family, the nuclear weapons reality, chemical dependency and addiction, the Holocaust, the common good, and salvation/redemption. There have been other joint Catholic-Jewish statements in the United States dealing with moral values in education, pornography, and a condemnation of Holocaust denial and historical revisionism.

Catholics and Jews will always differ on deeply held theological beliefs, and much of the American Jewish community differs with Catholic leaders on some church-state issues such as public funding of parochial schools, including vouchers or financial assistance to parents of such students. But increasingly, the two ancient faith communities are working together on a host of social justice concerns, including racism, immigration, world peace, bioethics, and human rights. There is also serious Catholic-Jewish work going on in the sensitive and important areas of health care, church-state relations, and public morality.

One of the proudest achievements of my career came in 1998 when the American Jewish Committee joined with Saint Leo University to establish the Center for Catholic-Jewish Studies on the campus of the University located north of Tampa, Florida. The founding agreement was signed by Bruce M. Ramer, the AJC's president, and Dr. Arthur Kirk Jr., SLU's president.

Joining Ramer and Kirk were Bishop Robert Lynch of the Saint Petersburg, Florida diocese. SLU is a Benedictine school founded in 1889. Many Catholic and Jewish laypeople of the region as well as local priests and rabbis have contributed to the Center's growth and success.

While there are about thirty academic centers of Christian-Jewish relations in the United States, before 1998 none existed south of Baltimore, Maryland. At the same time, the state of Florida continues to experience the rapid growth of both Jews and Catholics as more and more Americans become residents of what is currently America's third largest state in population. Dr. Matthew Tapie is the CCJS Director as well as a tenured member of the University's theology department.

At the graduate level, the CCJS teaches the History and Theology of Catholic-Jewish Relations. The students include priests, deacons, and Master of Arts theology students.

And at the undergraduate level, courses focus on learning World Religions through dialogue. They conclude with introducing Saint Leo students to basic knowledge and skills of interreligious leadership.

Since 1999, the Center for Catholic-Jewish Studies' Eternal Light Award is presented to a scholar or interreligious leader who has made outstanding contributions to Catholic-Jewish relations, and it is one of the most prestigious awards in the world of Catholic-Jewish relations.

Eternal Light Award recipients include: Professor Jan Karski, the Rev. John Pawlikowski, Rabbi Irving Greenberg, Professor Deborah Lipstadt, Bishop John J. Nevins, Rabbi Sanford Saperstein, Cardinal William Keeler, Rabbi A. James Rudin, Professor James Buchanan, Rabbi Abie Ingber, Professor William Madges, Dr. Amy-Jill Levine, Dr. Arthur F. Kirk Jr., Dr. Mary C. Boys, Rabbi Abraham Skorka, Dr. Philip Cunningham, Dr. Ruth Langer, Sister Celia M. Deutsch, and Rabbi David Novak.

In addition, the Center hosts local rabbis as visiting faculty who teach Judaism to hundreds of Saint Leo students. The CCJS leads workshops on Catholic-Jewish relations for diaconate continuing education programs in the Diocese of St. Petersburg, Florida, and in the Diocese of Charleston, South Carolina. All of this means Judaism is accurately taught and respect for Judaism is cultivated among thousands of students in a world where religion is sometimes neglected as a field of academic study.

The CCJS and other Christian-Jewish centers guarantee that the significant gains in interreligious relations are anchored at academic institutions and are not allowed to become merely beautifully worded documents, statements, and declarations. It is imperative that college and university students gain knowledge of the remarkable gains in this area so that they too will become participants in the effort to build mutual respect between Jews and Christians.

For more than four decades, I have been privileged to work closely on a myriad of issues with many cherished Catholic partners. They include the Rev. Edward H. Flannery, Dr. Eugene J. Fisher, the Rev. John T. Pawlikowski of the Catholic Theological Union in Chicago, the Rev. Dennis McManus of Georgetown University, Sister Dr. Mary Boys of Union Theological Seminary, Sister Dr. Rose Thering of Seton Hall University, Professor Thomas Bird of Queens College, Sister Gloria Coleman of the Philadelphia Coordinating Council on the Holocaust, Sister Ann Gillen of the National Interreligious Task Force on Soviet Jewry, Sister Margaret Traxler of the National Coalition of American Nuns, the Rev. Dr. Lawrence Frizzell of Seton Hall University, Dr. Leonard Swidler of Temple University, Dr. Elena Procario-Foley of Iona College, Dr. Philip Cunningham of Saint Joseph's University, Dr. Matthew Tapie of Saint Leo University, Dr. Carol Rittner of Stockton University, Dr. Eva Fleischner of Montclair University, Dr. Richard Lux of Marquette University, Sister Ann Patrick Ware of the National Council of Churches, and so many more men and women who have helped transform Catholic-Jewish relations.

But I want to pay special tribute to three American Cardinals who early on grasped the meaning and the challenge of *Nostra Aetate*: Cardinal Joseph Bernardin of Chicago, Cardinal William Keeler of Baltimore, and Cardinal John O'Connor of New York. Sadly, they are gone from our midst, but they have left a host of imperishable permanent achievements. They were my constant guides, warm friends, and superb mentors. The trio left a rich legacy of Catholic-Jewish relations for later generations to study and emulate.

As the AJC's Interreligious Affairs Director, I was joined by a number of outstanding associates and colleagues including Judith Banki, Rabbi Jody Cohen, Rabbi Lori Forman, Benita Gayle-Almeleh, Inge Lederer Gibel, Rabbi Alan Mittleman, and Dr. Amy Rosenbaum.

I owe special thanks to Shulamith Bahat who served for many years as the AJC's Associate National Director. It was Shula who first sent me to Poland in 1989, just as the Communist regime was collapsing and the Solidarity movement came to power in Warsaw. In 2000 she immediately understood the importance of Pope John Paul II's visit to Israel. She made certain I would be present in her native Israel to witness firsthand a significant and never-to-be-repeated moment in Catholic-Jewish relations.

I made many personal trips to the Vatican during my career. Most of the time, such occasions were serious events and quite formal in nature. But in 1998, during my final official AJC visit to Rome, "a funny thing happened on the way" to meeting with Pope John Paul II. My wife captured that moment in her brilliant remembrance of our three nights at the Vatican:

> *I will always have memories of the three nights I spent in St. Martha's House (Domus Sanctae Marthae) inside the Vatican Gates near St. Peter's Basilica. The cardinals who come to Rome to elect a new Pope sleep at St. Martha's, a facility built especially for such an occasion as well as for visits by prelates and other important church officials and guests. Before St. Martha's was built*

in 1996, the cardinals journeying to Rome to elect a Pope slept on cots in the Sistine Chapel.

The beautiful building inside Vatican City is five stories high and has 106 suites, 22 single rooms, and one apartment. There is a lovely lobby with a majestic winding staircase and a very large bar. It cost $20 million in 1996 dollars. The facility is operated by the Daughters of Charity of St. Vincent De Paul, and it replaced St. Martha's Hospice built in 1891.

What was a nice Jewish girl like me doing in a place like St. Martha's House? In March of 1998, my husband, Rabbi James Rudin, who was Director of Interreligious Affairs for the American Jewish Committee, led a delegation of about forty rabbis, academicians, Protestant and Catholic theologians, and Archbishops, and our host in Rome was Cardinal William Cardinal Keeler of Baltimore. We came to the Vatican to meet with Pope John Paul II. A few wives came on the trip. One of the wives, Julia Walsh Cunningham, stayed with her husband, Dr. Philip Cunningham of Saint Joseph's University in Philadelphia, in St. Martha's, as did I.

Julia and I were apparently the first women to stay in this facility, completed only two years before our arrival. We heard that the housekeeping staff—all nuns—was very upset that women would be sleeping in St. Martha's. To make matters worse, one of these intruders was a Jew!

Others at the Vatican were apparently also nervous about a feminine presence there because at dinner on our first night one of our hosts gave a speech no doubt directed towards Julia and me asking us to please behave decorously at all times while at St. Martha's. Did he mean we should refrain from making mad, passionate love in our bedrooms, screaming in ecstasy during our magnificent orgasms? Or perhaps refrain from running through the corridors in our bikinis or, even worse, in the nude?

Neither Julia nor I would look good in a bikini and even worse wearing nothing, so we shared a hearty laugh over those possibilities. The Swiss Guards who inspected our passes necessary to enter Vatican City to access St. Martha's House also seemed startled that women were given permission to enter the Holy See's inner sanctum.

Jim and I were assigned a suite in St. Martha's overlooking a lovely garden court. The second room was a small bedroom with, of course, its own bathroom. The entry room was a living area with a beautiful oak desk and chair. What most impressed me was an entire oak-paneled wall in that room containing floor-to-ceiling closets. These closets were necessary, one of the archbishops explained to me, so the prelates could hang their long robes and other elaborate vestments without creasing them.

We left St. Martha's after meeting Pope John Paul II twice, once in a private meeting in a gold-laden room in the Vatican. Julia Walsh Cunningham and I did not disgrace ourselves during our stay there.

However, about a week after our visit, one of the young Swiss guards murdered another in their headquarters at Vatican City, apparently a gay love affair gone wrong. Some of my friends swear to this day the scandalous murder was a result of the bad Karma generated by two women sleeping in St. Martha's House.

I want to focus especially on the life, career, and achievements of my very close personal friend: Cardinal O'Connor. This is because he shattered many of the popular stereotypes about Catholics who successfully engage with Jews and Judaism. One stereotype is the belief that Catholics involved in building positive relations with the Jewish community always hold progressive theological beliefs.

Indeed, that is what many Catholics and Jews initially believed about Cardinal John O'Connor's religious views, but they were wrong ... very wrong. Although O'Connor was a major leader in strengthening the bonds of friendship and solidarity between Catholics and Jews, on many other issues he was a strong religious conservative. That fact alone makes O'Connor's significant achievements more remarkable and gives the lie to the idea that only religious progressives or liberals can build mutual respect and understanding between Christians and Jews.

During his tenure as Archbishop of New York (1984–2000), O'Connor was America's most prominent Catholic leader as well as being an outspoken and unwavering supporter of Vatican policies. He was appointed to his ecclesiastical post by Pope John Paul II, a man born in 1920, the same year as O'Connor. But their shared age was only the starting point of a close personal friendship that endured for nearly 20 years.

O'Connor defended his Church's opposition to abortion, homosexual marriages, capital punishment, divorce, contraception, and sex education. The Cardinal, like his papal friend at the Vatican, also supported celibacy within the priesthood and rejected the idea of either married or female Catholic clergy.

But O'Connor's faithful allegiance to the basic positions of Roman Catholicism is but one part of his record. As Archbishop of New York, he also strongly supported the trade union movement, demanded a decent minimum wage for workers, and pressed for equal employment opportunities for all workers regardless of religion, race, or ethnic identity.

O'Connor and the Archdiocese's many institutions aided and gave succor to AIDS victims and offered New York's African Americans increased access to Catholic parochial schools even though most of that student community was not Catholic.

Despite his years as a high-ranking US Navy military chaplain, when O'Connor retired from the service as a Rear Admiral, he was not a priestly "rubber stamp" for massive military spending. In fact, he was a critic of many conventional military ideas, and O'Connor publicly questioned the morality of using nuclear weapons on civilian targets.

Like many other people who gained international fame and recognition in New York City, O'Connor was born somewhere else and came to the Big Apple later in his life. The future Cardinal O'Connor was born in Philadelphia on January 15, 1920, about one-hundred miles south of Manhattan's Saint Patrick's Cathedral, the site of O'Connor's sermons as New York's Archbishop and the location of his burial crypt beneath the cathedral's altar following his death on May 3, 2000.

John Joseph was the fourth of five children born to Thomas and Dorothy Gomble O'Connor. His father, a painter in the building construction business, was a lifelong member and advocate of labor unions, a belief the Cardinal carried with him his entire life. Indeed, in 1986 during a Labor Day Mass at Saint Patrick's, O'Connor declared: "[S]o many of our freedoms in this country, so much of the building up of society, is precisely attributable to the union movement, a movement that I personally will defend despite the weakness of some of its members, despite the corruption with which we are all familiar that pervades all society, a movement that I personally will defend with my life."

Fourteen years after his death, O'Connor's sister revealed the fact that their mother was Jewish but converted to Catholicism years before her son John was born. As a 10-year-old, John suffered a major trauma when his mother was temporarily blinded for a year. Even though Dorothy O'Connor's sight returned, her affliction and suffering sensitized the youngster to the special needs of the physically disabled, and this cause became one of O'Connor's lifelong commitments.

John O'Connor attended a public elementary school in Philadelphia, but later transferred to West Catholic High School for Boys. When he was 16, O'Connor entered Philadelphia's Catholic seminary, St. Charles Borromeo, and was ordained in 1945 at age 25. Because he was a divinity student during World War II, O'Connor was exempt from serving in America's military.

His first years after seminary were typical for many young Catholic clergy of the post-war era. It was a time of rapid Catholic growth and newly ordained priests frequently were given multiple assignments. O'Connor served a parish as an assistant pastor and also taught parochial high school classes in Chester, Pennsylvania, a city near Philadelphia.

After seven years of such work, everything changed for O'Connor in 1952 during the Korean War when Cardinal Francis Spellman, the prelate in charge of the United States Catholic military chaplaincy, issued a call for more priests to join the American armed forces. The 32-year-old Philadelphian responded to Spellman's request, and O'Connor became a Navy chaplain, a career that lasted 27 years.

During that time, O'Connor served in both Washington, DC, and at sea on a guided missile cruiser. Because the US Marine Corps is a combat-only fighting organization, all its support services are provided by the Navy, including medical staff, lawyers, and chaplains. In 1964, O'Connor saw combat duty with the Third Marine Division in Vietnam, where he earned a Legion of Merit citation and warm praise from Marine General Lewis W. Walt: "It is my opinion that no single individual in this command contributed more to the morale of the individual Marine here in Vietnam than Father O'Connor, who spent the majority of his time in the field with the men."

Like many other military chaplains during the 1960s—Catholic, Jewish and Protestant—O'Connor initially supported the US military involvement in the Vietnam War, although years later he changed his position. He was not alone in turning away from the American war effort in Southeast Asia. Other chaplains of that era, including myself, went through a similar process, but O'Connor's was one of the more publicized reversals because he had written a book in 1964 defending the US military intervention in Vietnam. However, years later he said: "That's a bad book, you know. It was a very limited view of what was going on. I regret having published it."

Following his tour of duty in Vietnam, O'Connor earned a master's degree in ethics and psychology at the Catholic University of America and a doctorate in political science from Georgetown University. One of his instructors at Georgetown was Dr. Jeanne Kirkpatrick, who later served as the US Ambassador to the United Nations between 1981 and 1985 in the George H.W. Bush Administration. In 1972, O'Connor was appointed Senior Chaplain at the US Naval Academy in Annapolis, the first Catholic to hold that position since the Academy's founding in 1845.

In 1975, thirty years after becoming a priest, O'Connor was named Chief of Navy Chaplains and promoted to the rank of Rear Admiral. He retired from the Navy in 1979, and by then, because of his long military experience and his advanced degrees, O'Connor had gained the attention of the leadership of the United States Conference of Catholic Bishops. In the same year, he was consecrated as a bishop and was assigned the same position held by Spellman a quarter century earlier: overseeing Catholic chaplains in the US armed forces.

In 1980, O'Connor became a member of a five-person committee comprising American bishops that was headed by Cardinal Joseph Bernardin of Chicago. The committee's task was difficult and controversial: it was instructed to draft a pastoral letter, that is, a Roman Catholic public statement, on the subject of nuclear arms, and the ethics and morality of using such weapons. O'Connor was an excellent choice because he was the only member of the five-person drafting committee who had served in the military and had actually experienced wartime combat.

His appointment to the drafting committee caused consternation among antinuclear Catholics, including some fellow bishops, who labeled Admiral O'Connor a "hawk" on arms limitation, nuclear warheads, and the role of the military. Critics worried whether O'Connor truly represented the Church's commitment to the cause of peace itself. They also fretted that O'Connor, because of his personal involvement with the military, might overly influence the other members of the drafting committee. It was a misplaced anxiety; they did not need to worry about O'Connor.

In May 1983, after several years of extensive debate and deliberation, the American bishops formally approved a lengthy pastoral letter of sixty-four tightly worded pages that included 127 footnotes, many of them citing the teachings of John Paul II. The document attacked the use of nuclear weapons against civilian populations and asserted that such horrific weapons could only be employed as deterrents and should not be used in an offensive way.

Although nearly forty years have passed since the document was adopted, and it has been more than thirty years since the end of the Cold War with the former Soviet Union, the pastoral letter entitled "The Challenge of Peace" has stood the test of time, even in the current age of asymmetrical warfare that takes place between established nation-states and amorphous decentralized terrorist foes.

O'Connor's colleagues agreed he had been a constructive member of the drafting committee because by the early 1980s, the former Navy chaplain and Vietnam veteran had moved away from his earlier pro-military stance. Like any good chaplain, O'Connor always expressed public admiration and support for the men and women in the armed forces, but during the last decades of his life he became a critic of America's interventions in many parts of the world including the Contra guerilla campaign in Nicaragua, the missile attacks in Afghanistan, and the US bombings of Kosovo in the Balkans.

Because of his important work in the creation of "The Challenge of Peace," O'Connor was called to a meeting in Rome with Pope John Paul II in 1983, and it is clear the two men quickly discovered they shared many similar values and interests. Not only were they almost the exact same age, but they were both spiritual conservatives with warm winning personalities that appealed to many people, including those outside the Church who did not share the religious beliefs or views of the two Catholic leaders.

John Paul II and O'Connor were religious conservatives who were aware of and open to the pluralistic world of the late twentieth century. Both were able to build human bridges of solidarity with Jews while maintaining impeccable Catholic credentials. It was a unique combination that benefited the cause of improved Christian-Jewish relations.

Not long after his meeting with O'Connor, the Pope appointed him Bishop of the Diocese of Scranton, Pennsylvania, a hardscrabble economically depressed area with a large Catholic population that is perhaps best known today as the birthplace in 1942 of Joseph Biden.

Scranton marked a kind of homecoming for the Philadelphia-born O'Connor, who was formally installed in his new position on May 6, 1983. Three months later, Cardinal Terence Cooke (1921–1983), the Archbishop of New York, publicly announced he had a terminal case of leukemia, and on October 6, he died at the age of 62.

O'Connor always liked to tell people, including myself, that after nearly thirty years in the Navy, he had been content to finish his priestly career as the bishop of Scranton. At least that's what he said to his frequently gullible listeners. But the Vatican had been aware of Cooke's deadly illness since it was first diagnosed in 1965, and it is likely John Paul II had his new American friend in mind to succeed Cooke when the time came to choose a new Archbishop of New York.

As it turned out, O'Connor was Scranton's Bishop for only eight and a half months before being called to New York in early 1984. When in May 1985, he received his cardinal's red hat in a Vatican ceremony, John O'Connor had reached another pinnacle in his career: first as a Rear Admiral and Chief of US Navy Chaplains with an earned academic doctorate and then as a member of the Roman Catholic College of Cardinals.

At age 65, the age when many Americans retire and start to collect monthly Social Security benefits and enter the Medicare health program, O'Connor was only beginning the most important part of his life—the sixteen-year period between 1984 and 2000 when his legacy would be permanently shaped. It was a tumultuous decade and a half that transformed him, his Church, and Catholic-Jewish relations.

Looking back, more than twenty years after his death and before the mists of legend envelop the record and achievements of Cardinal John O'Connor, it is important to note that two factors in his life and career played major roles in preparing him for his extraordinary work in building positive Catholic-Jewish relations and making real the hopes and ideals of the Second Vatican Council and its historic 1965 Declaration, *Nostra Aetate*, that addressed the Church's tangled troubled relations with Jews and Judaism.

The first factor was an obvious one: because of his military career, O'Connor knew Jewish men and women as actual human beings and not as an archaic ancient "Old Testament" people nor as a metaphysical/theological construct devoid of flesh and blood reality. Many of the Navy personnel he worked with, including other chaplains, were Jews.

Jews had lived in the Philadelphia area in the years before 1682 when it became a proprietary colony of William Penn and his family. The city's historic Sephardic (Spanish Portuguese) Synagogue, *Mikveh Israel* ["The Hope of Israel"], was formally established in 1782. One of the congregation's best-known early members was the Polish-born Haym Solomon (1740–1785), who was a strong supporter of the American War of Independence against Britain and a friend of many leaders of the new nation.

Like other American cities in the Northeast and the Midwest, Philadelphia's Jewish population greatly expanded in the four decades between 1882—the era of harsh discriminatory antisemitic laws and lethal *Pogroms* in Czarist Russia—and 1924—the passage of a restrictive American immigration law.

It is estimated that over 200,000 Jews lived in Philadelphia in 1920 when O'Connor was born, and the number was even larger a few years later when the young O'Connor attended public elementary school with Jewish classmates. The city's largest concentration of Jews at that time was in West Philadelphia, the location of O'Connor's Catholic high school.

Such demographic facts are sometimes overlooked, but they should not be minimized. While the Jewish and Catholic communities of that era frequently lived in close-knit communities amongst themselves and often in a hostile co-existence with one another, both faith communities suffered discrimination and bigotry from the established Protestant community that controlled and dominated the "City of Brotherly Love."

The second factor was O'Connor's long career in the US Navy where he served men and women of all religious persuasions as well as those who professed no specific religious identity. He had years of contact with members of many faith communities including Jews, all of whom were often thrown together in combat situations, a rare experience for any clergyperson. Religious pluralism was not a sociological theory or an abstract concept for O'Connor. It was what he experienced on a regular basis during his twenty-seven-year military chaplaincy.

A Philadelphia childhood and a long Navy career provided excellent preparation for his years as Archbishop of New York, the city with America's largest Jewish community. It was in that white-hot religious and political arena where O'Connor exhibited the head and heart that made him a major leader in Christian-Jewish relations.

O'Connor's commitment to the survival and security of the State of Israel, his understanding of the evil of the Holocaust, and support for the freedom of Soviet Jewry were dominant in his life. Antisemitism, hatred of Jews and Judaism, was for O'Connor not simply an ugly example of bigotry and prejudice, but rather, it was an affront to the Catholic faith. The Cardinal often told me, sometimes with a twinkle in his eyes, of the hate mail he received whenever he denounced antisemitism from the pulpit as he often did at Sunday services. The hostile letters were an indication he had struck a nerve among Catholics, and he was pleased to have goaded members of his flock.

When O'Connor became Archbishop, he used the electronic and print media to establish himself as a refreshing new personality in a celebrity-crazed city. He conducted weekly news conferences at St. Patrick's every Sunday following Mass, a practice he continued until 1990. Because O'Connor was witty and articulate, he and the sophisticated New York City media were made for each other. His off-the-cuff style contrasted with his predecessor, Terence Cooke, who shunned the public spotlight as much as O'Connor reveled in the center ring of New York's media circus.

The O'Connor era started well, especially when he stood on the front steps of Saint Patrick's Cathedral to personally welcome the thousands of marchers who paraded down Fifth Avenue each spring on behalf of Soviet Jewry. Although it was a simple gesture of solidarity with the international and interreligious movement to bring freedom to the Jews in the Soviet Union, it was widely recognized as a sign of the Cardinal's support for the cause.

But when O'Connor publicly equated abortion with the six million Jewish victims of the Holocaust, a firestorm of criticism immediately erupted. He compounded his public relations problems during the 1984 election campaign when he vigorously criticized two pro-choice Catholic political leaders: New York's Governor Mario Cuomo and Representative Geraldine Ferraro, the Democratic vice-presidential candidate. Both held pro-choice views on abortion.

At first, I dismissed O'Connor's Holocaust analogy as hyperbole. While the inappropriate analogy was painful to hear, I believed it would soon disappear from O'Connor's rhetorical arsenal. But I was wrong.

The Cardinal repeated the analogy, and the intense criticism ultimately resulted in a critical editorial in The New York Times. Because O'Connor was America's premier Catholic leader, his linkage of abortion with the Holocaust angered the Jewish community. Even Orthodox rabbis who frequently agreed with O'Connor's anti-abortion stance were offended.

Holocaust survivors sensed something ominous, even threatening behind the buoyant smiling O'Connor persona: for many survivors, he was an Americanized version of the antisemitic bishops they had encountered in Europe prior to and during World War II.

As the American Jewish Committee's Interreligious Affairs Director, I became concerned about the abortion-Holocaust link not only because it was inaccurate, but because it negatively affected Catholic-Jewish relations. The new Archbishop was arousing tensions, and I believed something had to be done to prevent permanent damage to those relations.

The opportunity to act came in 1984 during a private dinner at which O'Connor was introduced to Protestant clergy and rabbis active in interreligious activities. The otherwise friendly evening turned tense when the topic of linkage between abortion and the Holocaust was raised.

Several Christians and Jews at the dinner believed such a connection overloaded the compassion circuits, causing anger and confusion. One Protestant minister urged O'Connor to focus solely on abortion and not pair it with the Holocaust: "You are blurring two important issues." The Cardinal replied that such an analogy helped draw attention to the increasing number of abortions in the nation, a trend he abhorred.

At dinner's end, I had a private conversation with O'Connor. I mentioned my own military service as a United States Air Force chaplain in Japan and Korea where a highlight of that experience was the mutual respect that existed among chaplains of various religions. Because military chaplains work in close quarters, collegiality, consultation, and shared goals are imperative.

O'Connor replied that Navy chaplains serving at sea also depended upon one another for cooperation and friendship. I suggested that New York City was similar to a large military base with many religious, ethnic, and racial groups. Mutual respect and understanding were necessary if New York was to survive as a world-class city and a positive symbol of the remarkable American experiment in religious liberty and pluralism.

The Cardinal nodded his head in approval, and then spoke about the Holocaust with emotion. While in the Navy, he had been traumatized by a visit he had made to the Nazi concentration camp in Dachau, near Munich. That confrontation with radical evil "changed my life forever," he told me. It was a theme he came back to many times.

O'Connor was gripped by the horrors of the Holocaust, a genocide carried out by baptized Christians in the heart of "civilized" Europe. It was a feeling also shared by John Paul II who personally witnessed the Holocaust as a young man when his native country, Poland, was occupied by the Germans during World War II.

During our conversation, I told O'Connor his analogy connecting abortion with the Holocaust was particularly hurtful to Holocaust survivors. Abortion is a matter of choice, however painful or regrettable. The murdered Jewish victims during the Holocaust had no choice. They were killed solely because they were Jews. I remember O'Connor's immediate response: "I would never want to harm the survivors in any way!" I urged O'Connor to "detach" his concerns and focus on abortion without attaching them to the Holocaust, and I used a military phrase we both understood: "Fight a two-front war."

O'Connor thanked me for the "advice and counsel." I thought he was merely being polite, but as later events proved, that dinner encounter was the "start of a beautiful friendship." Over the next sixteen years we often sought out one another for "advice and counsel" on many issues involving Catholics and Jews.

Shortly after that dinner, O'Connor quietly abandoned the Holocaust-abortion equation in his public speeches, including sermons. His critics—they were always numerous—believed he was simply being expedient. Perhaps. But I believe our one-on-one conversation helped shape O'Connor's private thinking and public advocacy. He never weakened his anti-abortion position, and at the same time he became a passionate champion of Holocaust education and remembrance. He did "fight a two-front war."

A few weeks after our private conversation, Cardinal O'Connor accepted my invitation to speak at the American Jewish Committee's 1984 annual meeting in Manhattan.

It was O'Connor's first public appearance before a major Jewish organization since becoming New York's Catholic leader earlier that year. In his address, he denounced antisemitism and expressed his personal pain about the Holocaust. Many AJC members in the audience were surprised by O'Connor's openness, charm, and his visceral hatred of antisemitism, but I was not. I already knew that O'Connor intended to make constructive Catholic-Jewish relations a centerpiece of his work as Archbishop.

A year later, in October 1985, O'Connor and I were keynote speakers at a convocation in New York City's Temple Emanu-El marking the twentieth anniversary of the *Nostra Aetate* Declaration. O'Connor began his formal remarks by reading a prepared text a staff member had written. After ten minutes into the unimaginative speech, O'Connor literally tossed away his typewritten text and announced, "Enough of that. Now I want to really talk from my heart about Catholics and Jews."

O'Connor's ad-lib remarks stirred the audience of nearly 3,000 as he spoke of the immense debt Christians owed to Jews and Judaism, and he declared one "cannot be a faithful Christian and an anti-Semite. They are incompatible because antisemitism is a sin."

In June 1987, our friendship was again tested and strengthened when Pope John Paul II received Kurt Waldheim, the president of Austria, at the Vatican with full diplomatic honors. At the time, the Austrian leader and former United Nations Secretary General was living under an ugly public shadow because he had deliberately hidden his World War II record as a

German officer in the Balkans. Waldheim was charged with being involved in the mass murder of Jews and Eastern Orthodox Christians.

Because he had lied about his record for decades, the American government had placed him on its watch list and barred him from entry into the United States. The warm Vatican welcome for Waldheim displeased many Jewish and Catholic leaders, including O'Connor.

At the time of the Waldheim visit to the Vatican, I was in Hamburg, Germany, participating in an international Lutheran-Jewish conference. One night, while soundly asleep in my hotel room, the phone rang. Thinking the caller was someone from the front desk, I lifted the receiver and in a groggy voice mumbled, "Hullo."

"Sorry if I woke you," said the familiar voice with the distinct Philadelphia accent. "Jim, I really wish you were in New York now. You could be of big help to me with the problems created by the Waldheim visit. You know, the Holy Father is planning to come to the United States in three months and plans to meet with Jewish leaders in Miami. The fallout from Waldheim's visit is all bad. It might even cancel the Pope's meeting. When are you coming back? We need you here."

O'Connor expressed his pleasure when I replied: "In two days." He continued the surprising trans-Atlantic conversation, telling me he did not understand the lavish Vatican reception for Waldheim. With some laughter, he said: "I intend to take it up with my friends at the Vatican." Whenever O'Connor said those words, I knew he meant only one "friend" in Rome: Pope John Paul II.

The Cardinal told me the Pope was also planning to visit Austria in the near future. I joked: "It's like a home and home sports event. First Waldheim comes to the Vatican, and then the Pope flies to Austria." I offered one specific suggestion: "I know the Pope will visit the Mauthausen death camp near Linz, where thousands of Jews died. When he goes there, Waldheim must not accompany him, even if he is the Austrian president. The TV and photo images of the two men walking together would be a disaster. When the Pope goes, he should visit the camp alone."

O'Connor liked the suggestion and said he would mention it to his "friends" in Rome, and apparently that is what he did. Waldheim did not escort John Paul II to the death camp in Austria, and the solo visit to Mauthausen along with the Pope's meeting at Castel Gandolfo with Jewish leaders that summer eased the tensions created by the Waldheim visit. In September 1987, John Paul II had a successful meeting in Miami that was attended by several hundred American Jewish representatives, including myself.

I remember the other times the Cardinal and I worked together on the critical issues faced by our two communities. Our friendship was a concrete result of the Second Vatican Council.

Nostra Aetate urged Catholics to develop "mutual respect and knowledge" about Jews and Judaism, but it still required dedicated leaders like O'Connor to make the document come alive as a dynamic force within Catholicism. Without such leadership, the positive work of the Second Vatican Council regarding Jews and Judaism could easily have been relegated to the dustbins of history.

The extraordinary efforts of so many Catholic and Jewish leaders could have been erased because of inaction and indifference on the part of Catholic leaders.

In November of 1988, the Cardinal spoke at a New York City synagogue commemorating the fiftieth anniversary of the *Kristallnacht* Pogrom in Germany and Austria when, in a single night, hundreds of synagogues were burned, and Jewish-owned stores and shops were destroyed to the sound of shattered glass windows. During *Kristallnacht*, thousands of Jews were arrested and placed in concentration camps. It marked the beginning of mass violence and murder against Jews living under Nazi rule or occupation.

In his address a half century after those terrible events, O'Connor acknowledged that centuries of systematic anti-Jewish Christian teachings helped provide the poisonous seedbed for Nazism. He did not flinch from the truth or attempt to pass the blame for Nazism away from traditional Christianity and lay it instead on paganism.

On December 31, 1993, forty-five years after Israeli independence, the Jewish State and the Holy See finally set in motion the process that ultimately led six months later to full and formal diplomatic relations. To celebrate the occasion, O'Connor invited Jewish and Catholic leaders to his Manhattan residence on Madison Avenue located behind Saint Patrick's. For more than nine years, the Cardinal had spent many hours in private, off-the-record meetings in his spacious living room as part of his campaign to bring about the establishment of formal diplomatic relations between the Vatican and the State of Israel, linking Rome, the Eternal City, with Jerusalem, the Holy City. It was widely known that O'Connor repeatedly pressed this issue with his Vatican "friend," Pope John Paul II, each time he traveled to the Vatican.

At the Cardinal's residence, the Cardinal asked me to offer a New Year's toast to celebrate the accord that had been announced a few days earlier. Raising a glass of champagne, I called O'Connor "the chief architect" of Vatican-Israel diplomatic relations, but after the toast was concluded, O'Connor modestly demurred from my words of praise. With a sly smile, the Cardinal said: "No, no, Jim. The Pope deserves the credit." Of course, we were both right.

In the mid-1990s, Cardinal O'Connor and I were involved in a pioneering interreligious project that was co-sponsored by the American Jewish Committee and the Archdiocese of The Catholic-Jewish Educational Enrichment Project or simply C-JEEP. A rabbi became a faculty member at a Manhattan Catholic parochial high school where a course on Jews and Judaism was offered to the students. At the same time, a Catholic priest taught classes at a Jewish high school in New York City.

C-JEEP initially met some resistance from both Catholic and Jewish parents whose children attended the two schools. However, the faculties, and, above all, the students, were enthusiastic about C-JEEP because it provided personal firsthand information and academic content about "The Other" to an important group: high school teenagers. The project could not have happened without the leadership and full support of Cardinal O'Connor.

The humorous, jovial O'Connor was able to carry out his duties and responsibilities with a deft touch. Each time I was with the Cardinal I asked how things were going, and he always replied, "Every day's a holiday!" It was his way of saying how much he relished his role as one of the world's major religious figures.

But "every day" was not a "holiday" as O'Connor neared the end of the 1990s. He had a brain tumor that required chemotherapy and other invasive treatment. O'Connor continued his many activities despite his bleak prognosis, perhaps drawing upon the courage of his blinded mother, his own religious faith, and the sense of duty he learned and practiced in the Navy.

We last spoke with one another in January 2000 at his residence. It was his eightieth birthday, but Cardinal O'Connor's face was bloated from the chemotherapy he had received in his long fight against brain cancer. He was forced to sit in a chair as he greeted me. His once forceful handshake was no more; and when we embraced, we both knew he was terminally ill, with little time left. When O'Connor repeated his cheerful mantra about every day being a holiday, I turned away in tears.

Before O'Connor died on May 3, 2000, the Cardinal was awarded the Congressional Gold Medal with these words: "For more than fifty years, Cardinal O'Connor has served the Catholic Church and our nation with consistency and commitment ... Whether it was the soldier on the battlefield or the patient dying of AIDS, Cardinal O'Connor has ministered with a gentle spirit and a loving heart. Through it all, he has stood as an advocate for the poor, a champion for workers, and an inspiration for millions."

But O'Connor always described himself with only four words: "I am a priest." Maybe so, but O'Connor is the benchmark by which all present and future Catholic priests must be judged vis-à-vis Jews and Judaism.

One meeting with both Cardinal O'Connor and his Vatican "friend" took place in early October 1995 when Pope John Paul II was in the midst of his sixth of seven visits to the United States. While visiting New York City, he was a house guest at the Cardinal's residence.

I was honored when O'Connor invited me as his only Jewish guest to "come over to the residence around dinner time and visit with the Pope and me." I was, of course, happy to accept the invitation.

Because O'Connor had sent my name to the security folks who ringed the area on Madison Avenue, I was able to pass through the many guard rails and barriers and entered the residence. I was quickly led to the dining room, where the Cardinal warmly welcomed me and introduced me to John Paul II who had already begun his evening meal.

After shaking hands, I reminded the Pope we had met during Catholic World Youth Day two years earlier in 1993 when he was speaking in Denver's mile high Cherry Creek State Park. The photo of that meeting is the computer "wallpaper" on my Facebook account.

That night I saw how fatigued the Pope was because of Denver's high altitude, and in an act of chutzpah, I offered a rabbinic prayer for the Pope: the Hebrew words from the first chapter of the Book of Joshua: "Hazak V'amatz" ... "Be strong, and of good courage." When I concluded my prayer, the Pope smiled and said: "Thank you Rabbi Rudin." In fact, I met John Paul II eleven times in Rome, the United States, and Israel.

As a guest in Cardinal O'Connor's residence, I sat down at the table with the two famous Catholic leaders and requested only a cup of coffee because I had eaten my dinner earlier at home.

I thanked both John Paul II and O'Connor for successfully completing the complex process that resulted in the Vatican's full diplomatic recognition of the State of Israel. The Pope said: "It was my pleasure." And O'Connor again denied he had played a part in achieving that notable result. But, of course, he was a major factor in making those diplomatic relations a reality.

Finally, I thanked the Pope for hosting the Vatican concert in Rome in April 1994 that commemorated the *Shoah* [Holocaust]. I was a special guest at that memorable orchestral event where Pope John Paul II spoke movingly about the Jewish victims of the Holocaust concluding with the words: "Do not forget us!"

After finishing both my coffee and our conversation, a papal aide came into the dining room and reminded the Pope and the Cardinal about that evening's schedule of public events.

I expressed my thanks and appreciation, left the residence, and walked to my home about thirty blocks away. "Coffee with the Pope" was an unforgettable half hour.

CHAPTER 10

Bitter Memories: Auschwitz Convent Crisis

FRANCIS POULENC'S OPERA, "The Dialogue of the Carmelites," was completed in 1956. The first performance of the work about the martyred Roman Catholic sisters who were executed during the French Revolution took place the following year.

Today Poulenc's work is a standard in many opera houses, and each time I attend a performance and see the religiously faithful women slowly walking one by one to their deaths carried out by what the French called "the national razor"—the dreaded guillotine—I am deeply moved by the devotion of the doomed sisters. Nor am I alone. The Carmelites are widely respected for their piety and spirituality.

That is perhaps why, in 1984, when the Carmelite order established a new convent at the infamous Auschwitz death camp in Poland for the announced purpose of remembering those who were murdered by the Germans, there was little or no initial attention.

But that response quickly changed, indeed, a major crisis erupted, when it was learned the nuns had located themselves, not in a building outside the camp perimeter, but rather inside an original building: the camp's two-story theater. It was the warehouse site where the Nazi occupiers of Poland stored the lethal Zyklon-B gas used to speed up the mass killings during World War II. Holocaust scholars have determined that 1.5 million people were murdered at Auschwitz and nearby Birkenau; 1.1 million of them were Jews, about ninety percent of all victims. The remaining number were Soviet military prisoners of war, Polish Christians, and Roma people.

I was directly involved in the long, drawn-out crisis that lasted nine years, and I made five visits to the horrific place my wife called "The very Vortex of Evil." My goal on those journeys into hell was to learn about the convent situation firsthand and to interpret and share my findings and concerns with American and European Catholic leadership.

But in 1984 "Auschwitz" was just a name for many Americans; a place few Westerners had visited because the post-war Polish Communist regime was still in power. Travel was limited to Poland and other Soviet bloc nations of Eastern Europe.

If I was to build a strong negative Christian reaction to the presence of the Carmelite convent within the world's largest Jewish cemetery and a place of unique Jewish suffering, it was necessary to travel to Auschwitz and gain on-site knowledge of the situation.

Thanks to the vision of my American Jewish Committee bosses, I was dispatched to personally visit Poland in 1989. It was a harrowing experience, and I shall never forget the day I spent seven hours traversing both Auschwitz and Birkenau with a remarkable and knowledgeable guide: a Catholic priest who shared his name with one of America's sports heroes: Father Stanislaus Musial.

When I first met him, he laughed and quickly told me he was not related to the St. Louis Cardinal Baseball Hall of Famer. But Father Stan was an all-star for me because he provided an extraordinary amount of information about the neighboring twin killing sites of Auschwitz and Birkenau.

As he took me around the grounds on an extensive private tour, I constantly felt my body shudder, and I was filled with a sense of dread, and yes, even fear.

However, my chief "take away" that day was the fact that the poorly worded English language descriptions of the various grim sites were devoid of any reference to the fact that the overwhelming majority of the murdered men, women, and children in the two Nazi death camps were Jews.

In 1989, the signage and captions on the various grisly exhibits repeatedly stressed that the victims were all "anti-fascist, anti-Hitlerite," labor, political, academic, and cultural victims of the mass executions. Father Musial told me the word "Jew" nowhere appeared in either Polish or English.

Over the next decade and a half, I made four more visits to Auschwitz. On my final trip in the late 1990s, I was accompanied by my wife, Marcia. On our private tour led by the camp's museum director, it was clear the convent crisis, the collapse of the Communist government, and the worldwide publicity that emanated from the crisis brought about significant, systematic, and important changes in the signage and captions at the two camps. It was made clear to visitors that Jews, no longer blanched out of history, were ninety percent of the 1.5 million victims.

Father Musial told me that during the 1920s, the original Auschwitz buildings were used as barracks for the Polish army. That is why first-time visitors are often surprised that prisoners were housed in solid brick structures.

But in 1941, Nazi SS Chief Heinrich Himmler, believing the original death factory at Auschwitz needed to be expanded, ordered the construction of many shabby wooden barracks just three kilometers from the Auschwitz camp. The Nazis chose a peaceful sounding name for their new killing center: Birkenau, meaning "beech trees" in German. Birkenau was more "efficient" in first gassing Jews and then burning their bodies in crematoria that filled the sky with human ash and smoke.

After the war, only the concrete chimneys of the poorly built wooden Birkenau barracks remained. The poet Nellie Sachs, herself a Holocaust survivor, won the 1960 Nobel Prize for literature with her haunting poem "O, the Chimneys!" which ends "And Israel's body dissolves in smoke through the air!"

The name "Auschwitz" is a German variant of the Polish "Oswiecim," the name of a small town located less than forty miles from the intellectual capital of Poland: Krakow. By 1984, the harsh sounding name "Auschwitz" had become the collective singular name for the thousands of Nazi German concentration camps and killing sites used between 1933 and World War II's end in 1945.

The Carmelites' presence inside the camp and the erection of a large wooden cross near the warehouse/theater created an international furor, a toxic flashpoint between Christians and Jews.

The Carmelites at Auschwitz were financially supported by a Belgian Catholic group: "Aid to the Church in Distress." The organization declared the sisters "are doing penance for us who are still alive. They [the nuns] build with their hands the sacred sign ... which will witness the victorious power of Jesus. The convent will become a spiritual fortress, a token of the conversion of brothers [sic!] from various countries who went astray."

In February 1987, there was an attempt to cool the tensions that were sharply escalating among millions of Catholics and Jews throughout the world. Cardinals from Belgium, France, and Poland, including Frantiszek Macharski, the Archbishop of Krakow, Pope John Paul II's successor in that clerical position, signed a joint Catholic-Jewish public agreement.

The Catholic signatories were joined by France's Chief Rabbi Rene-Samuel Sirat, Dr. Tulia Zevi, the leader of the Italian Jewish community, and several other European Jewish leaders. Their joint declaration called for the construction of a new building outside the camp that would provide a home for the Carmelites and an interreligious center for "information, education, meeting, and prayer ... *outside* [emphasis added] the Auschwitz-Birkenau grounds." They were to move in two years: July 1989.

But as the deadline neared, the nuns remained in their convent refusing to leave, and were backed in their resistance by Poland's Catholic Prelate, Cardinal Józef Glemp, and many Poles who perceived any move to vacate as a surrender to "outside anti-Polish" pressure generated, they believed, mostly by Jews.

But they were wrong. Thanks to my efforts and those of many other Jewish leaders, many Christians became more and more incensed at the nuns' refusal to vacate the Auschwitz building.

There were constant reports they would not even move to a temporary convent until their new facility was constructed. In addition, there was a widespread belief that the entire controversy could be ended if the Pope simply "snapped his fingers."

It was not only the Cardinals in Europe who signed the agreement, but they were supported by American Cardinals John O'Connor of New York, Bernard Law of Boston, William Keeler of Baltimore, and Roger Mahony of Los Angeles; all of whom had long and fruitful working relationships with the American Jewish community.

Rising anger spilled over in July 1989 when Rabbi Avraham "Avi" Weiss, the leader of a large New York City congregation and the founder of a modern Orthodox rabbinical school, traveled with six other Jews to confront the Carmelites in person.

Weiss, a longtime activist, and his companions, dressed in the striped prison garb worn by Auschwitz prisoners. They appeared at the convent's entrance and sounded the *shofar*, the ram's horn used in Jewish services. Angry Polish workmen who were in the area attacked the seven Jewish protesters with paint and water, physically assaulted the rabbi and his followers and dragged them away from the convent.

Predictably, these events drew immediate international attention and a month later Cardinal Glemp delivered an emotional outdoor sermon to an audience of 100,000 people telling Jews throughout the world "not to talk [to] us [the Polish people] from the position of a superior nation," and to cease demanding terms surrounding the Carmelites "that cannot be fulfilled." Many Catholics and Jews considered his remarks antisemitic.

Weiss' action and Glemp's words created a critical dispute in Catholic-Jewish relations; an international controversy that threatened to undermine the important gains achieved since the conclusion of the Vatican Council in 1965.

It was a dangerous, potent, "radioactive" combination for many reasons. Many American and Israeli Jews trace their family roots to Poland and its extraordinary vibrant thousand-year-old Jewish civilization that was destroyed during the Holocaust in Auschwitz and other German death camps. In addition, for centuries, Poland was occupied by the Kaiser-led Germany, the Austro-Hungarian Empire, and Tsarist Russia.

Polish national independence was finally gained only at the end of World War I. As a result of that painful history, many Poles saw the convent crisis in nationalistic terms. A retreat by their beloved nuns would be interpreted as a sign of Polish national weakness.

At the same time, Jews, correctly perceiving Auschwitz as the ultimate location of Jewish suffering, pressed the nuns to carry out the 1987 agreement: leave the place of Zyklon-B gas and continue their devotional prayers elsewhere: outside Auschwitz' perimeter.

Complicating matters even more was the obvious public split between the two Polish cardinals; Macharski, who signed the 1987 interreligious agreement, and, in whose Archdiocese, Auschwitz was located, and Glemp, the country's Primate who was accused of being an antisemite. Of course, a third major Catholic leader, the Pope himself, was a Pole.

When Glemp visited the United States in September 1991, he met with a group of Jewish and Catholic leaders in Washington, DC. I was there and vividly remember the raw emotions and anger when Glemp spoke.

His words were far different from his sermon in Poland two years earlier. Glemp told us he was committed "to combating antisemitism at its very roots." He said "I have learned that certain of my own statements may have caused pain to the Jewish community and were seen as fostering stereotypes of Jews and Judaism, but were, in many aspects, based on mistaken information." He regretted the "difficult and highly emotional events of the summer of 1989 [Weiss' action and Glemp's sermon]."

It was a tough, tense meeting, but Glemp's words, obviously prompted by people like Cardinal O'Connor and others, did lower the emotional temperature.

Finally, in April of 1993, on the eve of the fiftieth anniversary of the Warsaw Jewish Ghetto Uprising, and after a long, painful clash of religious symbolism and historical memory, Pope John Paul II directly intervened. He wrote a personal letter to the Carmelites telling the fourteen nuns they must leave the Auschwitz camp building. They had a choice of moving their convent 1600 yards to the structure outside the camp or leaving the area.

The new building cost two million dollars to construct and contained a private convent and an interreligious conference center. Years later, I delivered several public addresses in that center, a piece of personal history that is part of my memory bank.

Despite widespread support in Poland for the nuns to remain inside the camp, the Carmelites reluctantly obeyed the Polish-born Pope and the majority moved to the new convent.

James Carroll, an acclaimed author and former priest, wrote some powerful and fitting words on the lengthy bitter convent crisis. In a unique coincidence, both Carroll and I were raised in military families in our shared hometown: Alexandria, Virginia.

He described the Auschwitz convent crisis this way:

Once, for Christians to speak among ourselves about the murder of six million as a kind of crucifixion would have seemed an epiphany of compassion, paying the Jews the highest tribute, as if the remnant of Israel had at last become, in this way, the Body of Christ. Yet such spiritualizing can appear to do what should have been impossible, which is to make the evil worse: the elimination of Jewishness from the place where Jews were eliminated.

The Body of Christ? If Jesus had been bodily at Auschwitz, as protesting Jews insisted, he would have died an anonymous victim with a number on his arm, that is all. And he would have done so not as the Son of God, not as the redeemer of humankind, not as the Jewish Messiah, but simply as a Jew.

Jewish sensitivity to Auschwitz was also recognized by the new Polish regime which succeeded the Communists. A special commission was set up with the participation of Jewish scholars to prepare completely new texts for the information, signage, and inscriptions presented in Auschwitz-Birkenau and the literature available there. Due prominence was given to the Jewish aspects of the site and the fact that of the then-current figures of 1.3 million victims of Auschwitz, 90 percent were Jews.

CHAPTER 11

Two Earnest Attempts to Confront the Holocaust: One Catholic, the Other Jewish … Did They Succeed?

AS A DIRECT result of the bitter Auschwitz convent crisis, both the Vatican and Jews involved in Catholic-Jewish relations were compelled to confront the *Shoah* or Holocaust in ways they had never before attempted. But the presence of the Carmelite sisters in the German death camp building created a global interreligious crisis that required responses from both faith communities.

The Vatican's formal effort to confront the Holocaust came in 1998 when it issued a statement entitled "We Remember: A Reflection on The *Shoah*." Two years later, nearly 200 rabbis and Jewish scholars published their document called "Dabru Emet" [Hebrew for "Speak Truth" from Zechariah 8:16].

I commend Catholic Church leaders for using the word *Shoah* rather than Holocaust, and I salute their efforts. The term "Holocaust" can be easily expropriated and used for a host of other disasters and horrific events. However, *Shoah* can never be expropriated. It can only mean one thing in modern usage. I believe we should follow the Vatican's lead. *Shoah* is the proper expression.

The pair of carefully crafted public statements—one Catholic, the other Jewish—represented sincere collective efforts, but, alas, I found both documents inadequate and each in its own way fell short of their authors' intended goals.

Here's why.

In March 1998, when the Vatican published "We Remember," the Holy See's long-awaited statement on the Holocaust, my wife and I were in Rome the day it was released at an international Catholic-Jewish conference. Joining us at the Vatican was Cardinal William Keeler of Baltimore and Dr. Eugene Fisher, the American Catholic leader charged by the US bishops with the responsibility of relating the Church to the Jewish community.

I and many of my Jewish colleagues had long urged the Vatican to publish its statement on the Holocaust. The final document, the product of many hands, was an outgrowth of Pope John Paul II's public address before a large group of American Jewish leaders in Miami in September 1987.

That appearance attracted wide attention because it followed the Pope's official but controversial meeting earlier that year with Austrian President Kurt Waldheim, who was accused of committing war crimes when he was a German army officer stationed in Greece during World War II.

As a result, the Vatican City meeting between John Paul II and Waldheim triggered consternation and public wonderment whether the Pope, who was scheduled to visit the United States that same year, was going to be welcomed by the American Jewish community. There were serious questions regarding whether he should even come to Miami for his announced formal speech before a large group of American Jewish leaders.

At that critical moment in Catholic-Jewish relations, a commitment was made by Vatican authorities: a document on the *Shoah* would be issued. Happily, the Pope's excellent speech (most of it written by Gene Fisher) reassured Jews throughout the world when he condemned the *Shoah* and asserted: "Never again!" The Pope declared: "This is the century of the *Shoah*."

The Jewish official response in Miami to John Paul II's address was written mostly by me and delivered by Rabbi Mordecai Waxman, then President of the Synagogue Council of America, an organization representing Orthodox, Conservative, and Reform rabbis.

Eleven years later, "We Remember" finally appeared. I praised part of the tightly composed document. My remarks were printed in a New York Times article written by Gustav Niebuhr:

"There were very high expectations on the Jewish side, even talk of an encyclical," said Rabbi A. James Rudin, interreligious affairs director of the American Jewish Committee.

Rabbi Rudin found more to praise than to criticize in the document, saying that it emphasized remembrance of the Holocaust, repentance for those who allowed it to happen, and a resolve to fight antisemitism. Missing, he said, is a sign that the church is taking responsibility for having helped to create a climate, through anti-Jewish teachings, in which lethal antisemitism could flourish.

But despite my praise, I found several sections of the well-intentioned Vatican document highly problematic. It asks, "did Christians give every possible assistance to those being persecuted and in particular to the persecuted Jews? Many did, but others did not." That little phrase, "many did, but others did not," gives readers the false feeling that it was a 50/50 moment in human history.

That is, fifty percent of Catholics helped Jews during those terrible years from 1933–45 and perhaps fifty percent didn't.

The grim reality was not 50/50. Not at all. There needs to be a robust exploration and discussion about the actual behavior of individual Christians, not merely Catholics, but of all Christian institutions and Christian bodies during the twelve years of Nazi German rule along with an analysis of why the overwhelming majority of European Christians were either perpetrators of anti-Jewish genocide or merely bystanders or onlookers.

Another area of discussion in "We Remember" is the difference between anti-Judaism and antisemitism, a centerpiece of the Vatican document. It makes the distinction, which I do not find acceptable, that yes, the Church did, for centuries, reflect anti-Judaism, that is, teachings against the Jewish religion and Jewish religious tradition, but that antisemitism, and I certainly would agree, is a modern, non-Christian invention of the nineteenth century.

However, I don't think we can make such a clean distinction between antisemitism, which I define as hatred of Jews and Judaism, and anti-Judaism which is contempt for the Jewish religion. Unfortunately, the Vatican document really stands or falls on this critical point because it seemingly "walks away" from antisemitism while acknowledging the existence of ancient anti-Judaism within the Roman Catholic Church.

One of the most overlooked issues in the 1998 document speaks about the dawn of Christianity, the crucifixion of Jesus, when there were disputes between early Church and Jewish leaders who in "their devotion to the law, on occasion violently opposed the preachers of the Gospel and the first Christians." That historically loaded statement is open to so many interpretations—I'm not clear why it belongs in a document on the *Shoah*.

The provocative words, "violently opposed," and "devotion to the law," skirt close to affirming the kind of false dichotomy dedicated Catholic and Jewish leaders have tried for decades to eradicate—Christianity is love,

Judaism is law; one is static, one is dynamic. And that is supposedly the difference between a superior Christianity and an inferior Judaism.

There is this sentence in the Vatican statement which most people overlook because it doesn't relate to World War II, but is an area that always generates intense discussion: what and when were the partings of the ways between the Nazarenes (the early Christians) and the Jewish community?

Another problematic area: why did the Vatican document describe flashpoint issues including the plight of Armenians, and a host of other appalling episodes of massacres and slaughter, and why the use of the elliptical and elusive phrase, "nor can we forget the drama of the Middle East, the elements of which are well known."

I think all of us know what the Vatican is talking about, but does it really belong in this document that is focused on the *Shoah* and the years 1933–1945?

However, there are Bishops' statements from several nations which are positive and strong, particularly those of the European conferences of bishops—France, Germany, Poland, and others, not to mention the American bishops' statements. But the Vatican document is written in a lawyer-like way, apparently to protect the Church from criticism or controversy.

Interestingly, I found the introductory letter from the Pope stronger, albeit much briefer, than the tortured writing of the document itself.

I am well aware "We Remember" is addressed to the global Church; it is intended for the one-billion-plus Catholics, many of whom live in areas without a Jewish community or without any involvement in the European massacre of the Jews. But *precisely* because the document was written for a worldwide Church, it should have been made much stronger.

The year 1998 was a unique moment in history to make the case, once and for all, eternally and universally, at all times and in all places, whether it's in Kenya or Papua, New Guinea; Amsterdam or Berlin; Rome or Hartford; or anywhere else on the planet. Because it's a declaration of the global Church, I believe the Vatican must assert as clearly and powerfully as possible, with all the strength that comes from speaking to the entire Roman Catholic family.

I regret the document mentions Pope Pius XII in such an apologetic manner. A defense of Pius XII, which is, of course, appropriate for the Vatican to make, should not have been included in this document. There are other arenas and venues to make that case, but not in "We Remember."

Unfortunately, the document prominently mentions Pius XII and then cites congratulatory statements from four prominent Jews to buttress his defense. It is a peculiar way to defend the wartime Pope.

Because the Vatican document is rooted in history and depends so much on historical analysis and primary source documents, it opens the proverbial door for historians who may have other documents and hold differing views to join the Catholic-Jewish encounter. Once history is employed, everybody can employ history, and everyone does.

I am certain the question of Pope Pius XII's policies and actions during the *Shoah* will continue to be a major topic simply because that question is prominently mentioned in this document.

But I am pleased Pope Francis opened the Vatican Archives to scholars in March 2020, seventy-five years after the end of World War II. That most welcome papal action will allow a full exploration and review of all the records of the period, beginning in 1933, which includes the pontificate of Pope Pius XI, through the post-World War II years.

I am aware eleven Vatican Archives volumes were released some years ago, numbering about 5,100 pages. But Pope Francis' action now permits teams of competent scholars to have full access to all the relevant documents of that critical period.

Despite my critique of "We Remember," I am confident the Catholic-Jewish dialogue can certainly endure. That is because those relations are strong, and since the promulgation of *Nostra Aetate*, we have developed a mature, sturdy relationship that makes it possible to address difficult, painful, and often haunting issues together.

In 2000, two years after "We Remember" appeared, nearly 200 rabbis and Jewish scholars signed a Statement on Christians and Christianity called "Dabru Emet." The Baltimore-based Institute for Christian and Jewish Studies provided the impetus for the document and my dear friend and esteemed colleague Rabbi Michael Signer who taught at the University of Notre Dame was one of the principal authors of the document.

Just eight paragraphs long, Dabru Emet was an ambitious attempt to present a "thoughtful Jewish response" to the "dramatic and unprecedented shift" in Christian-Jewish relations. When the statement's sponsors asked me to join the other signatories, I declined because the statement failed to adequately and accurately address the critical issue of Christianity and the Holocaust.

In 1997, the Interdenominational Group of Catholics and Protestants in Milan, Italy correctly recognized that the Holocaust is now central in all religious encounters. The Italian Christians declared: "The starting point for the question of God today can be no other than Auschwitz, a point behind which there is no return."

The signers of Dabru Emet declared: "Nazism was not a Christian phenomenon. Without the long history of Christian anti-Judaism and Christian violence against Jews, Nazi ideology could not have taken hold, nor could it have been carried out." A high school English teacher taught me to beware of long sentences filled with "coulds." She urged us to write straightforward declarative sentences.

Unfortunately, my teacher's sage advice was not followed in Dabru Emet. The result was an inadequate and surprisingly diffident description of an undeniable clear and sobering historical reality: *Many Christian teachings and actions throughout the centuries prepared the seed bed—the moral, spiritual, and intellectual climate—for the rise of genocidal Nazism.*

Why didn't the statement's Jewish authors address this significant point with the same accuracy and power that many Christians have done? Why is the United Methodist Church's 1996 General Conference Declaration on Christian-Jewish relations clearer and stronger about Christianity and the Holocaust than Dabru Emet?

The UMC asserted: "Especially critical for Christians...has been the struggle to recognize the horror of the Holocaust as the catastrophic culmination of a long history of anti-Jewish attitudes and actions in which Christians, and sometimes the Church itself, have been deeply implicated."

And the Milan Interdenominational Christian Group was even stronger: "The *Shoah* is an event, which happened in modern and Christian Europe, that was planned and executed by baptized persons. Christians cannot escape this fact. They must confront the challenge that here in Europe people tried 'to kill God by killing God's people.'"

I did not sign Dabru Emet in 2000 because of another problematic sentence dealing with the Holocaust: "If the Nazi extermination of the Jews had been fully successful, it would have turned its murderous rage more directly to Christians." I believe this is an inaccurate and dubious assertion.

Christianity was an anathema to many Nazi leaders, and there were attempts to co-opt the authentic Church by creating a Nazi-based Christian puppet church that attracted some clergy and lay people. The Nazis murdered "inferior" Slavs, including many Polish Catholic priests, as well as Christian intellectuals, the most famous being the German Lutheran pastor Dietrich Bonhoeffer.

But I find Dabru Emet is misleading at best, and dangerous at worst, because it sets up a moral equivalency between the undeniable Nazi attempt to kill every Jew in the world and an unprovable historical prediction that the same "murderous rage" would be aimed at "Christians" in general. The language is too sweeping and self-assured in its prediction, and it makes no distinctions about the kind and number of Christians the Nazis might have murdered.

Because the Baltimore statement has been widely read in Christian churches and institutions of higher learning throughout the world, in 2005 I asked several young Protestant seminarians to study the Holocaust section of Dabru Emet. They unanimously and independently agreed the document sends the message that Jews and Christians were both primary targets of the Nazis. That is simply not so.

Elie Wiesel wisely noted, "Not every victim of the Nazis was a Jew, but every Jew was a victim."

The troublesome paragraph concludes: "We do not blame them (Christians) for the sins committed by their ancestors." No argument here. But beyond rejecting blame there is a need for genuine responsibility on the part of Christian churches to search their past regarding the Holocaust. That specific call is lacking in Dabru Emet.

Fortunately, one religious leader has urged Christians to "examine themselves on the responsibility which they too have for the evils of our time."

His name? Pope John Paul II.

CHAPTER 12

"Mainline" Protestants and Jews! It's Complicated!

ONE OF MY first AJC tasks in 1968 was to develop a series of interreligious projects and programs with America's liberal Protestant church bodies, many of whom were members of the then-influential National Council of Churches (NCC), headquartered in New York City. At that time, the Council numbered nearly thirty-five Christian denominations representing over forty million Americans.

Back then, white Anglo-Saxon Protestantism represented the establishment expression of Christianity in the United States, and, indeed, it dominated our nation's religious, political, economic, cultural, and academic life for centuries. I quickly discovered that most NCC leaders and professional staff belonged to one of seven major Protestant denominations—"mainline" churches—that shaped the Council's agenda and provided much of its financial support: American (Northern) Baptist, Congregationalist, Disciples of Christ, Episcopalian, Lutheran, Methodist, or Presbyterian.

Those denominations long ago acquired that term because many residents of Philadelphia's affluent western suburbs who lived along the "mainline" suburban train route were members of those churches.

The Protestant national leaders I worked with for over thirty years on a myriad of issues and public policies were similar in their personal religious backgrounds, beliefs, practices, and observances to my family's Christian neighbors in Virginia who years before had requested the Rudins' assistance in judging holiday house decorations.

Unlike most adult American Jews in the late 1960s, I had decades of up-close-and-personal experiences with white Anglo-Saxon Protestants. While I neither idealized nor envied their dominant position in our national life, I clearly recognized that many of them frequently felt a sense of majority privilege and preeminence in all things American.

As a youngster growing up in Alexandria, Virginia, I was a longtime member of a close-knit group of Christian classmates, most of whom were "mainline" Protestants. As an insider, I was an elected student government officer in my public high school of 1800 students, a newspaper editor, and a member of several honor societies. At the same time, I was also aware of being an outsider as a Jew. I strongly believe this youthful ambivalent set of relationships was helpful in my later interreligious work.

That is because my double identity made it easy to understand the values, traditions, and backgrounds of "mainline" denominational leaders, as well as presidents, deans, and faculty members of Protestant seminaries, and, of course, local congregational pastors. In addition, I recognized the attitudes, opinions, fears, concerns, and hopes of individual church members—the laity, the proverbial "men and women in the pew"—who often differed sharply from the public policies and positions of the National Council of Churches and their specific denominations.

The youthful interreligious encounters in Alexandria combined with my Christian-Jewish experiences in the Air Force chaplaincy provided me with a sense of professional self-confidence. As it turned out, my work with the NCC and "mainline" churches, albeit complex and often frustrating, helped build my professional reputation as a successful and effective interreligious relations rabbi.

Recent decades have seen a continuing steep decline in both membership and influence of liberal white Anglo-Saxon Protestant churches while Roman Catholics, white Evangelical Protestants, African Americans, Jews, Muslims, and other faith communities have moved forward to play major roles in the American religious and political arenas.

A 2019 Pew Research Center study showed that all Protestants—"mainline," white Evangelicals, and Black church members—today number less than 50 percent of the general US population, and less than one of five Americans identifies as a member of a "mainline" church and one of four Protestants—26 percent—is a white Evangelical.

Indeed, in recent years the national percentage of Christians has shrunk to 65 percent, the first time in US history it has dropped below 80 percent, and that figure is rapidly decreasing; a result of smaller families, church membership losses, and millions of religiously indifferent young people. Protestants, liberal and conservative, Black, and white, will soon become a minority faith community in the United States. Clearly for them, the future will not be what their past was.

Surveys indicate a growing number of Americans are turning away from organized religion in general and opting for nebulous forms of "spirituality," creating serious problems for all faith communities. As result, economically stressed clergy and laypeople are concerned with basic existential questions of institutional survival and they frequently view Christian-Jewish relations as a luxury that is best pursued by a few professional "ecumaniacs."

A striking example of this downward trend was the 2012 US presidential election. For the first time in American history, none of the four major candidates—Barack Obama, Joe Biden, Mitt Romney, and Paul Ryan—was a white Anglo-Saxon Protestant.

But in 1958, white Anglo-Saxon Protestant hegemony was physically exemplified in the imposing nineteen-story limestone office building at 475 Riverside Drive on New York City's Morningside Heights. Nearby was Columbia University, founded by the Episcopal Church in 1754; Riverside Church, a flagship congregation of white Anglo-Saxon Protestantism; and Union Theological Seminary, a leading Protestant seminary.

In 1958, President Dwight Eisenhower laid the "475" cornerstone of the building that was officially called the Ecumenical Center but was quickly nicknamed the "God Box." The Rockefeller family contributed much of the cost required to construct the new religious edifice.

In 1968, several major Protestant denominations maintained their national headquarters at "475," and the NCC itself occupied three floors and employed a large professional and support staff. During my thirty-two years with the AJC, I spent a great deal of time inside the "God Box."

The NCC was established in 1950 and its membership included, in addition to "mainline" churches, many historic Black denominations, Mennonite "peace churches," Quaker groups, and several Eastern Orthodox churches.

For decades, the NCC's broad-based agenda was a long menu of liberal domestic and international policies and programs. While the Council's member communions were administratively independent and theologically diverse, they were able to work together on several basic core issues including Christian unity, religious education, social justice concerns, international relations, and worldwide relief efforts.

Since the end of World War II, the NCC and major segments of the US Jewish community, including the American Jewish Committee, often worked cooperatively on many shared domestic social justice issues. Indeed, until the conclusion of the Roman Catholic Second Vatican Council in 1965, interreligious relations in America usually meant a coalition of "mainline" Protestants and Jews pressing for such issues as civil and voting rights for African Americans, fair housing legislation, and the separation of church and state.

Perhaps most visible were the numerous pastors and rabbis throughout the country who participated in joint community services on Thanksgiving and other national holidays. In February 1964, I participated in a Presbyterian-sponsored clergy voting rights drive in Hattiesburg, Mississippi.

Protestant-Jewish issues frequently included opposition to antisemitism, racism, ageism, and sexism, disapproval of Christian conversion campaigns targeting Jews, opposition to mandated prayers and Bible readings in public schools, South African *apartheid*, and religious fundamentalism.

But because the NCC was a loose confederation with different, even contending constituencies within its membership, the Council's public positions on many issues were frequently controversial, but generally reflected the liberal views and policies of "mainline" Protestant churches.

Throughout its seventy-plus years of existence, the NCC has supported the rights of countless minority groups, underdogs, victims, dissidents, and nonconformists. However, because of the conservative theological positions held especially by Eastern Orthodox communities and Black churches, the NCC has never adopted a pro-choice position on abortion, and in the 1990s, after long debate and study, the Council did not admit to its membership a church body whose membership was openly homosexual.

While the AJC has been generally compatible with the NCC on many domestic policy issues, that was not true on a series of international concerns. For instance, I publicly criticized the Council whenever its staff leaders or Governing Board members spoke favorably about or publicly condoned the former Soviet Union's harsh treatment of its religious minorities, especially Jews who sought to emigrate to Israel and other lands of freedom, and Evangelical Christians in the USSR who demanded the right to worship free of state control.

But most of all, there was a wide and permanent public abyss between the NCC and the AJC on the Israeli-Arab conflict. For over thirty years, I continually, consistently, and correctly denounced as "one-sided" and biased many NCC Middle East public positions. I regularly accused the Council of employing an unfair anti-Israel double standard of judgment that it did not apply to any other nation in the region, especially Syria.

A typical example of the NCC's bias at work occurred in October 1973, during the Yom Kippur War that Egypt and Syria began on Judaism's holiest day. The two Arab nations mounted a coordinated series of armed attacks against Israel.

The bitter conflict, which threatened the very existence of Israel, lasted more than three weeks. During the midst of the intense fighting, the NCC's Governing Board, meeting in a New York City hotel ballroom, called upon both the US and the USSR to "use the full weight of its influence" to end the war. The Council further urged the two superpowers "to immediately halt arms shipments to the belligerents."

Of course, the NCC leaders undoubtedly understood the Soviet Union had no intention of stopping its massive deliveries of sophisticated arms to Egypt and Syria. The real target was our own government, the main source of arms the beleaguered Jewish state required for its national self-defense. Fortunately, President Richard Nixon quickly ordered the Department of Defense and the US Air Force to resupply Israel's depleted military arsenal with tanks, ammunition, and weapons. In addition, the NCC Board members failed to denounce Egypt and Syria for starting the war.

My AJC colleague Gerald Strober and I were official "fraternal observers" at NCC Governing Board meetings. As soon as the Middle East resolution was adopted, we called an emergency press conference to denounce the church body's one-sided actions. As we spoke to the media, including the New York Times, some NCC officials sat in the same room and glared at us as we assailed the NCC for its failure to deal with the "realities" of the war and "its total inability to morally condemn" Egypt and Syria. I described the National Council of Churches as a "forum for militant pro-Arab and anti-Israel bias."

But the NCC's anti-Israel/anti-Zionist animus was nothing new. It began years earlier among many American Protestant leaders long before the Council's founding in 1950 and before Israel's independence in 1948. It reached its peak following the 1967 Six-Day Arab-Israeli War, and the NCC's troubling 1973 resolution was but another chapter in that organization's long, biased relationship with the world's only Jewish state. The NCC, with a few exceptions, has been a consistent critic of Israel's alleged human rights violations and other supposed negative policies and actions.

In addition, over the years some individual "mainline" churches have adopted similar unfair anti-Israel positions. I attribute much of this negativity to the persistent pressures exerted by Arab churches in the US and by Middle East Christians themselves.

However, this is only a partial explanation of the NCC's long record of hostility to Israel. Several "mainline" churches have sent missionaries to the Arab Middle East during the past 150 years and established institutions such as the American Universities in Beirut and Cairo, Bir Zeit University in Ramallah, as well as hospitals, hospices, orphanages, and schools in the region. These extensive missionary programs created a natural affinity between the American host churches, such as the United Church of Christ and the Presbyterian Church, and Middle East Arabs, both Christian and Muslim.

On the other hand, I worked closely for many years with NCC staff members as well as leaders of member churches who were strongly supportive of Israel. The Jewish state's peace treaties with Egypt and Jordan, and the 1993 Oslo Accords between Israel and the Palestine Liberation Organization (PLO) muted some, but not all, of the anti-Israel feeling within the NCC and its constituents.

In my many public critiques of the NCC, I demanded the Council apply equal standards of judgment to all countries of the Middle East on questions of human or minority rights, and to resist singling out only one nation for particular focus without due recognition of other continuing human rights problems and violations throughout the turbulent region.

I also pointed out that deeply embedded theological antisemitism continues to exist among some Middle East churches and is still being employed for contemporary political purposes.

Even though the AJC and many other Jewish organizations have backed a "two-state (Israeli and Palestinian) solution," religious prejudice has remained strong among some leaders of the Arab churches that are NCC members.

As noted above, I was a longtime official "fraternal observer" at the NCC's twice-yearly Governing Board meetings. At nearly every one of those sessions that usually involved over a hundred delegates from member church bodies, a representative of the Antiochian Orthodox Church, a denomination composed primarily of Arab members, would present a one-sided resolution condemning Israel for what I termed Israel's alleged "crimes du jour."

There was usually a contentious floor fight when such one-sided anti-Israel resolutions came before the Governing Board for a vote. They were often "tabled for further study" or amended by Israel's friends on the NCC's Board and/or staff to achieve a fair balance. Happily, I had developed the support of many allies who participated in such meetings; some were NCC staff members while others were Governing Board members who had warm and constructive working relationships with local Jewish communities.

However, one positive result did emerge from the 1973 criticism that Gerry Strober and I publicly hurled at the National Council of Churches. Because many NCC staff and Governing Board members had little or no personal knowledge of or experience with modern Israel, I proposed a two-week interreligious "fact-finding" study mission sponsored by the AJC and the NCC that included Lebanon, Jordan, and Israel.

The NCC leadership accepted my idea, and in November 1974, I co-led a unique joint study mission consisting of twenty-five American religious leaders: fourteen Jews and eleven Christians.

When I first suggested the project, some AJC colleagues voiced concern about our group's physical safety, especially in a religiously divided Lebanon that was then lurching toward civil war between Christians and Muslims. In addition, the PLO was based in Beirut. But reassurances came when the NCC arranged for officials of the Middle East Council of Churches to be our sponsoring and protective guides in both Lebanon and Jordan. The AJC Jerusalem office was our guide in Israel.

While some AJC colleagues expressed serious misgivings about visiting Arab countries, other staff members expressed concern that Israelis, famous for their well-known gruff "tell it like it is" style, could not match the legendary reputation of warm "Arab hospitality." Worst of all, they worried, a depressed Israel, recovering from both the devastating war of a year earlier and the recent death in December 1973 of Israel's "Founding Father," David Ben-Gurion, would fail to provide a positive experience for the Christian members of our mission.

But I believed otherwise and convinced the skeptics and nay-sayers among my AJC colleagues that Lebanon and Jordan had to constitute one-half of our fourteen-day itinerary if we were serious in our interreligious efforts. Finally, I was very confident a carefully organized visit to Israel, with its warts and all, would be a powerful positive emotional and spiritual experience for the Christian leaders in the delegation. I was correct in my prediction. As Martin Buber declared: "All real living is meeting."

A well-planned, in-person visit to the Jewish state almost always overcomes negative reading material or hearing anti-Israel rhetoric. At its heart, positive interreligious relations are built upon human relationships, shared experiences, and a sense of self-confidence about one's deepest personal beliefs and commitments. I had no fear that Israel would, at best, shatter many false assumptions about the Jewish state and Zionism, or at worst, call into serious question previously held negative beliefs about Israel. That is exactly what happened on our journey.

In an ironic historical twist, our journey took place at the same time PLO Chairman Yasser Arafat, carrying a pistol on his hip, addressed the United Nations General Assembly in New York City. His November 1974 speech concluded with the ominous prediction that Zionism and the Jewish state it created would "perish."

As a direct result of Arafat's UN appearance, tensions and emotions remained high throughout our unique journey. We maintained a rigorous schedule that usually lasted eighteen hours a day and featured an extraordinary number of interviews with a series of public officials and spokespersons and a host of intense personal encounters.

We met with numerous political, religious, educational, media, and cultural leaders while still leaving time to attend worship services and visit Jewish and Christian holy places and historic sites that included Baalbek in Lebanon, Petra in Jordan, and Masada in Israel. Naturally we spent time visiting with ordinary Lebanese, Jordanians, and Israelis in their homes.

However, a tragic event marred our journey because it brought forth from one of the Christians in our group an example of anti-Israel venom and animosity that nearly ended our trip.

It occurred on November 19, 1974, just hours after our group crossed the Allenby Bridge that spans the Jordan River and entered Israel. That morning as our private tour bus headed north to the Galilee, we passed through the Israeli city of Beit She 'an.

Only a few hours before we arrived, three Palestinian terrorists posing as laborers crossed the border from Jordan and carried out a murderous attack on several apartment apartment buildings, killing four Israeli civilians and wounding another twenty. Israeli security forces were quickly alerted and killed the three terrorists.

Among the twenty wounded survivors were frightened young children who jumped out of apartment windows to save their lives.

When our bus, enroute to a northern *kibbutz*, stopped in Beit She 'an, we expressed our collective horror and shock at the terrorists' deadly assault on innocent civilians. The NCC co-leader of the mission, the Reverend Nathan VanderWerf, joined me in expressing to municipal officials our sense of revulsion about the act of terrorism and sympathy for the victims. But as Nate and I discovered, the empathetic sentiment from a group of American religious leaders was unfortunately not unanimous.

Nearly five decades later, Dr. Jeffrey Stiffman, a prominent St. Louis rabbi, was still able to describe in detail the obscene anti-Israel bile that was expressed that bloody day in Beit She 'an by one of the Christian ministers in our group:

> When we got to Beit She 'an, Israeli police had already killed the terrorists. Our interreligious group from America was told that the terrorists shot at the police through the windows of the residential building they had earlier seized, and where they murdered the four Israeli civilians. Everyone in our group was upset, except one pastor who asked: "Did the police shoot first? Then the terrorists had a right to fight back."

> As I remember, that was his attitude—anti-Israel—during the entire two-week trip. Another minister [the Rev. Dr. Robert Huston of the United Methodist Church] said that he didn't agree with that view, but felt it was better to keep peace in the group. I told him about the Jewish tradition of "Shalom Babayit" (maintain peace in one's home). As I remember, my roommate and a number of other Christians in the group were pretty shaken by it all.

> I also remember that when we were in Jordan, we met with a group of Protestant missionaries. To a person, they placed all the blame on Israel and none on the Arab side. Some of us were furious and started to argue vociferously with them. The same peace-making minister [Huston], who a few days later helped calm the scene in Beit She 'an, patted us on the shoulders, and said, "Calm down. Have a tea or coffee and let me take care of this." He then gently and forcefully told the missionaries in Amman that they had better study more about the region and not spout off as if they were part of the PLO and other anti-Jewish, anti-Israel groups.

Two years after our successful interreligious Middle East mission, another crisis erupted that threatened NCC-AJC relations. The Romanian Orthodox Church named Archbishop Valerian Trifa to the NCC Board of Governors. At first, Trifa's selection seemed quite routine ... except for the fact he was a Nazi supporter during World War II, and in January 1941 was the leader of the fascist Romanian Iron Guard that murdered 6,000 Jews in Bucharest. Clear evidence directly linked him with that infamous anti-Jewish *pogrom*.

In 1976, Trifa, living in Detroit, was under investigation by the US Immigration and Naturalization Service on charges of having lied about his Iron Guard connections when he applied for citizenship after World War

II. Membership in such groups prohibits a person from acquiring American citizenship.

When Marc Tanenbaum and I brought this incriminating information to the NCC leaders, they at first refrained from acting against Trifa on grounds that it might prejudice his right of due process.

The Romanian Orthodox Episcopate fully supported Trifa and the NCC leadership told us it relied on the confidence placed in him by his religious constituency, a church body with roots in the former Soviet Union and Eastern Europe. The AJC demanded Trifa's immediate removal from the Governing Board.

After our constant pressure, Trifa was ultimately removed from his NCC position, but it took the US government another eight years of litigation before the Romanian Iron Guard killer of Jews was stripped of his illegally acquired American citizenship and deported. In 1984, he turned up in Portugal where he died three years later.

Because Trifa was an archbishop of the Romanian Orthodox Episcopate of America, his case attracted worldwide attention. In 1984, *The Christian Science Monitor* published my op-ed that concluded:

> *There must be justice for the murdered victims of the Holocaust, men and women who cannot offer testimony on their own behalf. They cannot press their case in a court of law, but we can and must do so to honor their memory. And US citizenship is too precious to be granted to people like Trifa, who lied to obtain it.*

A final note: during the 1976 NCC Governing Board meeting in Detroit, I rode, by accident, nearly 15 floors on a hotel elevator alone with Trifa who was dressed in his full ecclesiastical regalia. When he noticed my NCC guest observer badge that noted I was a rabbi, the Nazi war criminal moved away from me. He asked: "Do you know who I am?" I immediately replied: "I know exactly who you are and what horrible things you did to my people!"

The elevator door then opened on the lobby level, and we both walked away from one another. It was one of the proudest moments of my life.

In 1996, 190 churches, most of them in the Southeast with African-American membership, were burned by racist arsonists. In response, the NCC and the AJC were part of a major interreligious effort that also included the National Conference of Catholic Bishops, and working closely together we raised $9 million to help rebuild burned houses of worship.

In August of that year, I joined the Rev. Dr. Joan Brown Campbell, the NCC's General Secretary (the Council's CEO) on the site of Salem Baptist Church in Fruitland, Tennessee, which was burned to the ground. Joan and I presented the church with a check for $105,000, and in a powerful show of concern, *both* President Bill Clinton and Vice President Al Gore participated in the interreligious event.

Four months later, in December 1996, I accompanied AJC CEO David Harris when he presented a sizable donation and participated in the ceremonial groundbreaking of the reconstruction of the Gay's Hill Baptist Church in rural Georgia. AJC volunteers from Atlanta assisted in the reconstruction of the new church building and were present at the dedication in July 1997. AJC Chicago members joined with Catholics, Lutherans, and other Christians in a successful fundraising effort to aid burned churches.

In a news interview at the time, I said: "People don't realize a church is more than just the physical building. It's replacing the organ, the robes, the Bibles, and the school rooms that were destroyed. In a way, synagogues and Black churches play a similar role in their respective communities. For African Americans, a church is often a community center providing daycare for children, senior citizens' programs, and a place to receive personal counseling."

During my decades of interaction with the NCC, there was an abundance of confrontation and cooperation and shared successes and permanent problems. There was also a tacit understanding that while the NCC and the AJC were often active partners for Christian-Jewish understanding, they remained apart on issues central to the safety and security of Israel, the Jewish biblical homeland that represents the culmination of 2,000 years of Jewish longing, prayers, hopes, and dreams.

Today, the National Council of Churches is greatly shrunken in size from the heady years when it was a major actor on America's religious stage. In 2013, severe financial problems compelled the Council to leave the "God Box" on New York City's Riverside Drive. With a much smaller staff, it moved to reduced office space in Washington, DC, and no longer attracts the support and attention of the past. Most observers believe the NCC will never regain its once prominent position in American society.

But the weakened Council is as controversial as ever when it relates to the Israeli-Palestinian issue. Its 2020 website called for "the right of [Arab] refugees to return to their homes, the dismantlement of the [Israeli] settlements, and the establishment of Jerusalem as a shared international city."

Plus, ça change, plus c'est la même chose! [The more things change, the more they remain the same!]

Chapter 13

Black Churches

During my years at the AJC, I devoted considerable energy and time to building positive relations with the large African American Christian community in the United States. The effort was complex and difficult, but highly satisfying work.

But before describing that decades-long effort, a question needs to be asked: what's in a name? Quite a lot, as it turns out.

When I was growing up in Virginia, the commonly used term for African Americans was "Colored," a usage preserved in the name of one of the country's legacy civil-rights organizations: the National Association for the Advancement of Colored People, better known as the NAACP.

But by 1964 when I participated in an interreligious voting rights drive in Hattiesburg, Mississippi, "Colored" had been replaced by "Negro." Unfortunately, some racist bigots deliberately slurred the pronunciation of that noun and their uttered word sounded much too close to a hateful epithet. "Negro" was generally abandoned by the 1970s and replaced by "Black" spelled with a lowercase "b."

That group name is still used today by many people, but after the racist events in 2020, journalists began employing the uppercase "B" in print to identify the nearly fifteen percent of the total American population, or approximately 45 million people. The Rev. Jesse Jackson is generally credited with introducing the term "African American" into the national lexicon.

I have chosen to use both "Black" and "African American" interchangeably in this book. Interestingly, the phrase "people of color" is currently being employed in both the public media as well as in private conversation.

A somewhat similar name game took place thousands of years ago with another people. There are three names for the people of the Bible—Hebrews, Israelites, and Jews. Although the trio of scriptural names had diverse linguistic roots and were used during distinct periods of ancient history, each name, while different from one another, identified the same people.

The historic Black churches represent one institution that has wide credibility within the African American community. The church has always remained with its people in the inner cities, and like the synagogue of pre-1939 Eastern Europe, the Black church remains a central political, cultural, social, and, of course, spiritual center of an entire community.

It is no accident that many Black civic and political leaders in the United States were ordained ministers—in addition to Martin Luther King Jr., and Jesse Jackson, we are familiar with Elijah Cummings, Floyd Flake, Benjamin Hooks, John Lewis, Al Sharpton, Raphael Warnock, Andrew Young, and a host of other Black preachers. Despite its many problems, the Black church remains the one place where Blacks can be completely "at home" with their own unique religious traditions and style of worship.

The analogy with the synagogue is obvious. For Jews, the most direct means of relating to Black Americans is through the churches. While Jews have been the world's greatest victim group, sadly, Blacks hold that tragic distinction in America that began when the first African slaves were brought to the British colonies in 1619.

Jews, victims of antisemitism, and Blacks, victims of racism, are bound together in the shared agony of victimization. African American churches frequently have progressive positions on the major social justice issues, but they are often conservative on theological questions.

Official relations between Black churches and the Jewish community are generally good, but I quickly discovered in my work that Black-Jewish relations do not occupy a major place on the Black churches' program agenda. Not surprisingly, their key issues include affordable housing, quality education, voter suppression, fair employment opportunities, prison reform, lethal police and white vigilante violence aimed especially at young Black men, strengthening the family, opposition to racism, and other similar concerns.

Historically, *apartheid* in South Africa was a major international concern of Black churches. Because Blacks constitute a significant percentage of America's armed forces, the community's leaders are especially sensitive to the use of US military force in the world.

While most Americans speak of the "Black church," it is important to understand the origins of the various faith communities, their unique histories, their differences, and their leaders. All five historic major Black national church bodies described below are members of both the National

Council of Churches (NCC) and the Geneva-based World Council of Churches (WCC).

During a high point in American Christian ecumenism in the 1960s and early 1970s, there was a drive led mostly by white Protestant leaders to form one large united religious body that would hopefully include the Roman Catholic Church and African American churches. It was an extraordinary effort that sought Christian unity, an elusive goal since Martin Luther's break with the Catholic Church in 1517. The drive for a "super church" was spearheaded by the famed global ecumenist, Dr. Eugene Carson Blake, a Presbyterian leader.

While many critics dismissed such a giant merged body, serious discussions at the highest ecclesiastical level took place over a period of several years. I knew and worked with many Christians who ardently believed such a goal was possible, but while I admired their zeal, I remained skeptical of their chances for success.

Ultimately and not surprisingly, Black leaders were cool to the concept of such an unwieldly creation. They were especially wary of a new "megachurch" that might mean an end to their spiritual distinctiveness. The proposed United Church never became a reality, and the Black churches' opposition was a key factor in deciding the outcome.

Those church bodies include three major Black Methodist denominations that have about 4.5 million members, and there are about 14 million members in Black Baptist churches.

Beginning in the seventeenth century, white slave owners in America transmitted their religion, usually Protestant Christianity, to their slaves. As a means of maintaining control, Blacks were often not taught to read, stripped of their unique African religious identity, native languages, and in many cases, their original names. As a result, Christianity was usually taught or, as some scholars argue, forced upon slaves via an oral tradition.

But in a remarkable way, enslaved Blacks transformed their masters' presentation of a passive and submissive faith into a liberation movement with a heavy emphasis on the biblical Exodus story. Indeed, Black slaves formed a spiritual affinity with the ancient Hebrews who were held in Pharaoh's bondage.

The white slave owners unwittingly provided their slaves with an extraordinary spiritual weapon that became a central feature of the Black freedom struggle. Because of their long identification with the Hebrew Bible, many African American Christians today have a special affinity for the Land of Israel, and they are regular visitors or religious pilgrims to the modern Jewish state.

At the same time, some Black church leaders also identify with the Palestinians as fellow victims. This bifurcation must be kept in mind when Jews engage Black Christians in interreligious dialogue.

The African Methodist Episcopal Church (AME) was officially organized in 1816. However, its original "defining moment" came earlier in 1787 in Philadelphia when Richard Allen, a Black Methodist pastor, was forced in the middle of prayer to move to a balcony of St. George's Methodist Church. Allen refused to do so and in protest, he started the Bethel Chapel, now the mother church of the AME.

In 1793, nearly 40 percent of all American Methodists were Black, but the twin issues of slavery and racial segregation divided the Methodist faith community as they did many other churches. Allen became the first Black bishop in any church in the United States. He died in 1831 and is widely revered as one of the major leaders of the early Black church in America.

Today, the AME numbers about 2.5 million members with approximately 8,000 churches throughout the country. Following Allen's lead, the AME stresses concern for poverty and the ongoing struggle for social, political, and economic justice.

The AME retains a church polity involving bishops. The AME General Conference meets every four years, but congregations are highly individualistic and independent. A worship experience that includes preaching, singing, prayer, testimony, and conversion is a key element in church life.

The African Methodist Episcopal Zion Church (AME Zion) began in 1796 in New York, when James Varick, the son of a slave and a Dutch slave owner, formed the first Black church in that city. Varick, AME Zion's first bishop, was a strong abolitionist, and Harriet Tubman and Frederick Douglass were church members. Today the AME Zion membership numbers about 1.2 million, and there are congregations on five continents. But church members are especially concentrated in the eastern part of the United States.

Like the AME, the AME Zion has a general conference every four years. It, too, retains the office of bishop, but its 3,200 churches are independent. The AME Zion Church is an active participant in Christian ecumenism.

The Christian Methodist Episcopal Church (CME) is the smallest—with 850,000 members—of the three historic Black Methodist church bodies. Most CME members live in the South. The church was founded in 1870 in Jackson, Tennessee, five years after the Civil War. Unlike the AME and the AME Zion, the CME was established in full cooperation with white Methodist churches. Like the other two Black Methodist churches, it supports congregations overseas in Africa and the Caribbean area. The church follows the Methodist pattern of holding a general conference every four years. There are 3,500 CME congregations.

The National Baptist Convention, USA, is the largest and oldest of the three major Black Baptist denominations. The Convention has eight million members in 21,000 churches. It holds an annual convention to transact church business.

A smaller Black church group is the National Baptist Convention of America, which was organized in 1880. The denomination meets annually in a national convention, and its membership is about 3.5 million.

The Progressive National Baptist Convention was founded in 1961 in Cincinnati, Ohio, and has a membership of 2.5 million. Its most famous leaders included Martin Luther King Jr., and Ralph Abernathy.

Beginning in 1971, I participated every Sunday from eleven o'clock at night until one o'clock Monday morning on an interreligious radio program, "Religion on the Line," that aired on WMCA in New York City. A Catholic priest, a Protestant minister, and I responded to questions from the program's listeners. Since the program was live, my two intrepid broadcast partners and I had to answer an extraordinary number of unpredictable religious questions.

The Protestant participant was the Rev. Dr. William A. Jones Jr. He was the pastor of Brooklyn's Bethany Church for 42 years. Bill was both articulate and irenic even when he was confronted by hostile questions from our unseen listeners.

I learned a great deal about the Black churches, their history, religious tenets, successes, and failures. Bill Jones didn't set out to be my mentor in all things dealing with the African American community, but that's what happened over a period of three years. And I, in turn, became his primary source of information about Jews and Judaism.

In the early 1970s, the AJC's Interreligious Affairs Department was led by Marc Tanenbaum. He designated Gerald Strober, our department's educational consultant, and me to develop a national conference on Black-Jewish relations.

I was delighted with the assignment and after much planning that included several trips to Fisk University, a historic Black college in Nashville, Tennessee, the four-day meeting took place in early June of 1974. We attracted fifty prominent Jewish and Black theologians, sociologists, academicians, clergy, and community activists to focus attention on the religious, historical, political, cultural, and social dimensions of Black-Jewish relations from the Biblical period to the present.

The conference was co-chaired by Dr. C. Eric Lincoln, chair of the Department of Religious and Philosophical Studies at Fisk, and Rabbi Tanenbaum. Lincoln was a noted Black sociologist who lectured extensively on religion and minority group relations.

Describing the rationale of the consultation, he declared: "The interest and destinies of Jews and Blacks have touched and, at times, ran together for thousands of years. Distresses incident to minority status in America have sometimes blinded Black Americans and Jewish Americans to their common interests and their common predicament. But each group has strengths the other can hardly afford to be without. Neither group has yet crossed so far into the promised land of the American mainstream as to be irretrievably secure."

Commenting on contemporary relationships between the two groups, he added: "Every Jew in America is somehow better off because of the 'Black Revolution' in the 1960s. The Black Revolution owes a great deal to Jewish involvement and participation. Jews are going to continue being Jews, and Blacks will remain Black. But when this conference is over, each should have a better understanding of what is involved in the self-perception of the other."

Marc added: "This is an important opportunity for both groups to sort out our history, theology, and culture with the clear intention of working together for our shared goals." He pointed out that "although Jews and Blacks have been of considerable help to each other on the basis of their common minority status as well as their common humanity, both groups have suffered because of misconceptions, distortions, and stereotypes about each other that have lain dormant in their collective consciousness."

"It is our hope," he declared, "that this consultation will be a step toward helping both Blacks and Jews restore their sense of mutual appreciation, put their relationship into true perspective, and enable us to go forward with the sense of common destiny that both groups need and want."

Topics included the Bible, Black and Jewish histories in Africa, including Egypt and Ethiopia, contemporary social issues, Blacks and Jews in Religious Thought and Experience, Blacks and Jews in American history, a discussion of affirmative action and quotas in hiring and educational opportunities, and a host of other key, often contentious issues.

The discussions and academic presentations were frank, open, and reflected areas of both congruence and conflict. The Fisk conference took place just six years after Martin Luther King Jr.'s assassination in Memphis, not far from Nashville, and emotions were still raw and painful among the participants.

One of the speakers was Tennessee State Senator Avon N. Williams Jr., a noted civil rights leader. As he began his remarks, he made several comments that angered many Jews and embarrassed the Black participants. In fact, the senator's remarks almost "blew up" the conference.

Nearly fifty years after the Fisk conference, Strober still recalls that explosive moment during the proceedings:

> *I vividly remember Avon Williams shocking the Jewish participants by beginning his presentation with the words, "I'm the product (he may have said, child) of a Jew rape." Was this just a personal pique or did his comments and tone represent the views of many of the Black participants? The Fisk meeting was unlike other dialogues where the Jewish and Christian participants would discuss and debate theological questions and biblical interpretation. But at Fisk we were dealing with contentious, real-life issues.*

Later that day, another Black speaker falsely asserted that Jews, not white Christians, were the major slave traders for hundreds of years and profited greatly from that tragic chapter of Black history.

Facing the possibility of an embarrassing and public collapse of the well-publicized conference, Lincoln and Tanenbaum rushed to assuage the anger of many participants and the conference concluded on a positive note. Both men called for further joint efforts to overcome misunderstandings.

Marc called the meeting "very sticky." He summed up the complex and difficult conference by declaring: "Enough sorting out of distortions on both sides had taken place [at Fisk] allowing for the close of the conference to be upbeat, with both Blacks and Jews searching for new ways to find common ground."

Twelve years later, I was the co-leader of another Black-Jewish national conference. The event's coordinator was Judith H. Banki, the AJC's Associate Interreligious Director. Joining me as co-chair was Dr. James Costen, the president of the Interdenominational Theological Center (ITC), a leading Black seminary located in Atlanta.

Unlike the Fisk Conference, there were fewer participants, scholarly addresses, and academic responses. Rather, I intended to bring young Jewish and Black seminarians together to discuss common issues and concerns.

We screened two films at the ITC meeting: one on the Holocaust and the other on slavery. A Black and a Jewish choir presented a joint musical program, and the conference participants attended two religious services, one led by ITC students and the other conducted by rabbinical students.

Dr. Costen hailed the Black-Jewish consultation as "a journey into understanding" that would "plumb the depths of historical, cultural, and religious roots" and forge relationships for the future. I said: "This pioneering conference takes on added importance in the light of the dramatic emergence of religion as a powerful force in American life. Nothing is more vital to the health of our nation than the fostering of religious and cultural pluralism. For the first time, future rabbis and Black ministers will systematically explore together the richness of our two traditions. What is the Black religious experience? The Jewish experience? Hopefully, the Atlanta conference will increase mutual respect and understanding between the men and women who will be our religious leaders of the twenty-first century."

Dr. Gayraud Wilmore, a prominent Presbyterian leader and professor of church history at ITC, spoke on "Black Liberation" and I delivered an address on "Zionism: The Jewish Liberation Movement."

By 1986, the Black and Jewish communities in Atlanta already had a long record of positive relations, and they were pleased with the conference. Both the ITC staff and Sherry Z. Frank, director of the AJC Atlanta, worked to ensure the conference's success. The New York Times carried a lengthy story complete with photos about the Atlanta meeting.

Ari L. Goldman, then a *New York Times* religion reporter and currently a professor at the Columbia University Journalism School, described the Atlanta conference:

> *Before the concert of sacred music was over, both groups joined hands and together sang a song of praise ... the formal two-day conference involving Jews studying for the rabbinate and Blacks studying for the Christian ministry had been organized to look at their common experiences and to learn about one another ... 'a clear indication that Blacks and Jews in this country are not on a collision course,' said Rabbi A. James Rudin, director of Interreligious Affairs at the American Jewish Committee' We hope to shatter more than a few stereotypes,' said Dr. James Costen, President of the theological center, which trains more Black ministers than any other school in the nation.*

> The seminarians—15 Jewish students and 18 Christian students—explored whether there were links between their separate histories and aspirations. What, they asked, is the relationship between slavery and the Holocaust? And are there parallels between the Black struggle for liberation and the Jewish quest for a Zionist state? But some of the richest learning experiences for the seminarians came in conversations over meals—both kosher and non-kosher food was served, and the Black seminarians took the rabbinical students out on the town Wednesday night.
>
> According to a study by the American Jewish Committee ... there is a paucity of courses at American rabbinical schools on Christianity and Jewish-Christian relations. Jewish and Black students said that they discovered more common ground than they imagined they would ... The students also found that they could learn from one another, especially after watching the other leading worship services.

I was pleased that successful follow-up Black-Jewish seminarians' conferences were held at ITC in 1989 and 1992.

A highlight of my work in Black-Jewish relations occurred in late January 1987. Once again, the scene was Georgia. I was a featured speaker at a large civil rights rally in Cumming, Georgia, located in Forsyth County north of Atlanta.

In fact, it was the biggest march—over 15,000 people—since the Selma, Alabama, civil rights march in 1965. The focus was on Forsyth County's discrimination against Blacks residing in the county.

The marchers were led by Mrs. Coretta Scott King and the Rev. Hosea Williams. Two-hundred buses brought us into Cumming, the county seat of the all-white county. I was in the second bus along with Mrs. King. We were met by several hundred counterdemonstrators, including Ku Klux Klan members.

It was one of the few times in my life I feared for my physical survival. We saw security forces on rooftops with automatic weapons. Then I saw about fifteen men covered in white sheets just outside our "leadership bus," some of them extending their arms in a Nazi salute. The folks on the bus became very quiet.

This was the first time I had ever seen the KKK up close. It was broad daylight and there were many Confederate flags amid the Nazi salutes. We had been warned about snipers who might want to hit the march's leaders, especially Mrs. King.

As we left the bus for the short walk to the dais at the county courthouse, I saw local police, state troopers, armed men with the large letters GBI (Georgia Bureau of Investigation) on the back of their jackets, and numerous FBI agents.

I was honored to be one of the featured speakers that included Black leaders and Senator Gary Hart (D-Colorado) who was then mounting a presidential nomination campaign.

When it was my turn to speak, I declared: "Bigots and racists everywhere must learn that Americans who stand for justice and equality will do whatever it takes, for as long as it takes, to eradicate racist hatred from our midst."

After the formal speeches, we marched through the streets of Cumming, and the counterdemonstrators on the other side of the very tight security line called out: "Nigger lovers ... Commie faggots." I was shocked to see one of the hooded KKK members hold up a sign reading "James Earl Ray, American hero." Ray, of course, assassinated MLK. Another banner proclaimed, "Trade with South Africa—Our Blacks for their Whites." Some of our marchers flashed the V for victory sign for love and peace and sang the civil rights "anthem:" "We Shall Overcome."

Rabbi Alvin Sugarman of The Temple in Atlanta also addressed the march and about forty members of the AJC-sponsored Black-Jewish coalition from Atlanta participated.

The most dramatic difference between my 1964 Hattiesburg, Mississippi, march and the 1987 Forsyth, Georgia, rally was the tremendous support and protection afforded by the security and law enforcement forces. In Hattiesburg, I looked on the local police and the sheriff as, at best, ambivalent toward the clergy marchers. In Cumming, there was no question that the entire state apparatus was on our side.

The success of the three Black-Jewish conferences paved the way for me to lead several groups of Black clergy and church educators on study missions to Israel. Such visits were usually about ten to twelve days in length. The daily schedule was grueling, as the Black leaders and I were "on the go" from seven o'clock in the morning to ten o'clock at night. Included in every itinerary were Jerusalem's Holy Places as well as meetings with Jewish and Arab Knesset members and other Israeli and Palestinian leaders; the Israel Museum; the Yad Vashem Holocaust Memorial Center; an absorption center for newly arrived Ethiopian Jews; the Martin Luther King Jr. Memorial Forest where the Christian visitors planted saplings; meetings with Jewish, Christian, and Muslim religious leaders; Masada; the Galilee (nicknamed

"Jesus land" by several Black ministers); Bethlehem, Nazareth, and an overnight visit to a *kibbutz* in northern Israel.

Many of the study mission participants said their exposure to Israel had taught them that the Middle East conflict is far more complex than they had previously believed. The Blacks also often praised Israel for the way it has absorbed Ethiopian immigrants throughout the country.

They were especially struck by seeing firsthand that the Ethiopians identify strongly with their Jewishness. But some expressed skepticism about the future of a Black community in the predominantly white Jewish state.

They feared that in a nation of new immigrants, Israel's small and vulnerable Black community may not be spared the resurgent racism which is striking roots in Europe and other parts of the world.

"I come from a country where, despite our constitutional Bill of Rights, *de facto* segregation still exists. I've also been told that Jewishness transcends racism. But I want to see how the Ethiopians have integrated, ten years from now," said Barbara Horsham-Brathwaite, director of the Ministry for the Black Catholics in the diocese of Rockville Center, Long Island.

The Rev. Reginald Tuggle, a Long Island Presbyterian pastor, said he was "encouraged by Israeli openness towards Ethiopian Jews, and hopeful of their successful integration in the Israeli society."

Modern Israel generally left a half dozen strong impressions upon visiting Black clergy and church leaders:

1. They were deeply impressed that Hebrew, the language of the Bible, was successfully revived and is the everyday language of Israel. They lamented that their own historic African languages, especially Ashanti, were lost because of a concerted effort by white slave owners.

2. A visit to a *kibbutz* always fascinated the Black pastors. They constantly questioned one another about the possibility of establishing similar Black collective communities in the US.

3. The Black visitors were amazed by the millions of new trees planted by Jews in Israel during the past century. They were often emotionally and spiritually moved when they personally planted young trees in the MLK memorial forest.

4. A common stereotype held by many American Blacks is that Jews are all wealthy upper-middle-class elites: physicians, dentists, lawyers, accoun-

tants, store owners, business tycoons, etc. They were frequently surprised to meet Israelis who fished, farmed, or worked at other modest, but difficult jobs for a living.

5. The public presence throughout the country of young male and female Israel Defense Forces soldiers also impacted the Blacks. Some still held the false belief that Jews are "cowards" and cannot be combat troops, fly jet fighter aircraft, or perform other hazardous military duties.

6. Shattering an often-held belief that all Jews reside in large homes were the *Shabbat* home hospitality meals the visitors enjoyed on Friday evening. The Christian guests were surprised by their hosts' small-sized flats or apartments in Jerusalem and other Israeli cities.

7. The visit to Yad Vashem was for many Black clergy a powerful, painful, and personal history lesson. A shared sense of victimization usually sparked an intense discussion of the Holocaust and human slavery.

Back in the United States, an "alumnus" of a mission to Israel asked me to speak to his congregation. I arrived at his New Jersey church early and was invited to join the youth group of teenagers who were nearing the end of viewing the classic film, *Gone with the Wind*.

When the lights came on after the screening, I witnessed a masterful cinematic dissection of the beloved movie. The minister pointed out the many racist images, tropes, and messages of *Gone with the Wind*. At the church dinner that followed, he told me: "I learned so much at Yad Vashem about how hatred and stereotypes can be transmitted by pictures, movies, and other images, and I applied that fact this afternoon to that hateful film."

A wave of church burnings, largely targeting Black church buildings, swept the nation in 1996. Jewish groups, including the AJC, mobilized and established funds to help rebuild the churches.

A group of Black and Jewish teens helped reconstruct an Alabama church over the Fourth of July holiday and, as noted earlier, in August 1996, President Clinton, Vice President Gore, and their families joined Rabbi Jody Cohen, my Interreligious Department Associate, the Reverend Joan Brown Campbell, the General Secretary of the National Council of Churches, and me to help rebuild a church in rural Tennessee.

In December 1996, I joined AJC CEO David Harris when he presented a sizable donation and participated in the ceremonial groundbreaking of the new building for the Gay's Hill Baptist Church in rural Georgia. AJC Atlanta sent volunteers to help in the construction of the new building who were present for its dedication in July 1997.

AJC in Chicago coordinated fundraising in the religious community, leading the Catholic archdiocese, the Lutheran Church, and other Christian bodies to instruct their members to send their donations for the burned churches to AJC.

Immediately following the devastating 2005 Hurricane Katrina, David Harris asked me to coordinate AJC's relief effort to help rebuild damaged synagogues and churches. I made a tour of the severe damage that took place in both Alabama and Louisiana, including the extensive damage suffered by Dillard University, a Black educational center in New Orleans.

In mid-December 2005, David, Brian Siegel, the Miami AJC Director, and I visited New Orleans to present a total of $575,000 in hurricane relief funds to four local institutions.

Dillard University received $200,000 to help rebuild its Information Technology Center, while $125,000 each went to Saint Clement of Rome, a Catholic church, and two synagogues—Congregation Gates of Prayer, a Reform synagogue next to St. Clement, and Congregation Beth Israel, an Orthodox *shul* in suburban Lakeview that was severely damaged by Katrina.

I consider my work with the African American community one of the highlights of my career. But of course, so much more needs to be done to bring these two great American communities closer together.

A major part of that work includes establishing Black-Jewish relations courses at rabbinical schools and historically African-American seminaries. Such classes could be team-taught by rabbis and Black ministers and would focus on how the Hebrew Bible, a.k.a. the Old Testament, has inspired both faith communities, especially the Exodus liberation story, the inspirational book of Psalms, and the prophetic teachings about justice, righteousness, and freedom—all themes central to both Blacks and Jews.

I urge an increase in the number of Black clergy educators' study missions to Israel. In some cases, rabbis and Jewish seminarians should be a part of such groups.

There is a pressing need for joint trips to a western African port where millions of Blacks were chained and then brutally placed on ships and "exported" to America where they were sold as chattel property. Then the interreligious group should travel on to Israel and especially a visit to the Yad Vashem Holocaust Memorial in Jerusalem.

Finally, rabbis and Black pastors should intensify their joint public opposition to systemic racism and covert and overt antisemitism and explore the historical uniqueness and particularity of both the Holocaust in Europe and the "Middle Passage" of slave ships from Africa to North America.

CHAPTER 14

Evangelicals and Jews: The Last Frontier in Christian-Jewish Relations

WHITE EVANGELICALS IN the United States were one of the most important and complicated Christian groups I worked with during my years at the American Jewish Committee. Unlike Roman Catholic and Eastern Orthodox clergy hierarchies and white liberal Protestants, Evangelicals have no singular organizational address like the National Council of Churches or clearly recognized national or international ecclesiastical leadership similar to the Pope in Rome or the Ecumenical Patriarch in Constantinople/Istanbul.

Despite these decentralized structural factors, I was easily able to relate to and interact with many Evangelical religious leaders and laypeople. That is because I grew up in a community during the 1940s and 1950s where white Evangelicals, led by Southern Baptists, dominated the Southern ethos of my hometown: Alexandria, Virginia. Back then, it was a small racially segregated city of thirty thousand people where Jews and Catholics were distinct minorities.

A second factor that aided my work with Evangelicals was my 1960s United States Air Force experience in Japan and South Korea. Some of my chaplaincy colleagues were Evangelicals, and, sadly, several of them still sought "the conversion of the Jews." However, a notable exception was Chaplain Earl Minor, a Southern Baptist minister stationed at Osan Air Base thirty miles south of Seoul.

As noted in an earlier chapter, I spent a great deal of time during an especially frigid South Korean winter interacting with Earl on a wide range of religious issues. Our shared conversations during many dinners at the

Osan Officers Club provided me with valuable insights into the beliefs, church polity, hopes, concerns, and theology of Evangelical Christianity.

The term "Evangelical" comes from the Greek word *evangelion*, meaning "good news." By this definition, all Christian churches are "Evangelical," that is, they seek to spread the "good news" of the Gospel to the entire world.

However, within the United States, the term "Evangelical" is generally associated with those Christians, mostly Protestants, who affirm that the Bible, both the Hebrew Scriptures and the New Testament, is the sole authority for religious belief and practice. Among some Evangelicals, this affirmation of biblical truth is termed "inerrancy."

Most Evangelicals have undergone a personal conversion experience, either instantaneous or one that evolved over a period of time. This phenomenon is sometimes called being "born again," and it involves the acceptance of Jesus as one's personal savior and Messiah.

A third striking feature of Evangelicals is the need to "go into all the world and preach the gospel," to evangelize either collectively or individually: the Christian "Great Commission."

An Evangelical scholar, Thomas A. Askew, has noted that: "...[E]vangelical Christianity has never been a religious organization, nor primarily a theological system, nor even a containable movement. It is a mood, a perspective, an approach grounded in biblical theology, but reaching into the motifs of religious experience...The Evangelical faith has roots that reach back to European Reformation theology...as well as to the Puritan tradition."

It is estimated there are over sixty million Americans who are Evangelicals, and they live in all sections of the country. Evangelicals are members of many different churches; indeed, almost every "mainline" Protestant church has within it an Evangelical component. For example, the United Methodist Church "continues its strong Evangelical heritage. Within each congregation is a vital center of biblical study and evangelism—a blending of personal piety and discipleship."

The Southern Baptist Convention is the largest Evangelical denomination in the United States, but one of the fastest-growing Evangelical bodies is the Assemblies of God (AG), headquartered in Springfield, Missouri. The Assemblies list about three million members and thirteen thousand churches.

I was a guest in Springfield in the 1990s and attended an AG service during my visit. As the prayers were invoked, several people began speaking in tongues: an integral component of the Pentecostal AG liturgy. The words uttered—a rapid-fire string of strange syllables—were completely foreign to me, but after the service, I was told what I heard were Hebrew verses from the Book of Psalms.

When I gently informed my hosts it was not Hebrew, they were at first skeptical of my remarks, and then they remembered I was a rabbi who knew Hebrew texts and the sound of that ancient language. I was told "speaking in tongues" spontaneously emerges from the power of the religious service and, indeed, is not a particular language.

Although smaller in membership, the Evangelical Free Church of America, based in Minneapolis is another center of Evangelical Christianity. While "mainline" church membership has sharply decreased, especially since 2000, the Evangelical numbers including members, new churches, and income have increased.

The noted church historian Martin E. Marty of the University of Chicago has described the current prominence of the Evangelicals as "the most significant religious trend in the United States."

Historically, Evangelical Christianity was the mainstream of American Protestantism until the 1890s, when it appeared to be eclipsed by theologically liberal churches. Indeed, Evangelicals were shunted aside after 1920, and especially following the famous 1925 Scopes "monkey trial" in Tennessee that pitted Evangelical William Jennings Bryan, a three-time Democratic nominee for US president, against the religiously liberal Clarence Darrow as contending lawyers.

The success of the play and film *Inherit the Wind* in the 1950s seemed to confirm liberal religion's victory over Evangelicalism. But it was not to be. Evangelical Christianity continued as the main spiritual expression of millions of Americans, particularly those residing in the South and Southwest.

But it was not until the 1970s that Evangelical Christianity reemerged as a strong and highly visible movement. Southern Baptist Sunday School teacher Jimmy Carter's election as president in 1976 and the enormous popularity of another Southern Baptist, the evangelist Billy Graham, were only two confirmations that some significant religious changes had taken place in America.

David F. Wells, an Evangelical professor, graphically describes those changes: "Liberal Protestants [e.g., the National Council of Churches and the "mainline" churches] had always taken it for granted that … there was a divine mandate securing for them their role as custodians of the culture." In the early 1970s this notion was unceremoniously abandoned, and the remaining heirs of the liberal Protestant tradition became contemporary culture's chief critics.

Indeed, many years ago I became personally involved in a liberal Protestant project that was highly critical of the contemporary American political culture of that era.

As noted in an earlier chapter, in February 1964 I spent a week in Hattiesburg, Mississippi, marching in front of the Forrest County courthouse in support of voting rights for African Americans who, in that era, were denied their constitutional right to cast ballots. I was joined in those demonstrations by rabbinical colleagues and Christian clergy. The marches were led by national leaders of the Presbyterian Church.

It was a challenging, frightening time, filled with threats of bodily violence and possible imprisonment. But thanks to the Presbyterian leadership, the marchers were well protected both physically and legally.

Back then, in the mid-1960s, the building of serious and constructive Evangelical-Jewish relations was not yet part of the interreligious mix. The reasons were both geographical and theological.

Until recently, most American Jews lived in the major urban centers of the Northeast or the Upper Midwest: New York City, Philadelphia, Boston, Hartford, Providence, Baltimore, Pittsburgh, Cleveland, Chicago, and Detroit. The Christian groups Jews encountered in those cities were often Catholics with family roots in Italy, Ireland, and Poland, and Eastern Orthodox Christians from Greece, Russia, Romania, and the Balkans.

Evangelicals, mainly the descendants of immigrants to the US from Great Britain and other western European countries, were the religious majority in the South and Southwest, areas—until recently—with small Jewish populations.

Those demographic patterns meant the formative American experiences for both Jews and Evangelicals took place in different sections of the country. Until the early 1970s, members of the two faiths were similar to Henry Wadsworth Longfellow's "ships that pass in the night," barely aware of one another and never truly encountering one another as vibrant and unique spiritual communities.

Geographical and emotional distance that bordered on a huge chasm was why many Evangelicals and Jews dealt in caricatures and stereotypes about the unknown "Other." Each group hurled verbal hand grenades at one another. Jews perceived Evangelicals as unenlightened "Elmer Gantrys," "rednecks," "crackers," even bigoted antisemites. Conversely, Evangelicals defined Jews as "Christ killers," "deniers of Jesus," and "Scribes and Pharisees."

There were two initial encounters between Evangelicals and Jews in the 1960s and 1970s. The first took place took place in 1969 at the Southern Baptist Seminary in Louisville, Kentucky, and the second six years later in New York City. I helped organize and participated in both conferences.

The American Jewish Committee cosponsored the events with several Christian institutional partners. In the early years of Evangelical-Jewish dialogue, I wrote that a "dam of pent-up interest, curiosity, and excitement burst" between Jews and Evangelicals, two communities that had been distant from one another, but soon discovered they had much in common.

Participants at the two conferences addressed the meaning of Messiah, biblical theology, the impact of modern Israel, conversion, witness, mission, and the long-held negative images each group had of the other. Also on the joint agenda was the plight of Jews and Evangelicals in the Soviet Union, the quest for global human rights, the roots of religious antisemitism, the Holocaust, church and synagogue polity, the shared American principle of church-state separation, and the appropriate role of religion in American life.

Participants from both communities felt they were spiritual pioneers pressing forward on a new interreligious frontier. Since then, numerous joint Evangelical-Jewish projects, conferences, and interchanges have taken place throughout America.

The Evangelical-Jewish encounter that began at that time was the "third wave" in interreligious relations in the United States.

The liberal/mainline Protestant churches were the first to enter into significant dialogues with Jews after World War II, and the Roman Catholic Church followed in 1965 after the conclusion of the Second Vatican Council.

Whenever Jews and Evangelicals meet in dialogue, they soon discover five major areas of mutual interest and agreement:

1. A similar congregational structure of independent synagogues and churches.

2. A deep respect and reverence for the integrity and authenticity of the Hebrew Bible.

3. An abiding commitment to the security and survival of both the people and the State of Israel.

4. A shared commitment to the principle of church-state separation in the United States, but this is changing with the rise of the Religious Right.

5. A common opposition to antisemitism in all its forms both here and overseas.

Evangelicals have been among the most public supporters of Israel within the Christian community. It is a theological commitment that runs deep and is not easily shaken by the international machinations of realpolitik.

Because many church leaders, especially within "mainline" Protestant churches, have been highly critical of certain Israeli policies, a growing number of American Jews and Israelis have warmly welcomed the Evangelicals' strong support of the Jewish state based upon the Christian belief that a Jewish "ingathering of the exiles" is a vital prerequisite for the eagerly anticipated Second Coming of Jesus.

Because of this belief, the largest number of American Christians who visit Israel each year come from Evangelical churches, and Evangelicals can be counted upon to petition US and UN officials regarding the pressing needs and concerns of Israel.

At the same time, many Evangelicals remain active in campaigns to convert Jews to Christianity. Unfortunately, Hebrew Christian groups, often called Messianic Jews, have sometimes been successful in gaining support, both financial and moral, from Evangelical churches and their leaders.

Many Evangelical leaders are pressing for mandated prayer and Bible reading in America's public schools, a position that is rejected by most American Jews. And most members of the Religious Right are also Evangelical Christians. Clearly, on some issues, such as vigorous public support for Israel, Evangelicals and Jews stand together. But on other key issues, it is the "mainline" churches that often act in coalition with the American Jewish community.

But one must be careful not to draw the dividing lines too sharply on such complex issues. Not all Evangelicals are strong supporters of Israel, and not all Evangelicals seek the conversion of the Jewish people to Christianity. Not all "mainline" church leaders are harsh critics of Israel, and there are conversionist elements within some of those liberal churches as well. Like all other religious groups, Evangelicals are not of one voice on all questions and issues.

For example, Dr. William S. LaSor was a leading Evangelical theologian, but he rejected attempts to convert Jews. LaSor declared: "Just as I refuse to believe that God has rejected his people [the Jews] [Romans 11:1] and that there is no longer any place for Israel in God's redemptive work or in the messianic hope, so I refuse to believe that we who were once not his people, and who have become his people only through his grace, can learn nothing from those who from of old have been his people."

And in 1973, Billy Graham, the leading evangelist of the twentieth century, publicly criticized the excesses of the Key 73 national evangelical campaign. Meeting at his Montreat, North Carolina, home with Marc Tanenbaum and Gerald Strober, Graham cited the New Testament book of Romans, chapters 9-11. He declared:

"I believe God has always had a special relationship with the Jewish people … In my evangelistic efforts, I have never felt called to single out Jews as Jews … just as Judaism frowns on proselytizing that is coercive, or that seeks to commit men against their will, so do I."

Clearly, Graham was the most significant and influential evangelical leader of the last sixty years. He was also the most controversial.

I attended the Manhattan press conference prior to Graham's June 2005 crusade. It was the last of his 714 public crusades that spanned many decades, and it was clear Graham still commanded attention. There were twenty-one television cameras and the familiar whirl of cameras clicking and flashing. Graham remained big news in America's media capital.

By then he had stopped commenting on political issues as he once did. "I went too far" in becoming entangled with political leaders and public policy, he said.

And he surely "went too far" in his 1972 secretly taped White House conversation with President Nixon.

Graham's anti-Jewish remarks represent the low point of his career when he told the president Jews control the American media: "This stranglehold has got to be broken or the country's going down the drain." Incredibly, Graham agreed with Nixon's previous bigoted words about Jews and their alleged influence in the United States.

"You believe that?" Nixon asked Graham after the "stranglehold" comment.

"Yes, sir," was the reply.

"Oh, boy," said the president. "So, do I. I can't ever say that, but I believe it."

In the same conversation, Graham mentioned he had Jewish friends in the media who "swarm around me and are friendly to me." But he told Nixon, "They don't know how I really feel about what they're doing to this country."

Tragically, Graham failed to stand up to Nixon by rejecting the president's obscene remarks. We expect important religious leaders to speak truth to power. Instead, Graham agreed with Nixon and added his own hostile remarks.

When the tapes were released in 2002, Graham begged the Jewish community's forgiveness for his mistake and offered personal repentance "on my hands and knees."

So, it was not surprising his first comments at the news conference were warm words of friendship and appreciation for the Jewish community. In a private conversation with me later, he repeated his words of contrition and hoped his public act of repentance would be accepted by the Jewish community.

His remarks set me thinking about Graham's long, often unknown, positive relationship with Jews, Judaism, and the State of Israel.

I first met Graham in 1977 in Atlanta when the American Jewish Committee presented him an award for his interfaith work. Many Christians were surprised by my organization's action, and some Jews, both lay and rabbinic, were critical. After all, Graham's single message always was the Gospel. But Graham deserved the AJC award.

In those years he worked effectively behind the scenes at "the highest levels" in Washington and elsewhere in support of Soviet Jewry.

At the same time, Graham produced the film *His Land*, a glowing cinematic tribute to modern Israel and its people. The movie attracted critical acclaim and large audiences of both Christians and Jews.

In addition to his 1973 statement mentioned above, Graham in 1996, was again critical when the Southern Baptist Convention, Graham's denomination, adopted a resolution to actively single out Jews for conversion.

I met Graham again in 1991 during an earlier crusade in New York City. He was very sensitive to the Jewish community and made clear he never targets any specific group for conversion.

No one knows how history will ultimately treat Billy Graham. But I am certain we shall never see his like again. That's the way it always is with a true original.

It is no secret that most American Jews differ with the public policy positions held by many Evangelicals, including their opposition to gun control, abortion, the Equal Rights Amendment, embryonic stem cell research, gay rights, and their support for mandated prayer and Bible reading in public schools.

Despite those differences, a major part of my job was to intensify AJC's contacts with conservative Protestant church bodies. It was a delicate balancing act fraught with pitfalls and conflicting responses to specific issues: we joined with liberal Protestants against Evangelicals on church-state issues, but we also welcomed Evangelical support for Israel while many liberal Christian leaders were cool, at best, or hostile at worst, towards the Jewish state.

Several Jewish leaders, including some prominent rabbis, gravitated toward Evangelicals and welcomed their support. The fact the AJC and other members of the US Jewish community worked closely with Evangelicals upset some prominent liberal Protestant leaders.

But my task of building relationships with both liberal and conservative Christian groups was based on the historic fact that Zionism was never looked on favorably by most "main line" Protestant leaders before 1948, and the State of Israel, Zionism's creation, has been a constant target of criticism and hostility from the same Protestant leadership cadre.

However, I was also well aware the proverbial men and women in the pews of "mainline" churches have favorably viewed Israel since its independence. Gallup polls and other opinion surveys consistently indicate American public support for Israel sits at about 70 percent and only 15 percent back the Palestinians.

This split between national Protestant leaders and their flocks is not limited to Israel; it reflects the grassroots' rejection of many public positions taken by the NCC and denominational leaders that were the creation of their top echelon professional staffs. The tension between leaders and churchgoers is real and one reason, among others, for the continuing decline in "mainline" membership.

However, many anti-Israel Protestant leaders constantly warned me about the dangers inherent in the so-called Religious Right. Unlike their negative stances on Israel, they were correct vis-à-vis the positions of the extremist branch of American Evangelicalism.

The presence of the Religious Right in the United States has important implications for the Jewish interreligious encounter with the total Christian community. Religious Right members are waging an aggressive war against theological and cultural modernity or what they term as "secular humanism." Interestingly, they entered the national political arena relatively recently.

For many decades, they followed a policy of strict separation from the world of politics. That estrangement was based on the conviction the world was sinful and unworthy of their involvement since Jesus's Kingdom would soon arrive. But in the 1970s, conservative politicians reached out to Evangelical churches in an effort to expand their political base.

They encountered several key Evangelical religious leaders who became active partners. Chief among them was the Rev. Jerry Falwell, Sr. who headed a large church in Lynchburg, Virginia. Around the time of the 1980 presidential election, he established the Moral Majority movement that urged the fundamentalists to abandon their old distrust of politics. Falwell, along with fellow Evangelicals Pat Robertson and Billy Graham, all supported a divorced film star, non-Evangelical presidential candidate, Ronald Reagan, in 1980. They turned their collective electoral backs on President Jimmy Carter and Independent presidential candidate Congressman John Anderson, both of whom were strong Evangelical Christians.

The organization's name, "Moral Majority," implied the rest of American society was the "Immoral Minority." The Religious Right believes the Founders [of America] never meant to separate the institutions of church and state or to prohibit the legal establishment of religion. Such a view is historically inaccurate and endangers our common welfare because it uses religion to divide rather than unite the American people.

At its heart, the Religious Right believes America has lost its moral compass as a nation. There are some leaders of the movement who constantly invoke "Divine Authority" for their policies and platforms, and who characterize their opponents as "sinful" or "ungodly." Behind the catchy rhetoric of "family values" and "moral tradition," the Religious Right is attempting to establish a "Christian America" that will embody its particular and exclusivist theological beliefs and supposedly solve our society's problems.

During my AJC career, I constantly articulated several significant points about the Religious Right. There is, of course, no objection to its participation in the American political process and I constantly asserted that separation of church and state does not mean the separation of religion and politics. However, many Americans, including Jews, do raise objections to an exclusivist, non-pluralistic vision of America.

In the Religious Right's attempt to "Christianize" America and the world, what is the place of non-Christians? What would be the status of those Christians who do not share such particular religious beliefs?

And although members of the Religious Right are strong public supporters of Israel, authentic interreligious relations are not a kind of a quid pro quo game in which Jews conveniently overlook the disturbing domestic political agendas of their dialogue partners because of support for Israel.

Because the Christian-Jewish agenda is a broad-based one, Evangelical support on one key issue—Israel—does not guarantee agreement or consensus on other vital questions, including financial vouchers for parents of private school students, capital punishment, student-led prayer in public schools, an abstinence-based sex-education curriculum, the teaching of scientific creationism in public school science classes, and a highly restrictive immigration policy for the United States that favors newcomers from northern and western Europe.

It is ironic that the Religious Right is seeking to project its exclusivist agenda at a time when recent American population studies indicate that the United States is increasingly becoming a multireligious, multiethnic, and multiracial society. Americans are more, not less, diverse in their religious identities. The attempt to create an exclusive and constricted "Christian America" flies directly into the face of these demographic facts.

Many Jews also suspect the presence of antisemitism within the Religious Right even though it is difficult to point to any explicitly antisemitic statements in its carefully worded official rhetoric.

But in 1998 Pat Robertson wrote: "The liberal Jews have actually forsaken Biblical faith in God and made a religion out of political liberalism … If someone attacks abortion-on-demand or asks for prayer in the schools, the liberal Jewish community reacts as if this stand were somehow antisemitic. They have anti-Christianity liberalism intermingled with Judaism to such a degree they can't distinguish anymore."

Almost twenty-five years after the founding of the Moral Majority, the 2004 election of George W. Bush to a second presidential term solidified and confirmed the extraordinary potency of key Evangelical issues in the political arena. Three of those issues can be conveniently lumped together as the "Three Gs"—God, guns, and gays—but, as noted above, they also include opposition to abortion and embryonic stem-cell research, attacks on popular culture, and support for unrestricted expressions and symbols of Christian faith in the shared communal square, especially in public schools and courtrooms.

In the past cycle of recent elections, these values—said to be the major concern of at least one-quarter of American voters—were more decisive than jobs, health care, education, and even terrorism as prominent issues. Political observers, many of them stunned by the high priority voters placed on religious issues, emphasized that white Evangelicals in 2004 supported Bush over his Democratic opponent Senator John Kerry by a four-to-one margin.

Donald Trump in both 2016 and 2020 received about 80 percent of the white Evangelical vote. Indeed, some Evangelicals sincerely believe Trump was anointed by God to save America.

It is clear the white Evangelical community supplies the religious and political ideology as well as the foot soldiers, a.k.a. voters, who fuel the current "religious/cultural war."

In addition to the issues mentioned earlier, Evangelicals are generally united in opposing same-sex marriages, and work for the appointment of "constitutionally and theologically sound judges" to the Supreme Court and all other legal positions.

A significant feature of my interreligious work was challenging many of the Evangelicals' public positions, while at the same time building support for Israel and Soviet Jewry and other traditional American values and law. Today, the strengthening of Evangelical-Jewish relations shows no sign of easing, even though ambivalences, ambiguities, and differences remain.

Are Jews and Evangelicals permanent domestic adversaries because of long-standing differences between them on the host of domestic issues mentioned above? The Jewish community rejects all Evangelical efforts to convert Jews to Christianity. The term, "completed Jews," used by many Evangelicals to describe a converted Jew, is odious because it implies Judaism is an incomplete religion, a belief Jews and many Christians deny.

At the same time, the two religious communities are linked together as international partners; both are committed to the survival and security of the State of Israel and the enhancement of human rights and religious liberty throughout the world.

The recent surge in antisemitic acts and language, especially in the United States, parts of Europe, and within many Islamic nations, is a cause of concern that hopefully will bring Evangelicals and Jews closer as part of a broad-based interreligious coalition that opposes hatred of Jews and Judaism and all other forms of religious bigotry and prejudice.

Because Evangelical missionaries are active in many regions of the world, it is imperative Evangelicals speak out against what the Vatican Council in 1965 called "hatreds, persecutions, and manifestations of antisemitism."

In the last decades of the twentieth century, Evangelicals and Jews were active partners as they demanded religious liberty and freedom of conscience for Jews and Christian believers—often Evangelicals—residing within the former Soviet Union. Evangelicals were highly supportive of the public campaign to allow Soviet Jews to immigrate to Israel, the US, and other lands of freedom.

It was a successful effort. Since the collapse of the Soviet Union, more than one million Jews have left the former USSR. However, others have chosen to remain in the three Baltic republics of Estonia, Latvia, and Lithuania as well as Russia, Belarus, and Ukraine.

While their situations are much improved from the grim days of the former USSR, Jews remain victims of antisemitism and discrimination. Today, another coalition of Evangelicals and Jews is required to monitor and actively oppose the continued persistence of antisemitism in Europe and Muslim nations.

Another area of partnership between Evangelicals and Jews is working to protect Israel. The creation of the Jewish state has placed Evangelicals and Jews in new theological and psychological territory. Neither community regards modern Israel as simply another nation.

Marvin R. Wilson, my longtime Evangelical colleague and interreligious partner, and distinguished Professor Emeritus of Biblical and Theological Studies at Gordon College in Massachusetts, has written:

"The concepts of 'land of promise' and 'return to Zion' are deeply grounded in biblical literature. The very last word in the Hebrew Bible [2 Chronicles 36:23] is a call to 'go up' to Zion … I also believe that the remarkable preservation of Israel over the centuries and her recent return to the land are in keeping with those many biblical texts which give promise of her future."

Millions of Evangelicals are aware the land of Israel was where Jesus taught, was executed by the Roman Empire, and where, they believe, he was resurrected.

For them, modern Israel is a powerful combination of biblical landscape and a sense that Israel reborn is part of a divine economy that calls for a Jewish ingathering of exiles as a prerequisite for the Second Coming of Jesus.

In my 2006 book, The Baptizing of America: The Religious Right's Plans for The Rest of Us, I note that:

"Evangelicals do constitute the largest group of Christians who are actively involved in politics and piety, and they lead the current effort to baptize America. But not all Evangelicals seek to permanently alter the historic communal fabric of American life. Such Evangelicals may, in fact, be devout Christians, but they do not want to shatter or even weaken the long-held American principle of church-state separation, nor do they desire the legal establishment of any religion, even their own, in today's America."

Evangelicals and Jews need to recognize that the Religious Right believes America is somehow morally and religiously lost as a nation. That is why some Religious Right leaders continually invoke "Divine Authority" to validate their own political policies and partisan platforms, and characterize their opponents as "sinful" or "ungodly."

Members of the Religious Right remain committed to changing the increasingly pluralistic America. Some zealots speak of establishing a "Christian America" that will embody the extremist movement's particular and exclusivist theological beliefs.

During an Evangelical-Jewish meeting some years ago at Gordon College, Marvin Wilson and I jointly issued a ten-point Conference Call. The words of the Call remain relevant and still form a basis for continued Evangelical-Jewish cooperation:

1. We are united in a common struggle against antisemitism. We are outraged by the continued presence of this evil and pledge to work together for the elimination of this and all other forms of racism. We are committed jointly to educating this present and future generations about the unspeakable horror of the Holocaust.

2. We categorically reject the notion that Zionism is racism. Zionism, the Jewish people's national liberation movement, has deep roots in the Hebrew Scriptures, no less than in the painful history of the Jewish people.

3. We are committed to supporting Israel as a Jewish state within secure and recognized borders. We also recognize that Palestinian Arabs have legitimate rights. We pledge our joint efforts on behalf of a just and lasting peace, not only between Jews and Arabs, but among all peoples of the Middle East.

4. No government is sacred, and no government's policies are beyond criticism. But we strongly object to the practice of holding Israel to a different standard of conduct and morality from that applied to all other nation-states, especially those committed to Israel's destruction.

5. We affirm the eternal validity and contemporary relevance of the Hebrew Scriptures as a primary source of moral, ethical, and spiritual values. And

we pledge to work together to uphold and advance these biblical values in our society and throughout the world.

6. We pledge to uphold the precious value of religious pluralism in our society. We strongly condemn those who would use unethical, coercive, devious, or manipulative means to proselytize others. Witness to one's faith must always be accompanied with great sensitivity and respect for the integrity of the other person lest religious freedom and pluralism be threatened.

7. We will seek to overcome any popular stereotypes, caricatures, and images that may contribute to one faith community falsely perceiving the other. To further this end, we pledge to continue to examine the rich spiritual legacy that Judaism and Evangelicalism hold sacred together as well as their profound differences of belief.

8. We share a common calling to eliminate inhumanity and injustice among all humankind. We also jointly resolve to work together to prevent nuclear annihilation and to pursue the path of world peace.

9. We share a joint commitment to uphold the principle of separation of church and state in the United States. We pledge to deepen our joint involvement in the struggle to achieve human rights and religious liberty for our coreligionists throughout the world.

CHAPTER 15

The Battle of Camp David: A Victory in 1991, But Could It Be Won Today?

BACK IN 1991, I was personally involved in a battle that focused on this nagging question: Is the United States a Christian nation? But despite its importance, the fight took place far from the public view, in a high-profile location with one of America's best-known addresses: Camp David, Maryland.

The important issues raised at the presidential retreat in the Catoctin Mountains were a preview, a foretaste, of what is currently taking place throughout the country. But now, years later, I wonder if the Battle of Camp David would have turned out the same way in today's highly polarized political and religious climate.

April 21, 1991 was a cold and rainy Sunday. Despite the miserable weather, my wife and I were excited because we were among the 150 guests invited to join President George H.W. Bush in the formal dedication service of the newly constructed interfaith chapel at Camp David, the presidential retreat.

Although the chapel dedication took place more than ten years before the 9/11 terrorist attacks, security was extremely tight as our car approached the entrance to Camp David. Metal detectors swept over every vehicle, including the area underneath each auto and truck. Car trunks, personal packages, and purses were examined, and armed guards checked and rechecked our names on a master list.

While the lengthy security procedure was taking place, I thought back to the day two years earlier when my friend Bishop James Mathews of the United Methodist Church had invited me to join the Camp David Chapel Committee, composed of clergy and lay people.

Since the days of Franklin D. Roosevelt, American chief executives have used the camp near Thurmont, Maryland, as a secluded, wooded retreat, free of the White House press corps and the general public. Originally built as a public works project in the 1930s during the New Deal, Camp David had been a Boy Scout campsite before April 1942, when Roosevelt chose it as a presidential escape from the brutal Washington summer heat.

FDR mischievously called it "Shangri-La" to make it sound remote and mysterious, although it is only seventy-four miles from the capital. The more prosaic President Dwight D. Eisenhower named the camp in honor of his grandson, David.

Surprisingly, in 1989, there was no permanent chapel at Camp David. Over the years, beginning with FDR in the 1940s, religious services had been held in the camp's kitchen or bowling alley. The lack of a chapel building at Camp David upset Kenneth Plummer, a devoted United Methodist layman from nearby Chambersburg, Pennsylvania.

In the late 1980s, Plummer began a personal campaign to build a permanent chapel. As a teenager, Plummer had participated in Boy Scout outings at the camp, and as an adult, his construction company had transformed the site into America's presidential retreat.

With the White House's official permission and encouragement, Plummer started his campaign by asking his fellow Methodist, Bishop Mathews, to assist him in putting together a working group of religious, civic, political, and business leaders to build what came to be known as "The Camp David Interfaith Chapel."

Besides Mathews, the fifteen-member "blue ribbon" chapel committee included Archbishop Iakovos, the Greek Orthodox primate of North and South America, Episcopal Bishop Theodore Eastman of Maryland, Cardinal James Hickey of Washington, DC, Methodist Bishop Fenton May, and former US Senator J. Glenn Beall Jr. (R-Maryland). I was the only Jewish member of the group.

Our committee's task was to raise private funds to construct a building that would be used for worship, study, and meditation by presidents, their families, Camp David's military support staff, Cabinet members, and visiting world leaders.

We were successful in our fundraising efforts, and the chapel was completed in the spring of 1991. On that gloomy Sunday, our committee was officially turning the facility over to the United States government as "a gift to the American people." The government would then be responsible for the building's maintenance.

In addition to raising money, our committee was also responsible for the chapel's architectural plans and the artistic designs of the eight stained-glass windows of the new building.

When I accepted Mathews' invitation, I had no idea that the committee's internal debate over the proposed window designs would become one of the most difficult and significant fights of my life. I call the chapel window dispute "The Battle of Camp David" because it raised issues central to American life that have extraordinary relevance today.

Even though the Battle took place out of public sight at a highly secret and secure location, a place 99.9999 percent of Americans will never visit, it reflected the tension between those who see America as a Christian nation and those who believe our nation has no established religion, but instead provides constitutional guarantees of freedom of religion and conscience for all its citizens.

These issues began with America's Founding Fathers in the late eighteenth century and have never been fully resolved or permanently settled. What is the proper relationship between religion, especially Christianity, and the state in our national political life? Should Christianity, the majority faith community, and its adherents receive preferential treatment?

During my service as a United States Air Force chaplain in Japan and Korea, the Christian clergy and I shared the same chapel building and support staff. I understood firsthand what an interfaith chapel was and how it operated.

During my tour of duty, I worked closely with priests, ministers, and pastors, and that working relationship made a deep impression upon me. I believed that military interreligious cooperation was a model to emulate in civilian life.

As a Camp David Chapel Committee member, I had the distinct sense of representing not only the American Jewish community, but I also felt an obligation to promote the mutual understanding and respect between Christians and Jews that I had experienced in the Air Force. I also believed that I was defending the Constitution's First Amendment, which guarantees freedom of religion and the historical church-state legacy of Thomas Jefferson, James Madison, and George Mason.

The committee work was both exhilarating and discouraging. It was exciting for a rabbi to participate in a history-making project at the world-famous Camp David. But it was disheartening because some committee members, despite the chapel's official interfaith name and announced purpose, insisted that we were building a Christian church and not an edifice of sacred space where all Americans would be comfortable, as well as the camp's international visitors.

The Battle of Camp David began when a highly patriotic and deeply religious Hungarian Christian émigré artist, Rudolph Sandon, and his wife Helen, of Little Valley, New York, presented their plans for the windows. When the designs were first laid out, I found them unacceptable but remained silent with my criticisms. There were "oohs" and "aahs" from committee members since it was clear that the Sandons were skilled artists.

However, I was dismayed by the initial drawings. Six of the eight windows contained the denominational logos of several major Protestant bodies, including the Presbyterian Church, the United Methodist Church, the United Church of Christ, and the Episcopal Church.

The seventh window featured a Christian cross representing Roman Catholicism, and the eighth window included symbols of Judaism, Islam, and Hinduism. The Sandons' original plan also called for a large Presidential seal and the famous words "We the People."

I was eager to hear the reactions of my Christian colleagues. Unfortunately, their responses were disappointing once the initial artistic praise subsided. It seemed that everyone was satisfied with the dominant Christian themes for the chapel windows. Everyone but me.

I waited in vain for a committee member to raise some of the issues that were churning within me. But as person after person lauded the window designs, I realized that any objections would have to come from me.

When my turn came to speak, I carefully presented my critique. I made it clear that my objections to the window designs were not aimed at the Sandons or their artistic skills. In fact, the Sandons remained the primary artists, and ultimately the final window designs were theirs.

I recognized that the Sandons' plans expressed a basic view held by many committee members. That is, the Camp David Chapel should contain specific Christian symbols reflecting the majority religious population of the United States, with one window only allotted to Jews, Muslims, and Hindus. There was nothing for Buddhists, Shintoists, and America's indigenous peoples.

And in the six Protestant windows, the artists went far beyond the mere use of the cross or other recognizable Christian symbols.

Incredibly, they planned to create stained-glass versions of the specific logo designs of six major Protestant church bodies; designs that usually appear on denominational stationery and in various church publications.

If the original designs had been accepted, the chapel windows would have reflected the corporate images of Protestant Christianity.

I said that even if one shared the Sandons' view of Christian triumphalism and dominance in the United States, their math was poor. Nearly one of every four Americans is a Roman Catholic; by that reckoning, Catholics "rated" two of the eight Camp David windows. Three-quarters of the windows were allocated to a half-dozen Protestant churches whose total membership was nowhere near 75 percent of the total US population.

But, naturally my strong objections to the initial window plans were not based on demography or the number of people identified with a specific faith community, no matter how large. I was outraged by the arrogant belief that Christianity, and indeed, only a part of that faith community, merited stained glass windows at Camp David's interfaith chapel. I especially objected to the not-so-subtle message that only Christianity and Christians deserved to be highlighted in the chapel windows of the presidential retreat. The implication would be obvious to any visitor to Camp David: Only Christianity and Christians truly merit the term "American."

I felt strongly the chapel should contain no permanent symbols or artistic representations of any particular faith. The key word was permanent. I knew from my Air Force experience that the Christian baptismal fount, the Crucifix, and the Holy Ark that houses Judaism's sacred Torah scrolls, the Menorah, and other religious objects were not a permanent part of the military chapels I had used in Japan and Korea. Rather, in a spirit of mutual respect and understanding, the specific objects required for liturgy and religious ritual were brought into the chapel area for use during a Christian or Jewish worship service and then returned to well-maintained storage areas.

Since this arrangement worked well in conventional USAF chapels overseas, I felt it was even more important that such procedures be followed at the presidential retreat chapel. I stressed to my committee colleagues that US presidents and their families will come and go, but the religiously diverse American people, the true owners of Camp David, will always remain. Even though few of them may visit the place, Camp David belongs to all Americans, and, I argued, the proposed chapel must reflect this fact.

I protested that the proposed designs ran counter to the spirit of American history and the Bill of Rights: i.e., there must be no *de jure* "establishment" of any single religion in America. Unfortunately, the proposed windows favored de facto one faith community of America for permanent validation.

Devoting seven of the eight windows to artistic representations of Christianity was a disservice to American traditions, values, and jurisprudence. I said it would be a serious error and a misreading of our nation's history if Camp David, of all places, did not reflect our long-standing national commitment to religious freedom and spiritual diversity.

I continued my litany of objections by pointing out that every religion known to the human family was represented in the United States, and that extraordinary demographical reality will not change. I added that because leaders from other nations, many of them not Christians, are frequently guests at Camp David, it was imperative their unique religious sensibilities be respected.

I reminded my chapel committee colleagues that Israeli Prime Minister Menachem Begin, an Orthodox Jew, and Egyptian President Anwar Sadat, a devout Muslim, had hammered out a peace agreement between their two countries at Camp David in 1978. In previous years, Soviet leaders engaged in high-level meetings with US officials at the camp, aimed at easing Cold War tensions.

We now know that some USSR diplomats, while outwardly professing atheism and Communist dialectic materialism, secretly practiced Eastern Orthodox Christianity, a faith community that was omitted from the original chapel window designs.

Finally, I urged that the original plans for the windows be scrapped and redesigned to express universal religious values common to all peoples. I told committee members that I had no problem with the presidential seal and the famous words from the Constitution: "We the People." It was, after all, the chapel for the American presidential retreat.

Because of my strong objections to the Christian symbols and themes in the Sandons' window designs, what had started as a polite aesthetic debate soon became a robust debate. I noted that the key issue, which is hotly debated today, is whether the United States is, in fact, a "Christian nation," or whether it is a religiously diverse country with no one "established" faith.

Until the Battle of Camp David, I had falsely, perhaps naively, believed that both issues had been definitively settled. Settled, I thought, more than two hundred years earlier by the adoption of the Bill of Rights containing the Constitution's First Amendment, which guarantees religious freedom and prohibits the official "establishment" of any religion by our government.

Established, I had mistakenly thought, in the early 1800s by President Jefferson's historic letter to members of a Danbury, Connecticut, Baptist church, asserting that a "wall of separation" exists between religion and state. Settled, too, by the many legal decisions, including US Supreme Court cases, that legally upheld the principle of church-state separation.

But the Camp David fight over the artwork of the chapel windows proved that I was wrong. I learned that nothing is ever really resolved when it involves the interplay between God and the United States, between religion and state, and between the American Eagle and the Christian Cross. It remains a neuralgic concern that never goes away, a divisive political and religious issue.

But despite the Constitution, Jefferson, and the decisions of various courts, each generation of Americans has been forced to redefine the issues of religion and state and the relationship between politics and piety. The Camp David Chapel debate between 1989 and 1991 was my turn. The fight involved what artistically represents a microcosm of the continuing political fights over such potent terms as "Christian nation," "mainstream America," and "religious pluralism."

Camp David was the perfect arena for such a vigorous debate. I believed then, and I believe even more strongly today, that what finally appeared on the Camp David Chapel windows reveals a great deal about who we are as Americans and how we perceive ourselves.

I would like to say that my words of criticism immediately swayed the views of the other committee members. They did not.

At first, the committee members were reluctant to abandon the carefully prepared designs that the Sandons had submitted for approval. Initially, there was resistance to my key points: that the Camp David Chapel, especially its permanent artwork, must represent the spiritual beliefs, strivings, and ideals of all Americans, and that the chapel must also reflect universal values even though various religious groups will use it for worship services, study, meditation, and rites of passage like weddings and funerals.

The issues that I raised were discussed at a series of committee meetings that took place over several months. Slowly, the tide turned, and interestingly, the Christian clergy on the committee were among the first to support my call to scrap the original window plans.

They clearly understood the need for the Camp David Chapel to be more inclusive in its design and construction. But it required more time and extensive debate to convince the lay people on the committee to request new stained-glass designs from the artists.

As we debated the issue, each of the committee members realized the significance and long-term importance of their decisions. Our animated discussions became an unanticipated seminar on church-state issues, religious diversity within the United States, and religion's role in American society.

We knew we were making critical decisions that would last for decades to come. At one point during the discussions, I told my colleagues that I recognized how difficult it was for people of goodwill to give up previously held beliefs and replace them with something different. But throughout the debate, I remained confident that I stood on principled American historical and religious ground. In the end, the Camp David Chapel Committee did request seven new window designs from the Sandons.

Instead of Protestant church logos and other uniquely Christian symbols, the artists came back to us with radically revised plans. The new windows featured visual representations of the sea and an anchor, a mountain, a globe, an open book, a tree of knowledge, a sheaf of wheat, seven flames, a dove, and a lamp with a flame. I was satisfied with the designs, and the committee unanimously approved the new submission.

After the final vote was concluded, many committee colleagues thanked me both publicly and privately for my efforts to make the chapel inclusive and welcoming. Some members admitted that it was their first encounter with an assertive advocate of religious pluralism.

The Battle of Camp David is long over. In retrospect, some people may view it as an insignificant debate, a minor skirmish over colored pieces of glass in a building few Americans will ever visit. I do not agree.

During the hours of debate at Camp David, I believed that I was fighting for a basic, even a sacred principle of American life. In a country of over 300 million people, no one faith community or religion can ever claim that it is legally, historically, or artistically "America's religion." The concept of religious diversity buttressed by constitutional guarantees of religious freedom is as old as the republic and as fresh as today's headlines.

While I was personally involved in many other interreligious confrontations and issues during my years with the American Jewish Committee, I consider the Battle of Camp David the high point of my career.

Once the issue of the windows was decided, the committee moved quickly and adopted a chapel dedication liturgy reflecting the religious pluralism for which I had fought.

In addition to Chapel Committee members and their families, the guest list at the dedication included prominent clergy and national, state, and local public officials, including two United States Senators, Howell Heflin (D-Alabama) and John Danforth (R-Missouri)—the latter is an ordained Episcopal priest.

Other guests were military chaplains and members of President Bush's family: First Lady Barbara Bush, their son and future president George W. Bush, his wife Laura, and some of the president's grandchildren.

The dedication events began with breakfast attended by the president, who spent an uninterrupted hour with us. Because the president was so casual and at ease during our breakfast, my wife jokingly whispered to me that the man sitting next to us was probably an actor impersonating the president, while the real George H.W. Bush was attending to the nation's business elsewhere. But, of course, it really was the American president.

Once the breakfast was over, Marcia and I walked around the grounds. Camp David's buildings are far from luxurious. The entire area resembles a well-maintained, slightly upscale summer camp. Perhaps its simplicity is why presidents have used Camp David as a respite, a place where they can walk, jog, or ride a bicycle in security and privacy.

The formal chapel ceremony began at eleven o'clock in the morning with our carefully crafted interreligious liturgy. My assigned task during the service was to read an English language selection from the Hebrew Bible, or what Christians call the Old Testament. I chose some verses from the prophet Isaiah.

During the service, I glanced at the eight stained-glass windows that dominate the beautiful chapel. The building's rich oak wood and the rugged stone blend perfectly into the building's rustic Maryland mountain setting. But my mind and my eyes constantly wandered back to the windows as I relived the Battle of Camp David.

Like most of the participants who attended the dedication service in 1991, today's visitors to Camp David will never know the intense struggle surrounding the choice of symbols that were used in the stained-glass windows.

That is true even when they read the official brochure describing the chapel. While I did not write the text, I take personal pride in the brochure's words: "The building's response to its site is expressed through the choice of materials and with the more obvious symbolism of the 'tree like' shapes of the exposed laminated wood columns and window designs. All symbols were selected and designed to be open to various understandings by persons of differing faith traditions.... For example, the mountains may be seen as the land God created or Mount Sinai, or Mount Moriah, or Mount Calvary."

I particularly like the words "designed to be open to various understandings by persons of differing faith traditions." That is what the fight was all about.

I like to think those earlier Virginians—Jefferson, Madison, and Mason—would have been pleased with another Virginian's efforts at Camp David. At least I hope so.

It is likely that if the Camp David Chapel was being built today, several clearly identified members of the Christian Religious Right would likely be members of the planning committee. They would surely press for the inclusion of specific Christian symbols on the chapel windows.

Nor would they be satisfied with the somewhat bland Protestant denominational logos and symbols that were first proposed. The Religious Right adherents would certainly object to the windows' final abstract pluralistic and universal designs.

Instead, they would likely prefer a stained-glass portrait of Jesus, several Christian crosses, some angels, perhaps a representation of the Last Supper, the New Testament, and John the Baptist's encounter with Jesus at the Jordan River. Who knows what else they would want on the windows, as well as inside the building?

The Religious Right leaders would want the chapel at the presidential retreat to make clear to all visitors that America is, in fact, a Christian nation.

It is said that in love and politics, timing is everything. And back in 1989–1991, the fierce polarizing campaign to assert Christian dominance and triumphalism in all aspects of American public life had not yet gained the strength that it has now achieved.

But that was then, and this is now.

CHAPTER 16

Two Passion Plays Convinced Me the Play's (Not) the Thing!

FOR MORE THAN fifty years, the American Jewish Committee's Interreligious Affairs Department has worked to rid the Oberammergau Passion Play (OPP) in Germany of its centuries-long antisemitic depiction of Jews and Judaism.

Passion plays originated in Europe in the twelfth century and have a long history of potent anti-Judaism. These theatrical performances that dramatize Jesus's week-long Passion—the period between Palm Sunday and Easter—were often filled with medieval anti-Jewish tropes, depicting the Jews of the first century as greedy, bloodthirsty, devilish (including costumes with horns), and exclusively concerned with the dry, formal, legalistic elements of religion.

Such plays were used to transmit the Passion story to the many Christians who were unable to read a text, but who clearly understood the messages conveyed by a dramatic stage performance.

In my interreligious work, I have several litmus tests for all passion plays:

1. While there surely must have been Jews who opposed or disagreed with Jesus' rabbinical teachings, the Gospels never provide us with precise numbers. Was the group huge or small in number? Instead, many passion plays have a large howling, bloodthirsty Jewish crowd on the stage, demanding his death. How the Jewish crowd is portrayed tells me a lot about a passion play.

2. How is Pontius Pilate, the vicious Roman prefect in ancient Jerusalem, portrayed? In most passion plays, he is a poor *nebbish* who can't help

himself. He appears as a Hamlet-like indecisive figure, so weak that he is controlled by Caiaphas, the cunning Jewish High Priest. Pilate is a pawn manipulated by the sinister venal Jewish establishment.

3. Is it made clear in a passion play that Pilate was a fearsome, brutal historical figure, who actually controls Caiaphas? And in history, the High Priest is usually perceived as a collaborator, a submissive tool of the oppressive and lethal Roman occupation.

4. Finally, is it clear the Jewish religious community of the time was extraordinarily diverse and dynamic? Is it evident to an audience that Jesus was Jewish, as was his immediate family, and his followers: all Jews living under a harsh occupation? They were a restive people who fought four losing wars with the Romans, the last armed conflict about a hundred years after Jesus' execution by the Romans, the only group that had the authority to carry out capital punishment.

With these guiding principles in mind, I have been personally involved with the world-famous Oberammergau Passion Play (OPP) since 1970. In 1984, I led a joint Christian-Jewish delegation to that picturesque town in the Bavarian Alps—fifty-eight miles south of Munich—to view a virulent, antisemitic, six-hour religious drama. I made return visits to Oberammergau in 1999 and again in 2010.

Most importantly, passion plays often explicitly or implicitly charged the entire Jewish people with deicide, which sometimes served as a motivating force for the Christian audiences to violently attack their Jewish neighbors, especially during Holy Week.

The OPP was particularly excessive in its negative portrayal of Jews and Judaism. The production was dominated by classic medieval anti-Jewish tropes. Additionally, Oberammergau's *tableaux vivant* (living images) used Old Testament stories, scattered throughout the play, that were portrayed as being superseded by New Testament stories.

According to Oberammergau village tradition, the OPP was first performed in 1634 as the fulfillment of a vow made by the townspeople. In 1633, Oberammergau was struck with the bubonic plague, and many died. The townspeople vowed that if the deaths would stop, they would perform a passion play every ten years to show their appreciation for God's intervention.

The plague ended, and the residents fulfilled their vow. In 1680, the decennial performance schedule was fixed to the beginning of decades

(1680, 1690, etc.), and in 1899, when a railroad line was constructed between Oberammergau and the rest of Europe, the play became an attraction for foreign visitors as well as Germans. Thomas Cook & Son, the famous British travel agency, heavily promoted "pilgrimages" to view the production.

Today, half a million people view the play during each decennial season when more than a hundred performances take place during the spring and summer. Additionally, passion plays all over the world look to Oberammergau as a leader in the field and design local passion plays with Oberammergau as a model and inspiration. The OPP has been rightly called the Grandparent of all passion plays.

A notable attendee of the OPP was Adolf Hitler, who saw the play in 1930 and 1934, during its three-hundredth anniversary season. Following the play's 1934 performance, Hitler proclaimed, "Never has the menace of Jewry been so convincingly portrayed."

Even after the Holocaust, the text of Oberammergau was not immediately revised. However, the Vatican Council's 1965 proclamation of *Nostra Aetate*, which positively transformed Catholic attitudes toward Jews and Judaism, put the unreformed play at odds with the Church, which meant that the play could no longer receive the *missio canonica*, or official Church blessing. *Nostra Aetate* rejected the idea that the Jews had been abandoned by God, and therefore the overt supersessionism in the play was no longer acceptable within mainstream Catholicism.

Additionally, *Nostra Aetate* stated that Jews could not be held collectively responsible for Jesus's death, which ran counter to Oberammergau's portrayal of the Jews, of all generations, as guilty of deicide. Change was needed.

At the same time and bolstered by *Nostra Aetate*, American Jewish groups intensified their efforts to reform Oberammergau. Under the leadership of Marc Tanenbaum, AJC submitted a report written by Judith Banki to German government authorities and church leaders detailing the problematic issues within the 1970 script.

Seven years later, AJC led the first dialogue session between Oberammergau leadership and Jewish activists. When many of the proposed revisions were not carried out in the 1980 performances, Tanenbaum publicly declared Oberammergau the international capital of antisemitism.

Among the many Christian scholarly critics of the OPP were Sister Mary Boys of Union Theological Seminary, Dr. Philip Cunningham of Saint Joseph's University, Dr. Eugene Fisher of the National Conference of Catholic Bishops, Dr. Eva Fleischner of Montclair State University, Presbyterian interreligious leader Dr. William H. Harter, Dr. Franklin Sherman of the Chicago Lutheran Seminary, and especially Dr. Leonard Swidler of Temple University.

The latter scholar early on recognized the textual and structural problems of the OPP, and for decades Swidler has led an international effort to rid the play of its anti-Jewish elements.

A year after I succeeded Marc as the AJC's Interreligious Affairs Director, I attended the 1984 performance of the play accompanied by AJC lay leaders Mimi Alperin, Irving Levine, and Kurt Kelman, Professor Fleischner, and Dr. Harter.

After attending the performance, I wrote an op-ed for the New York Times, calling out the play as "unmistakably antisemitic," in my attempt to push the townspeople to revise the production.

My 1984 New York Times op-ed included these words:

> The Oberammergau Passion Play … remains a serious obstacle to building better Christian-Jewish relations. Despite outside efforts to have changes introduced, the play still is unmistakably antisemitic. Unless, finally, it is purged of its bias, economic pressure should be brought to bear on those who profit from sending tourists to see it …. Over the centuries, the play has become a major international tourist attraction. The play is produced, directed, staged, and performed solely by the villagers. Certain key roles sometimes are handed down from generation to generation. There is elaborate staging with massive "living tableaux," a large chorus, and orchestral music.

> Hundreds of people form the cast, and the spectacular Alpine scene adds to the sense of grandeur. The audience anticipates an exalted spiritual and exhilarating theatrical experience. But the play remains marred by its fundamentally anti-Jewish orientation.

> It's an old problem. Anti-Jewish elements have been in the play from its inception, but with the end of World War II and the Holocaust many Christian and Jewish leaders have expressed profound concern about the bias, both in the script and staging. Comprehensive studies of the play and books about it have been published and high-level consultations have taken place between critics and Oberammergau officials. The critics have pointed out that the play perpetuates the pernicious belief that the Jewish people, then and now, must bear the guilt for the death of Jesus, and as a result of this "crime" they must suffer continuing collective punishment from God. Critics charge that the play

removes Jesus from his Jewish roots, portrays Jews as malicious antagonists, whitewashes the role of Pontius Pilate in the crucifixion, and entirely departs from the Bible in significant ways.

Oberammergau leaders have made some text changes. As a result of the criticism, it was hoped that the anti-Jewish elements would be eradicated in this year's production. Sadly, the changes, which are inadequate, have failed to remove the bigotry. Although I had read a great deal about the play, I was not prepared for the overwhelming power of the performance. It is one thing to read the script, something else to experience the play in person. The prologue and sixteen acts produce an incremental effect: Slowly, inexorably, the Jews emerge as a corrupt, brutal people, driven by harsh and cruel law—clearly the "bad guys" of the play.

The treatment of the Jewish priests and Temple money changers was grotesque. Their overly ornate costumes seemed decadent when compared with the simple flowing robes of Jesus and Jesus' followers. The priests' actions were always venal as they conspired to put Jesus to death.

Moses appeared twice, each time with long horns growing out of his head. In the Judgment scene, 250 men, women, and children shouted for Jesus' death. In calling for the crucifixion, they cried: "We take His blood upon us and upon our children."

The viewers with whom I spoke believed that what they saw and heard was historically accurate and theologically sound. Tragically, it was neither. Responsible New Testament scholarship has repudiated the medieval anti-Jewish theology that Oberammergau exemplifies. Vatican Council II and many major Protestant church bodies have developed new and positive theology toward Jews and Judaism. The play, in transmitting its traditional anti-Jewish images, fails to incorporate these significant advances.

When the next regularly scheduled performances take place, a great deal of work needs to be done. Alternate scripts that mitigate or remove the antisemitism have been suggested for possible use. Further changes in the present script also have been suggested. If this doesn't work, pressure ought to be put on airlines, travel agencies, alumni associations, and department stores that promote the play to refrain from such promotions until the bigotry is removed, once and for all ... I would like to believe that this tiny village did not survive a poisonous plague in order to transmit another poison: antisemitism.

Sixteen years later, I wrote another op-ed with the hope the 2000 production *"would at least be purged of all anti-Jewish elements. But a study of an English translation of the German language text reveals this will not happen, and I am profoundly disappointed."*

The elaborate production is nearly six hours in length and is produced, directed, staged, and performed by Oberammergau (population 5,350) residents. The performances will attract some 500,000 viewers from around the world and ticket sales will exceed $30 million.

Americans will comprise the largest number of visitors, and alumni associations of several U.S. universities, including Harvard and Wesleyan, have scheduled trips to the play.... And indeed, there will be many positive changes this year, including the elimination of the horrific judgment scene of earlier productions that had 250 men, women, and children on the large outdoor stage shouting for Jesus' death by crucifixion—a Roman form of capital punishment: "We take his blood upon us and upon our children." This chilling blood curse from the book of Matthew will not appear in the 2000 performances ... The American Jewish Committee urged Oberammergau reformers to create an entirely new play reflecting the positive gains in Christian-Jewish relations as well as modern biblical scholarship while still providing a spiritually satisfying experience for the audience.

Unfortunately, this did not happen and the 2000 Passion Play, despite the constructive changes, still reflects many of the problems of the basic text written in the mid-19th century.

While I am deeply appreciative of the positive reforms, the text remains deeply flawed and still contains anti-Jewish elements. Nor am I alone in this assessment. I formally requested eight prominent scholars of religion, including Catholics, Jews, and Protestants, to independently study the text.

The scholars welcomed the positive changes from previous scripts, but they also expressed serious concerns about the script's overall themes. The scholars understood the Oberammergau Passion Play is much more than a text. The production is akin to an opera with rich costuming, dramatic staging, com-

> plex scenery, and evocative music. While no script can convey the total theatrical experience, it is also true that the text is the central component of the play ... The scholars carefully analyzed the script. Their findings reflect a general dissatisfaction with the text, and several scholars were especially critical, including the Rev. John Pawlikowski of Chicago's Catholic Theological Union who attended a 1984 performance. After studying this year's text, he wrote: "The Jewish priests are portrayed as totally wicked and ultimately responsible for Jesus' death. While one can detect some effort to make it more acceptable... It is far too minimal. Christian visitors deserve something better."

I hope that "something better" will be in future OPP productions. But it seems in a passion play, some must be the good guys and some the bad guys. And the bad guys are always the Jews.

As a result of these and other efforts, real change to Oberammergau's script, staging, and costumes began to occur in 1990, when Christian Stückl and Otto Huber, both natives of the town, took over as directors of the play. At that point, the town's play committee did not allow Stückl to make significant changes to the script, but he was able to place greater blame for Jesus' death on Pontius Pilate. In past performances, Pilate had only agreed to Jesus's crucifixion because he was coerced by the Jewish High Priest, Caiaphas, and the Jewish masses.

For the 2000 performance, Stückl and Huber revised the script and staging extensively. In this version of the play, Jesus' Jewishness was highlighted. For instance, he wore a *kippah* [Jewish head covering], was referred to as "Rabbi," and prayed in Hebrew. Additionally, in this script, Judas betrayed Jesus for political reasons, while in earlier scripts he had done so for money.

Pilate was presented more fully as the villain, many supersessionist *tableaux vivants* were replaced by more positive biblical scenes, and the infamous verse from the Gospel of Matthew 27:25 that charged Jews in every generation with Jesus's death—"We take his blood upon us and upon our children"—was removed from the play.

Notwithstanding the progress, AJC remained committed to addressing the play's lingering anti-Jewish tropes through constructive engagement. The current AJC Director of Interreligious and Intergroup Relations, Rabbi Noam Marans; his predecessor Rabbi Gary Greenebaum; Rabbi Eric Greenberg, the Anti-Defamation League's Interfaith Director; and I worked with Stückl and Huber before, during, and after the 2010 production.

The most dramatic addition to the 2010 version was a new scene featuring Jesus holding aloft an open Torah scroll (in facsimile form), while all of the Jewish characters on stage sing a newly composed rendition of the *Shema*, Judaism's central prayer.

The Jewishness of Jesus and his followers was even further emphasized in the 2010 production, and the struggle between Jesus' camp and the other Jews was more vividly portrayed as an internal Jewish matter rather than a theological battle between Judaism and emerging Christianity.

Progress has happened at Oberammergau, but the process of constructive engagement and revision must continue. There are remaining concerns regarding the depiction of the power dynamic between the Jewish priests and Pilate. Pilate should be portrayed as more powerful than the priests, reflecting the historical reality.

There remain concerns about points within the play that do not accurately reflect the divided Jewish views of Jesus' leadership, as well as some of the *tableaux vivants* that remain supersessionist. It is important that attendees educate themselves on the history of Oberammergau, the progress achieved, and the remaining sensitive lingering issues that still need to be addressed.

The next performances are scheduled for 2022, a two-year hiatus caused by the coronavirus pandemic.

In February 2004, the movie star Mel Gibson released *The Passion of the Christ*, a two-hour and seven-minute film that he financed, produced, and directed. He was also a screenwriter for his production.

Gibson was born in 1956 in Peekskill, New York, but moved with his family to Australia when he was about twelve years old.

Gibson calls himself a "Traditionalist" Roman Catholic, one who rejects all or almost all of the reforms of the Second Vatican Council. Gibson also does not fully recognize the legitimacy of Popes John XXIII, Paul VI, John Paul II, Benedict XVI, or Francis. Gibson's ultraconservative Catholicism is pre-Vatican Council II, and because of his personal wealth, he has reportedly built a private church in Malibu, California. Many Catholic leaders have told me that Gibson is "off the charts religiously."

I was one of the few Jews who saw a rough cut in Houston of *The Passion of the Christ* in August 2003 along with Rabbi Eugene Korn, a prominent interreligious scholar, and a diverse group of Houston's religious and ethnic leaders. I later saw Gibson's final version in January 2004 at a special Winter Park, Florida screening with nearly four thousand Evangelicals in the audience.

One of the many reasons *The Passion of the Christ* is difficult to watch is because the actors communicate on-screen with one another in Aramaic (well, sort of), the language Jesus probably spoke. There are English language subtitles on the screen. Gibson used the Aramaic for "authenticity."

"Mel," as everyone called him, was present for the rough-cut Houston screening of his film. I went to the event with an open mind and did not read the script before seeing the movie. I did, however, know the sharp critique some Christian and Jewish scholars had voiced about the film, but based upon the changes achieved in Oberammergau and the recent positive teachings of the Catholic Church, I was hopeful about what Gibson produced.

Alas, what I saw was a huge disappointment. His rough cut was in the long tradition of passion plays infused with toxic anti-Jewish elements. It was also extremely bloody, gory, and sadomasochistic, filled with gratuitous violence.

In the Q&A session that followed the screening, a Protestant minister publicly chastised Gibson for the horrific violence and told the film star: "Your *Braveheart* movie was a kindergarten film compared to *The Passion*."

There was much more criticism from both Christians and Jews. An angry Gibson lashed out in response by declaring he did not care what scholars thought of his film and boasted he did not "have a lot of letters" after his name, a not-so-veiled criticism of those scholars holding graduate degrees in religion, history, or theology.

It was clear that Gibson is an absolute "true believer." The film is a cinematic testimony to his personal Savior. Gibson rejected any charge that his film is wildly inaccurate in many places and employs anti-Jewish images and teachings from an antisemitic German nun of the nineteenth century: Anne Katherine Emmerich.

Because of his wealth and celebrity, the film attracted a wide audience. *The Passion of Christ* moved many Christians to tears as they saw the lashings, beatings, blood, scars, and whippings on the "silver screen." Jews, not surprisingly, felt uneasy and even angry at the screen portrayal of Jesus' fellow Jews.

In many ways, Gibson's cinematic murderous Jewish mobs were worse than anything I saw in the 1984 Oberammergau production. When I told that to Gibson, he simply replied: "I have not been to Oberammergau."

To make the movie even more "radioactive" was the fact the negative verse from Matthew was not uttered in the rough cut, but it did appear in the final version I saw in Florida.

I quickly became one of the national Jewish leaders who publicly criticized *The Passion of the Christ* when the film was released to the general public. Charges and countercharges swirled in the public print and electronic media, and in many synagogues and churches.

Even Pope John Paul II became involved when he supposedly said "It is as it was" after a private screening at the Vatican, but a Holy See spokesperson quickly distanced the Pope from that quote and the film.

Nearly twenty years later, the fears expressed at the time of the film's release that it would trigger waves of antisemitic violence did not materialize. (Anti-Jewish bigots do not require a film to foster their hatred.)

In 2006, Gibson subsequently created some personal problems for himself, including an antisemitic rant when he was stopped for a traffic violation by a California sheriff's deputy who happened to be Jewish. Unfortunately, *The Passion of the Christ* is still used in some churches on Good Friday as a "sacred teaching tool."

Professor Philip Cunningham perhaps had the last word on the controversy when he edited the acclaimed *Pondering the Passion*, an important collection of scholarly essays about passion plays in general, Gibson's film, and other key issues on this vexing subject. I had the honor of contributing the article about the OPP.

For many people, and especially for those who saw either the Oberammergau play or the Gibson film, both productions are perceived as the "gospel truth" about the life, trial, and death of Jesus. Despite that perception, both the stage and film versions transmit to their audiences' pejorative perceptions and attitudes toward Jews and Judaism.

Those who seek improved Christian-Jewish relations must confront the continuing issue and problem of passion plays, whether medieval or modern. That is because the passion story, so central to the Christian message and Christian self-understanding, is familiar to hundreds of millions of people throughout the world. When passion plays emit anti-Jewish images and stereotypes to audiences, positive Christian-Jewish relations suffer.

For too many years, defensive, sometimes hostile Oberammergau community leaders, including some who were Nazi party members in the 1930s and 1940s, were locked into a harshly anti-Jewish production. Because of the town's conservative religious tradition, the strong anti-reform sentiment within the Oberammergau community, and the community's fear of losing lucrative tourist revenue, critics had little effect, even after World War II, in removing anti-Jewish elements from the world-famous play.

It required extraordinary time and talent by concerned Christian and Jewish leaders to develop a scholarly and religious critique of the play. Next came the task of building human bridges of mutual respect and understanding between the play's critics, led by the AJC and the Anti-Defamation League, with the Oberammergau officials directly responsible for the play.

Once a bond of mutual trust was established and once the people of Oberammergau voted for play reform, changes became possible. Even then, based on my personal experiences, reform came slowly in Oberammergau. While the 2010 production was a welcome and notable change from previous productions, the Oberammergau Passion Play remains fundamentally flawed. Further substantive reform is needed.

Yet, Oberammergau illustrates what can be achieved when both sides work together. The result of that effort is not only a more accurate, less poisonous anti-Jewish passion play, but it is also a significant achievement in the vitally needed area of positive Christian-Jewish relations.

CHAPTER 17

Special Assignments:
Things I Never Learned in Rabbinical School

Mr. Moon and Destructive Cults

DURING THE EARLY 1970s, I began to receive numerous questions from *Religion on the Line* radio listeners as well as from concerned parents who contacted me at my AJC office in New York City. All their questions focused on someone called Reverend Sun Myung Moon, a Korean, and his Unification Church. Who is he? Why are so many young people giving up their personal freedom, physically bowing before him, breaking all links and communication with their families, and joining his church?

The public concern grew more intense when in 1976, Moon rented Yankee Stadium for a well-publicized massive rally to celebrate himself—a self-proclaimed Messiah—and his cult-like religious group that attracted thousands of people who proudly called themselves "Moonies."

Moon's followers worshipped—there is no other way to describe the phenomenon—both him and his wife who boastfully called themselves the "True Parents" of all humanity. Moon, a presbyterian minister by training, further claimed his Korean-based Unification Church had superseded and replaced Judaism, Christianity, and Islam.

In addition to his demand for total submission and obedience from his mostly youthful followers, Moon, a multimillion-dollar business mogul, owned a series of media outlets that included a politically conservative newspaper in Washington, DC, as well as many lucrative companies, factories, and high-priced real estate properties, including his Church's headquarters in Westchester County, New York. He consistently refused to publicly reveal his finances.

I learned that many young Jews were attracted to Moon and his Church which spewed out a hard-right political agenda that strongly supported President Richard Nixon during the Watergate scandal.

As Moon's public image and conservative political power *increased* in public visibility, I undertook a systematic study of the basic text of the Unification Church: *Divine Principle*.

My AJC study charged that Moon's foundational theological book, *Divine Principle*, first published in Korean in 1966 and later expanded into a 536-page 1974 English-language edition, was "replete with hostile and vicious anti-Jewish stereotypes."

Moon employed the most hostile elements in the Christian tradition to describe the Roman crucifixion of Jesus. While welcome positive changes on this subject have taken place within the Christian community during the past fifty years, I discovered Moon continued to foster hatred of the Jewish people for their alleged role in the execution of Jesus.

My study contrasted Moon's doctrines with those of Protestants, Catholics, Evangelicals, and other Christians who encountered Jews "in love and mutual respect." But Moon, I wrote, "perpetuates only hateful, destructive and divisive teachings about Judaism and the Jewish people." Nowhere did Moon attribute any spiritual validity to Jews or Judaism, either ancient or modern. They are seen only as a people devoid of genuine faith and spiritual qualities and in severe need of abandoning Judaism and submitting themselves to the Unification Church's leader.

I concluded my detailed study asserting: "Rev. Moon's *Divine Principle* is a feculent breeding ground for fostering antisemitism. Because of Moon's unrelieved hostility towards Jews and Judaism, a demonic picture emerges from the pages of his major work. One can only speculate on what negative and anti-Jewish impact *Divine Principle* may have upon a follower of Rev. Moon."

My study sparked national attention, including extensive coverage in the major print and electronic media. I was pleased the Rev. Dr. Jorge Lara-Braud and Father James LeBar, representatives of the National Council of Churches and the Roman Catholic Archdiocese of New York, respectively, joined me at an AJC news conference to support my findings and to warn the general society about the dangerous anti-Jewish teachings and recruiting tactics of the Unification Church.

Of course, there was an immediate and strong response from Moon's followers, including several Christian theologians and sociologists who dismissed my findings and charges and spoke instead of the Unification Church as a new and religiously exciting faith group on the American scene.

The public controversy triggered my deep interest not only in Moon's church, but it strengthened my personal and professional commitment to counter the deceptive recruiting tactics and the mistreatment of many cult members. My wife Marcia, a former professor of religion at William Paterson College in New Jersey, and I were among the early founders of the counter-cult movement that focused on the physical, emotional, and spiritual abuses carried out by cult leaders on their members.

These tactics frequently included enforced family separation, physical isolation, malnutrition, sexual abuse, sleep deprivation, public humiliations, forced marriages, even physical beatings, and many other brutal actions—all to ensure members' total submission to the various cult leaders.

In 1980, two years after nine hundred people, one-third of them elderly and one-third children, died by suicide at leader Jim Jones's command during the infamous People's Temple Jonestown, Guyana, massacre, Marcia, and I coauthored *Prison or Paradise: The New Religious Cults*. The first general book written about cults, it drew praise from many reviewers, including Terry Eastland who wrote in Commentary magazine:

> *"Prison or Paradise?" is their [the Rudins] answer to those originally inquiring parents; that they have put the answer into a book indicates concern that it be read by a larger audience. It deserves to be. Simple and straightforward, the book is valuable not only for the information it provides on the cults but also for its suggestions on how to counter them.*

Now, more than four decades after our book was published, Marcia remains active in combatting destructive cults. In the 1990s, she founded and headed the International Cult Educational Program (ICEP), a project of the American Family Foundation, today known as International Cultic Studies Association (ICSA). The ICSA now includes a large global membership and shares its insights into psychological manipulation with organizations which help victims of physical and sexual abuse.

In 1977, I presented an academic paper at the San Francisco meeting of the American Academy of Religion (AAR). It was a comprehensive analysis of the Unification Church that included a description of its deceptive recruiting methods, its mistreatment of its members, the pervasive antisemitism within Divine Principle, and a call for the Church to make public its vast hidden financial holdings. The complete text of the AAR presentation can be found on my website: www.jamesrudin.com.

I concluded my address with words that still apply to all destructive cults that exist today: "I am deeply convinced that no new truth can emerge from a group whose teachings foster antisemitism, whose financial dealings are hidden from public view, and whose recruiting methods and cultic lifestyle violate the human rights of others."

1985 Farm Crisis

My interest in agriculture began when I was a youngster during World War II in Alexandria, Virginia. Like every male in my extended family above the age of eighteen, my father was in the US armed forces. He was an Army Major stationed at Fort Belvoir, and like millions of other American families, my parents and older brother, Bert, purchased savings bonds, saved kitchen fat to contribute to the war effort, and maintained a small "Victory Garden" near our house where we grew a variety of vegetables and tomato plants to relieve the demand on commercial food suppliers whose top priority was providing food for our military.

My assigned job was to use a heavy watering can to irrigate our tiny garden crop, and I still remember my excitement when carrots, a fast-growing vegetable, first appeared. Bert and I were thrilled to harvest our initial crop, and we immediately gave the fresh vegetables to our mother who added them to our dinner salad that very evening. I was proud of the food we produced during the war years.

When I was fifteen, Bert and I got summer jobs working for an Alexandria veterinarian, Dr. David Witter. It was my first paying job—fifty cents an hour that added up to twenty dollars a week!

I often accompanied my boss to nearby farms in Northern Virginia where Dr. Witter tended to the various illnesses and injuries that afflict horses, cows, and pigs. Years later, I joked that a future rabbi physically held many pigs and clipped their ears while Dr. Witter injected the fidgety animals with an anti-cholera serum.

During those farm visits, I learned firsthand about the vicissitudes of agricultural life: possessing the right topsoil, the need for fertilizers, planting the best crop at the right time, the reliance on both rain and sunshine, the difficult labor required to harvest a ripe crop, keeping stray animals from destroying a "money crop," and raising a physically and mentally healthy family miles away from a neighboring farm or a populated area.

Alas, many of the Virginia farms I visited as a youngster are long gone because the land became prime real estate as new suburban communities were created on agricultural acreage that had sometimes remained in a family for over a century.

Years later, I returned to the region of my youthful work and sadly realized that new highways, shopping malls, huge parking lots, apartment houses, and individual homes had replaced the farmlands I loved visiting when I was a teenager.

In 1968, I wrote an article describing a nineteenth-century Jewish farming colony in Hodgeman County, Kansas, located not far from the fabled "Wild West" town of Cimarron. The article appeared in the Kansas Historical Quarterly with the title: "Beersheba, Kansas: 'God's Pure Air on Government Land.'"

It described the attempt in 1882 to quickly move new immigrants from Eastern Europe to free homestead land in the American Midwest. The effort, sponsored by the Reform Jewish movement leadership based in Cincinnati, was a noble plan to acclimate the new Jewish arrivals to the United States. A less-praiseworthy motive was to keep the mostly Yiddish-speaking immigrants far away from the big cities where their unfamiliar embarrassing presence might undermine the security and status of the established Jewish communities.

The Beersheba settlers, forbidden to own land in the antisemitic European nations they had just fled, lacked any knowledge or experience as farmers. But they struggled for several years living in sod huts, built a sod synagogue, and sought to raise profitable wheat crops. The colony financially collapsed despite aid from Cincinnati, and many of the Jewish farmers moved to Kansas City, Missouri where they permanently settled and, in time, became leaders of the Jewish community in that city.

When I served as a rabbi in Kansas City following my US Air Force tour of duty, I met several of the grandchildren of the Beersheba, Kansas farming community. Today, a state historical marker near the site of the Beersheba colony is the only reminder of the failed farming community.

In 1972, I published an article about another Jewish farming experiment, and it appeared in the state historical journal Michigan History. In 1891, leaders of the Detroit Reform Jewish community established a Jewish immigrant agricultural colony in the small village of Bad Axe, which is in Michigan's "Thumb District." After several difficult years, like the earlier Beersheba farming experiment, the Bad Axe settlement also failed. Many of the Jewish immigrants who tried to make a success of the agricultural effort moved to Detroit. Both articles appear on my website: jamesrudin.com.

I enjoyed doing the historical research for both articles, and I learned once again of the difficulties all farmers face: the weather, financial concerns, fluctuating market prices, and physical and emotional loneliness. I appreciated the extraordinary efforts that are needed year after year to purchase seed and fertilizer, to maintain farm machinery, to plant, nurture, and harvest crops in the face of the often brutal and fickle forces of nature. And I grew to understand the economic unpredictability and psychological stress created by the constantly shifting global agricultural markets.

Many Americans today forget that our nation experienced a severe farming crisis beginning in 1985. Prices dropped sharply, many longtime farmers, especially in Iowa, Missouri, Wisconsin, and Kansas, were in danger of losing their land, even facing eviction, as unpaid debts and expenses—seeds, fertilizers, harvesters, tractors, taxes, and mortgages—piled up.

Anger, anxiety, and fear became a constant companion of many farmers who experienced family tensions, loss of self-esteem, domestic violence, and a staggering increase in mental health problems. American agriculture back then was situated on a delicately balanced fulcrum: disaster or recovery, realistic hope, or total destruction of a cherished way of life.

Not surprisingly, extremists rushed in to tell farmers their woes were the direct result of the Federal Reserve's monetary policies, "Eastern bankers" (a code word for Jews), the Internal Revenue Service, big-city politicians, the Department of Agriculture, "Big Government," and something called the Trilateral Commission. The latter group is a global think tank founded by David Rockefeller in 1973 in an attempt to bring Japan, North America, and Europe closer together.

Overt antisemitism increased in American farmlands: one 1985 poll of Midwestern farmers reported that 27 percent of that group blamed "the Jews" for the crisis. In response, the AJC's Executive Vice President, Dr. David M. Gordis, asked me to undertake a ten-day visit to Iowa to meet with farmers, religious groups, political leaders, law enforcement officers, local media, and a host of other people to gain a better picture of what ABC-TV's 20/20 program called "America's Farming Crisis."

In August 1985, I drove throughout Iowa and spoke with many owners of "Century Farms" who were about to lose their land, their very identity. My Jewish heritage and personal interest in farming helped shape my responses to the people I met in Iowa.

The people I encountered in the Hawkeye State were overwhelmingly democratic and nonviolent. I told them their dire situation sounded all too familiar; it resonated within me as a Jew whose family forebears fled antisemitic Eastern Europe.

In 1985, Iowans were being uprooted from their land, their children were fleeing the region in large numbers to escape a precarious existence, and once-valued members of a society were being called "surplus people."

A lifestyle, a cadence, a rhythm of life was not only being challenged, but was being destroyed. The New York Times in 1985 reported: "Around the clock through the year, 180 times a day now, another American farm disappears."

In Iowa, and during my similar trips to Missouri, Kansas, Colorado, North Dakota, and Wisconsin, I witnessed farming families literally being torn apart, husband against wife, parents against children, brother against sister, generation pitted against generation. Coming from a religious tradition that extolls farming, celebrates the agricultural seasons of the year, and with a Bible filled with agricultural images, I was pained to see people torn from their vine and their fig tree, their cornfield, their soybeans, their cotton, their dairy farm, and their wheat fields: modern exiles plunging into an uncharted Diaspora.

As a Jew with knowledge of the rich biblical theology of the land and with knowledge of how the Zionist movement successfully brought Jews back to the sacred soil of Israel, I shuddered as an eyewitness to seeing the fabric of the American agricultural community unravel.

I told my Iowa hosts to let the economists argue whether the family farm was economically viable or not. Whatever the merits of one economic theory or another, I was concerned by the seemingly inexorable destruction of the family farm.

The result was a wrenching experience for a talented and gifted people, the American farmers, from the land, all taking place at an enormous human cost. As a Jew with a long memory of antisemitism, I was outraged when I saw political extremists, white nationalists, neo-Nazis, and antisemites enter the agricultural scene in Iowa and provide false and easy answers for complex problems.

Tragically, the scapegoat (another Biblical image!) that was frequently offered to troubled and distressed farmers was the eternal scapegoat: the Jewish community, the "globalists," the "internationalists, the "Rothschilds." I learned that some extremist groups in the Midwest were militia survivalists, hoarding weapons and food.

Several groups were paramilitary and had armed militia training camps located in remote areas of the region. Many of them urged the violent overthrow of the US government. A bumper sticker seen in Iowa and attributed to the Posse Comitatus group read: "Know Your Leaders; They're Your Enemy."

At the time, the Posse Comitatus was the only white supremacist, paramilitary organization listed by the FBI as a domestic terrorist organization. Other extremist groups I encountered in Iowa were the Populist Party, The Order, The Covenant, The Sword and the Arm of the Lord, Liberty Lobby, and the National Agricultural Press Association.

I became especially friendly with Dixon Terry, a remarkable dairy farmer residing with his family in Greenfield, Iowa. Esquire magazine called him one of America's important young leaders under the age of forty. He was the state leader of a progressive farming group that opposed all extremists and antisemitism.

Other key allies were Thomas Kelly, the head of the Kansas Bureau of Investigation (KBI); Maurice Dingman, the Catholic Bishop of Des Moines; and leaders of a farmers' association and a Christian agricultural community group. They were all warm and welcoming to me and expressed opposition to the dangerous extremists who were roaming the Midwest spewing their lies and offering easy answers to complex problems.

During the same period, my colleague Jonathan Levine, the director of the Chicago AJC office, was also making fact-finding trips to battered farming communities in Illinois.

Upon my return to New York City, I wrote an AJC report about my findings. In September 1985, my organization hosted a well-attended news conference in Manhattan that drew national attention. The key speakers were Bishop Dingman; Rev. Donald Manworren, executive coordinator of the Iowa Interchurch Forum; KBI Director Kelly; Dixon Terry, chair of the Iowa Farm Unity Coalition; and me.

The speakers denounced the extremists' attempts to stir up antisemitism among Midwestern farmers, warning that such actions posed a danger to the farmers and to democracy as well as to Christian-Jewish relations.

The specific solutions offered by the speakers were varied, but all exhorted the Federal Government to move quickly to find answers to the farm crisis, and all called for programs to make farmers aware of the deceptiveness and viciousness of antisemitic propaganda.

Dixon Terry urged that the problem be attacked at what he considered its roots: the farmers' economic problems, and their isolation. "Farmers across the country and particularly in the Midwest," he said, "are now facing a greater economic upheaval than any we have seen in more than half a century. Because of economic dislocation, the loss of farms, and the financial pressures that farmers and their families are under, there is an atmosphere of despair and hopelessness, and in this atmosphere many farmers are blindly grabbing at anything that seems to provide an answer for them... The right-wing threat in rural communities is the greatest it has been in a long time ... I think the farmers' progressive movement has a much broader base, and the best hope for combating the right-wing anti-democratic movement lies with the more progressive forces."

Bishop Dingman said: "Desperate people will look for scapegoats. Farmers are desperate. Therefore, they are psychologically and emotionally prey to the hatemongers who would blame the devastating farm crisis on 'Jewish bankers.'"

He added: "There is, of course, absolutely no truth to this charge, and the obvious solution is twofold: first, remove the occasion for the hatred by giving the farmers a just price for their produce, and second, engage in a strong educational program to dispel the notion of the so-called 'Jewish conspiracy' of bankers allegedly trying to take farms away from family farmers. They make a mockery of Christianity by calling themselves Christian while spreading a patently un-Christian message."

I concluded the news conference expressing AJC's view and the consensus of the other speakers: "We pledge our continuing opposition to the destructive 'siren songs' of the radical right. We will not remain silent in the face of bigotry, and we urge all men and women of goodwill throughout our nation to join with us in a broad-based coalition of concern. The pernicious virus of hatred must not be allowed to spread."

In February 1987, I traveled to Chicago where I addressed the National Interreligious Conference on Rural Life. The text of my speech, "The Rural Crisis: A Jewish Perspective" can be found on my website: www.jamesrudin.com.

In the same year, 1987, I published an op-ed in the New York Times that described the farm crisis in great detail. It contained these words of warning:

> During this chill winter, when 180 family farms are disappearing every day, the agricultural crisis is getting worse. It is a long-term problem, and, as one farmer wryly said at the recent Interreligious Rural Crisis Conference in Chicago, "There is no light at the end of the tunnel, only an onrushing farm machine coming to destroy us." ... There are some people who will tell you

that they know exactly whose fault it is. Political extremists, anti-Semites, have entered the countryside with false and easy answers for complex problems. They blame "the international Jewish conspiracy" for the farm problems. Fortunately, the agricultural community overwhelmingly rejects this ancient canard, but the lie is still being spread.

Farmers traditionally "go it alone," but today they need to share their pain with the 97 percent of the American population not engaged in farming. Together, our society needs to establish more institutions and organizations of collective support and welfare. Farmers desperately need counseling centers offering extensive legal, financial, and psychological advice about survival. We can admire farmers' traditional independence, but personal independence alone is not a sufficient guarantee of group survival.

America is a collection of minority groups. No one profession, religion, race, ethnic group, or gender group can achieve its goals in isolation. Only by working together in pluralistic coalitions can real gains be made. We must respond effectively and compassionately to the cries and whispers of our suffering agricultural community.

In a bizarre, tragic twist of fate, in June 1989, Dixon Terry, only thirty-nine years old, was instantly killed on his dairy farm in Iowa when a lightning bolt struck the tractor he was driving. His family and his beloved Greenfield, Iowa, community were devastated by his tragic death. And American farmers lost a great champion.

I shall always remember his warm hospitality and sage advice when I was a welcomed guest in his home. May Dixon Terry's memory always be for a blessing.

New York State Task Force on Life and the Law

New York has a highly diverse population that speaks over 120 different languages, but it is precisely in the Empire State where enormous gains have been achieved on vital bioethical issues. That is because a unique and pioneering interreligious, interracial, interethnic group has been able to address those questions without the rancor and bitterness associated with the controversial question of abortion. I believe that group, the New York

State Task Force on Life and the Law, offers a model for other states to follow as they tackle key bioethical questions.

In 1985, New York Governor Mario Cuomo appointed me one of the founding members of the Task Force on Life and the Law, a twenty-six-member panel that included Christian and Jewish clergy, physicians, nurses, lawyers, ethicists, social workers, and hospital administrators. Task Force members represented many religious, political, medical, and cultural opinions. The Task Force, now more than thirty-five years since its creation, has been aided in its work by a superb professional staff.

For the next eighteen years I was involved in drafting legislation for New York State that included do not resuscitate orders (DNR) for hospital patients; a proxy healthcare law for people who cannot make their own medical decisions; laws affecting surrogate parenting, withdrawal and withholding of life support systems; medically assisted suicide; and a host of other complex bioethical public policy questions.

The lengthy debates needed to achieve Task Force consensus reflected the diverse religious and moral values of our society. My work as a Task Force member was among the most challenging of my entire career because it focused directly on matters of life and death and because those issues transcend all religious, racial, and ethnic borders.

The record of having our proposals approved by the state legislature in Albany has been quite high. But that came only at the end of a long and intensive process of public fact-finding and internal discussion among Task Force members.

At the outset, we received expert testimony, both oral and written, on a specific issue, and then debated the need to draft new regulatory legislation. It was invigorating work because we dealt with a series of real-life, critical concerns, including the legal definition of death, balancing patients' rights, and the state's interests.

This was especially true in establishing the validity of do not resuscitate orders issued in hospitals in cases of cardiac arrest, drafting laws relating to the status of unwanted frozen embryos (the result of multiple in-vitro fertilization attempts), and the determination of the safety of certain popular food and dietary supplements.

My years on the Task Force provided a unique vantage point to witness the rapid changes in medical technology since 1985. It also taught me the importance of applying deeply held religious teachings to modern bioethical questions. However, it often became clear to me that some long-held traditional beliefs must be updated or even abandoned in the face of twenty-first century medical advances.

One example was the need to determine when a person is legally considered dead. It sounds simple, but in many instances, it becomes a complicated question if a patient is kept alive by mechanical means—ventilators and respirators.

The definition of death is particularly important in cases of a possible organ transplant. When is it legally permitted to remove a heart or other vital organs from a person for use by another human being?

In the Jewish religious tradition, it is assumed death has occurred when a person's breathing stops. When that happens, the body must remain untouched for an eight-minute period to guarantee that breathing, pulse, and heart have actually ceased functioning.

During those eight minutes, a light feather is placed upon the lips of the presumed deceased person. If the feather does not move, the person is considered dead. Sometimes a mirror was positioned under the nostrils to see if condensation appeared on the mirror, indicating a person was still breathing.

But what happens if a patient's heart and breathing functions continue as the result of highly sophisticated support machines? Is such a person actually "alive?" Or is the patient "organically" dead, even though breathing, pulse, and a heartbeat are mechanically sustained?

The Task Force, after a thoughtful study of religious traditions and medical technology, determined that in New York State death legally occurs when there is "irreversible brain stem damage," a condition that can only be determined by modern medical tests, and not even by sharp-eyed witnesses observing a patient or by placing a feather on a person's lips.

In 1997, I testified before a US Congressional committee describing in detail the Task Force's definition of death. I also went to Albany, New York several times to meet with state legislators to press for adoption of some of our recommendations including surrogate parenting.

I supported our group's endorsement of a ban on surrogate motherhood contracts. In recommending legislation that would prohibit payments to surrogates and bar surrogacy brokers from operating in the state, we took a proper stand.

But we did not call for a total ban on surrogacy arrangements and would still permit surrogacy arrangements when they are undisputed and do not involve payment of a fee to a surrogate. The practice of paying women to serve as surrogate mothers has the potential to undermine the dignity of women, children, and human reproduction.

In case of disputes, the Task Force recommended that custody always be awarded to the mother, unless there is clear and convincing evidence that awarding custody to the father would be in the child's best interest. For me, commercial surrogate parenting is similar to baby-selling, and it also places a contractual price tag on human reproduction.

We also pressed for legislation that would give patients in New York the ironclad right to authorize other people to make life-and-death decisions about their medical treatment if they become incompetent.

Our proposal went beyond what is commonly known as living wills in which patients dictate the limits of their medical treatment if they become incompetent in the hope their families, physicians, and hospitals will honor them later. People dread the future loss of control over their lives and they fear becoming victims of runaway medical technology. Our recommendation allowed them to maintain control for the rest of their lives.

Under the proposal, any competent adult would have the right to designate a "health care proxy" who would be legally empowered to make medical decisions on the patient's behalf that could range from the routine to life and death. The proxy form would also allow patients to limit those decisions.

Dr. David Axelrod, the New York State Health Commissioner and Task Force Chair, said: "This proposal would assure patient autonomy and remove the unfortunate need for their families to go to court to sustain their wishes." The press called our proposal "To Die with Dignity."

Medical ethicists said it would strengthen patients' wishes to escape life-extending efforts when they face severe pain and suffering, and the quality of life has been seriously and irrevocably compromised. Task Force members said the proposal followed a series of court decisions and legislative initiatives across the country that sought to restore the right of patients to control their medical fate, even if it means that medical technology can forestall death.

My eighteen years of Task Force service revealed that the process of making realistic and sensible medical decisions is rapidly becoming the single most important aspect in a clergyperson's life. Those decisions are the most difficult and painful questions rabbis, priests, pastors, or imams face at the bedside of a dying individual.

And what a surprise! It's not abstract theological or metaphysical queries clergy are asked. Rather, most questions, usually asked in a hospital room, go like this: "My beloved family member is gravely ill. The doctors are recommending some extraordinary and complex medical treatments. I am confused and I am being asked to decide. As my spiritual leader, please tell me, what should I do?"

My Task Force membership provided a unique vantage point to witness the rapid changes in medical technology, but I also became aware of a larger issue our religious leaders have not adequately confronted: bioethical decisions about the allocation of vital but limited medical resources including health care professionals, mechanical devices, and organ replacements.

For decades, most Americans falsely believed that every needed medical resource would always be available to them 24 hours a day, seven days a week, no matter a person's age, gender, race, socioeconomic class, or place of residency.

Medical resources are always finite, and today they are becoming scarcer and increasingly expensive. The growing shortage of physicians, nurses, and other healthcare providers and the escalating costs of prescription drugs are additional signs of a health system at risk.

Tragically, the horrific COVID-19 pandemic clearly revealed that both human and medical facilities are quite limited and can collapse under the strain of a global deadly virus. Despite these obvious and ominous signs, most of the nation's spiritual leaders and seminary faculties have not addressed these key bioethical questions that require immediate attention.

For example, who is more entitled to the finite and often shrinking medical facilities? Children under three years of age or the elderly? What steps, if any, can be taken to deliver necessary quality health care to America's rural and minority communities?

But one thing is certain: medical science and technology will move forward with or without the religious community. Major decisions about health care in the US, including the overwhelming question of withdrawing and withholding life support systems from desperately ill or comatose patients, will be made with or without the benefit of clergy.

If the best thinkers within our faith communities do not address these issues in a thoughtful and informed way, others will decide for us, and that would be an abdication of religious leadership. If that happens, rabbis, priests, pastors, and imams will have no one to blame but themselves, and worst of all, desperately ill patients and their troubled families will be the losers.

In a painful twist of personal history, Dr. David Axelrod, the Massachusetts-born son of an Orthodox rabbi, suffered a debilitating stroke at age fifty-six. He was one of the most competent dedicated public servants I have ever encountered, and, alas, poor David died three years later. He was only fifty-nine years old.

I mourned when Governor Mario Cuomo died in early 2015. Lost in the extensive media coverage of his death was no mention of one of his most enduring achievements: the New York State Task Force on Life and the Law.

During his first term as governor, Cuomo established the Task Force because he was concerned that as developments in medical technology and science accelerated, neither society nor state government was prepared for the critical decisions required in the face of such rapid change. Cuomo's instruction to our group was to study the new frontier of bioethics and make specific public policy recommendations for state lawmakers in Albany.

Cuomo wanted us to focus on the right of patients to make informed decisions about their medical conditions. One result of the Task Force's efforts was to shift the center of the medical universe to the patient—something that especially pleased the three-term New York governor.

Cuomo opposed those who sought preferential treatment as they waited in line for an organ transplant. He deplored the rich and/or famous celebrities who demanded a place at the front of the organ replacement queue.

Cuomo will likely be remembered for many remarkable political achievements, but the enduring success of the Task Force he created in 1985 remains one of the crown jewels of his political career and the standard by which all similar efforts in the other forty-nine states must ultimately be judged.

Biafra Relief

Just two months after joining the American Jewish Committee staff, I became deeply involved in the Nigerian civil war that had begun a year earlier in 1967.

The Ibo tribe, a minority in that large oil-rich African nation, broke away from the Nigerian Federal Government that was dominated by anti-Ibo Hausas. Biafra was the name of the Ibo-led new nation, and as the war dragged on, the Ibo people faced the twin horrors of mass famine and the threat of genocide. Many Jews throughout the world, remembering the Holocaust, personally identified with Ibo suffering and rallied to the Biafran cause.

In August 1968, Marc Tanenbaum responded to the desperate situation in Biafra and organized the American Jewish Emergency Effort for Biafran Relief that included twenty-one Jewish organizations. Over $350,000 was quickly raised for vital humanitarian aid that would be funneled through the Protestant Church World Service and the Catholic Relief Service.

I became the coordinator, the "point person," of the Jewish campaign for Biafran relief as well as the liaison to the two well-established international Christian relief agencies.

In late October 1968, an interreligious rally in support of Biafra was held at Saint Patrick's Cathedral in New York City, and I was honored to be a featured speaker as the representative of the American Jewish community.

This is an excerpt of what I said in that world-famous Catholic house of worship:

When the fires of the Nazi crematoria were finally extinguished, a stunned and traumatized Jewish people cried from the very depths of its being: mass human destruction must never happen again to any people at any time in any place.

Some of us who spoke those words have now forgotten that pledge; we have forgotten as we live in our affluent and self-indulgent society, but we come together today in this sanctuary to remind ourselves and to remind the world that a people is dying today in Biafra.

As I speak, as we pray, children die of starvation and men and women are killed, and the lush rich countryside of Biafra becomes dark with the blood of massacres. In my mind's eye, the crematoria smokestacks of the Nazi German death camps blur into the cities and the bush country of Biafra.

In my wakeful and terrible visions, I see the mass Jewish graves of Europe rapidly filling with starving and dying Biafrans. I come as a rabbi to this place for the sake of life, to save lives. I come to remind us of that universal and demanding pledge: genocide must never happen again to any people at any time in any place. Jewish sages have said one who permits an innocent person to be killed is responsible for all the victim's potential descendants until the end of time. We are responsible.

I come today to remind the princes, and the presidents, and the prime ministers, and the premiers that oil can never be thicker than blood, that Russian jet aircraft and Egyptian pilots cannot destroy a people's will to live in Africa, the Middle East or Central Europe, that the State Departments and the For-

eign Ministries of the world cannot stand idly by in the face of mass starvation and murder.

We cannot be silent; we cannot be passive. We may not be prophets, but we are descendants, the spiritual children of prophets, and our message will be heard.

Alas, the Ibo-led nascent nation of Biafra lost its bitter struggle for independence in 1970, but the multifaceted effort to bring vitally needed food, medical supplies, and other humanitarian aid to the Ibo people was my "initiation" to such interreligious efforts, and it was not to be the last.

Music for the Vatican Holocaust Concert

On April 7, 1994—Yom Ha Shoah (Holocaust Remembrance Day)—a widely televised orchestral concert to commemorate the Holocaust was held in the modernistic Pope Paul VI auditorium in Vatican City. Pope John Paul II was the host of the special event that attracted an audience of 7,000, including 150 Holocaust survivors.

The American conductor, Sir Gilbert Levine, led the London Philharmonic Orchestra and the Vatican's Cappella Giulia Choir in specially chosen musical selections to mark the solemn occasion.

Levine, whose mother-in-law was a Slovakian Holocaust survivor of Auschwitz, had served for four years as the conductor of the Krakow Symphony Orchestra beginning in 1987. While in that Polish city, he became friendly with Pope John Paul II who had earlier been Krakow's Archbishop.

I worked closely with Gilbert in New York City as we prepared for the special concert. The music included Kol Nidrei by Max Bruch played by the cellist Lynn Harrell, the Adagio of Ludwig van Beethoven's Ninth Symphony, and Psalm 92. Cantor Howard Nevison of Congregation Emanu-El of New York City sang the biblical text in the original Hebrew. Franz Schubert set the Psalm to music to mark the inauguration of a new synagogue in Vienna in 1826.

Concluding the concert were selections from Leonard Bernstein's Kaddish Symphony, which includes the recitation of the Jewish prayer for the dead. It was read by the actor Richard Dreyfuss, and the orchestra and chorus performed two of Bernstein's Chichester Psalms, which also contain passages in the original Hebrew.

While Bernstein's compositions are among my favorites, I suggested that Gustav Mahler's Kindertotenlieder, the mournful ode to dead children, be included in the concert. Interestingly, I was told our Vatican partners did not want the piece performed despite its appropriate theme. It was rejected because in 1897 Mahler converted from Judaism to Catholicism, an unfortunate necessity in that highly antisemitic era in order to become the musical director of the Vienna Court Opera.

I was told Vatican officials did not want to be accused of fostering or encouraging Jewish conversions to Catholicism, and the Bernstein pieces were added instead to the program.

Thanks to Gilbert Levine, I was one of the three honored guests at the Vatican concert that included Rome's Chief Rabbi, Elio Toaff, and Italian President Oscar Luigi Scalfaro. Pope John Paul II spoke that day with eloquence about the evils of the Holocaust:

> We are gathered ... to commemorate the Holocaust of millions of Jews ... This is our commitment. We would risk causing the victims of the most atrocious deaths to die again if we do not have an ardent desire for justice, if we do not commit ourselves, each according to his own capacities, to ensure that evil does not prevail over good as it did for millions of the children of the Jewish people ... [The victims cry out] 'Do not forget us.'

Attending Good Friday Services

Jesus' pilgrimage to Jerusalem to celebrate *Pesach*, the eight-day Passover festival marking the Hebrew slaves' exodus from Egyptian bondage, was a religious requirement for Jews of his day. After his execution by Roman crucifixion, Passover became an integral part of the Easter story, and Jesus's Last Supper has been considered by some scholars an early version of what later became the holiday *Seder* meal.

During my career, I anonymously attended Good Friday services in New York City and sat alongside Christians as they commemorated the death of Jesus as recounted in the New Testament Gospel of John. I alternated each year between Roman Catholic and Protestant churches because I was interested in how preachers handled John's seventy one references to the Jewish people, a text often called "radioactive" because of its negative teaching about Jews and their alleged culpability in killing Jesus.

I attended the most solemn Christian service of the year knowing it had often been a day of dread and even death for many Jewish communities. On some Good Fridays in the past, especially in Eastern Europe, worshippers stormed out of churches filled with hatred and venom for their Jewish neighbors. Many preachers provoked their congregations with sermons saying that "The Jews killed our Lord," the infamous "Christ killer" or deicide charge that has long poisoned relations between Christians and Jews.

John's Gospel introduces more problematic themes and hostile descriptions about Jews and Judaism than the other three Gospels of Matthew, Mark, and Luke. Some contemporary scholars have attempted to mitigate or soften John's negative description of "The Jews."

One explanation is that the Greek word *Ioudaioi* refers only to the obsequious Jewish leaders who collaborated with the Romans, not the entire people. Another approach is to translate the word as "Judeans," the residents of Judea, the Roman name for the region. Yet for most people, these are linguistic differences without any real meaning or significance.

A more plausible explanation is that John describes a bitter intra-Jewish family feud, an internal clash between the followers of Jesus and those who remained faithful to the older faith. Vigorous angry debates took place within the *mishpacha*, the Hebrew word for "family." Truth be told, people often utter or write more derogatory words and phrases in family disputes than they would ever use with those outside the family circle.

Such finely crafted academic opinions, however, were rarely heard at the Good Friday services I attended. Some preachers made "The Jews" into the chief adversaries, the eternal enemies of Jesus. They preached that the Jewish people merited eternal divine punishment because of their alleged "crime."

The decisive and central role played by the cruel Roman authorities—the only ones with the power to carry out capital punishment—was frequently minimized or omitted. Jesus' killers were "The Jews," full stop. Such anti-Jewish Good Friday services were painful and distressing.

But I also attended Good Friday services in both Catholic and Protestant churches where the death of Jesus was portrayed in broad universal terms without placing the blame on "The Jews" or even the Romans: no condemnation, no divine punishment. Such sermons focused less on "who" killed Jesus than on the meaning of his death for our age. Those positive sermons reflected the Second Vatican Council's 1965 repudiation of the deicide charge and the call for "mutual respect and knowledge" between Christians and Jews.

After Passover and Easter concluded, I always contacted the various preachers and suggested we meet to discuss my Good Friday experience. Almost all accepted my invitation.

The Christian clergy, including those who did not verbally criticize the Jews, usually asked:

"Rabbi, why didn't you tell me you were coming to the Good Friday service?"

My response:

"Would that have changed your preaching?"

The answer from even those who had spewed anti-Judaism from their pulpit was invariably something along the lines of:

"Knowing a rabbi was present would have made a real difference. I would have changed my message, so I didn't offend you."

My response:

"It's not a matter of politeness. Before you again falsely condemn Jews as 'Christ killers' and cursed by God, imagine that Jews, the kinsfolk of Jesus, are physically present at all your services, not just on Good Friday."

Good Friday services remain a point of contention that must be fully addressed in Christian schools, especially seminaries. The death of Jesus, so central to Christian belief, needs to be presented and taught in both the spirit and letter of *Nostra Aetate*.

CHAPTER 18

The Interreligious Struggle to Free Soviet Jewry

EVEN THOUGH CHERISHED personal memories of Sister Ann Gillen are forever embedded within me, I am in great debt to my friend, Fred A. Lazin, Professor Emeritus at Ben Gurion University of the Negev in Israel. Fred's carefully crafted and meticulously researched book *American Christians and the National Interreligious Task Force on Soviet Jewry: A Call to Conscience* is the definitive work describing an underreported aspect of the Soviet Jewry advocacy movement: the Christian component of that long but ultimately successful struggle.

Fred's detailed book brilliantly describes the important role Sister Ann and her many Christian colleagues played in the epic story of freeing Soviet Jewry. Thank you, Fred!

Following the end of World War II and the Holocaust, a sense of collective guilt enveloped many American Jews.

They asked themselves some painful questions: Did we do all that we could have between 1933 and 1945 to save our brothers and sisters from the murderous genocidal Nazis and their collaborators? Why did we not demand more effective refugee rescue and immigration policies and actions from our political leaders, especially President Franklin Roosevelt? Where was the public outcry and support from our Christian neighbors and their religious leaders?

Feelings of shame combined with anger haunted American Jewish organizations and their leaders in the late 1960s when another catastrophe was unfolding; this time it was the fate of three million Jews living in the Soviet Union. Fifty years after the 1917 Communist revolution, it was clear the utopian promise to end all forms of antisemitism in the "workers' paradise" was a cruel mirage.

Irrefutable evidence revealed a systemic antisemitic campaign that discriminated against Soviet Jews in many aspects of daily life including the practice of religion, emigration, education, and employment. So strong was the USSR's anti-Zionist, anti-Israel, anti-Judaism campaign that even the study of the sacred Hebrew language was termed "counterrevolutionary."

Although the Stalinist Soviet regime voted in favor of the United Nations Partition Plan for Palestine in 1947 and diplomatically recognized the newly independent nation of Israel (Golda Meir was the Jewish state's first Envoy to Moscow), all of that changed in later decades as the Soviet Union provided Israel's hostile Arab neighbors with modern weapons and strong diplomatic support.

The Soviet Jewry advocacy movement that emerged in the early 1970s was preceded and fueled by three major events that revealed the paranoia and brutality of Soviet leaders. One of Joseph Stalin's final anti-Jewish acts before his death in 1953 was the infamous "Doctors' Plot" in which nine physicians, seven of them Jews, were accused of treason. They survived only because the Soviet dictator died before the executions could be carried out.

A year earlier, a parallel Stalinist campaign was the "liquidation" of many Jewish authors: "The Night of the Murdered Poets." Thirteen Jewish literary figures were executed in the Soviet secret police's Moscow prison. Even after Stalin's death, Jews were still forbidden to emigrate from the USSR to lands of freedom, especially Israel and the United States.

A final major catalyst for the rise of the Soviet Jewry movement in North America and Europe was the June 1970 "Leningrad Airplane Hijacking" in which sixteen Russian Jews attempted to seize an aircraft at the Leningrad (now St. Petersburg) airport in a futile attempt to escape the USSR by flying to Sweden. Eleven members of the group were arrested and placed on trial. Two of the hijackers were sentenced to death and nine received lengthy prison terms.

I remember the extraordinary international attention the event attracted. My AJC assignment was to gather public support for the prisoners from lay and clergy leaders of the American Christian community. It was an easy task for several reasons.

The bravery of the Jewish hijackers amazed millions of people because the Soviet Union was then perceived as an impenetrable closed society whose citizens were beaten down and obedient to the Communist state. Yet, the young Jews carried out an audacious act that stunned the Soviet leadership and impressed the outside world.

In addition, the arrests, trials, and harsh sentences were recognized as a gross human rights violation. Finally, I believe there was an unspoken feeling among numerous Christians that their various denominations and church leaders had been too silent three years earlier during the Israeli-Arab Six-Day War when the Jewish state was existentially threatened by a host of neighboring belligerent states.

The Leningrad events were for many Christians free of any ambiguity and without the need to "balance" their responses, unlike the Middle East conflict. And finally, there was widespread anti-Communist sentiment extant among many prominent American Christians.

Because of the powerful and rapid international reactions to the trials, at the end of December 1970 the Soviet Union blinked and reduced the prison sentences and commuted the executions. That action exposed the reality that the USSR was not immune to outside international pressure. This important fact was again proved true during the two decades of the Soviet Jewry movement.

The dramatic Leningrad episode and its aftermath spurred the creation of several national organizations in the United States, including the National Conference on Soviet Jewry and the Union of Councils to Free Soviet Jews. Both the Israeli government and many prominent US congressional leaders joined in the effort. Chief among the latter were US Senator Henry Jackson (D-Washington), and US Representatives Charles Vanik (D-Ohio) and Father Robert Drinan (D-Massachusetts).

The year 1970 was only twenty-five years after the end of the Holocaust, and memories from that horrific event were still fresh in the collective memory of the American Jewish community. When they rallied to the Soviet Jewry cause, countless Christians and Jews told me: "This time we will not fail! We will not be silent!" The biblical words from the Book of Exodus took on real meaning: "Let My People Go!" became a battle cry.

And unlike the 1930s, in 1970, American Jews were sure-footed in their political actions, less fearful of taking public positions, and of course the USSR was a longtime adversary of the United States. All those pieces began to fall into place to create a powerful advocacy movement on behalf of Soviet Jews.

One remarkable Catholic nun in Chicago, Minnesota-born Sister Margaret Ellen Traxler, grasped both the importance and the possibility of the moment, and changed the history of Christian-Jewish relations. Sister Margaret was a post-Vatican Council II activist, deeply committed to her faith and the cause of civil and human rights throughout the world.

In 1965, Sister Traxler marched with Dr. Martin Luther King Jr. in the historic iconic civil rights journey from Selma to Montgomery, Alabama. Traxler was a cofounder of the progressive National Coalition of American Nuns (NCAN), and in 1971 she became the Executive Director of the National Catholic Conference on Interracial Justice (NCCIJ). It was only natural she championed the Soviet Jewry cause.

That year, Sister Traxler publicly expressed her support in an NCCIJ newsletter article that drew the attention of AJC Midwest Director Eugene DuBow and his assistant Judah Graubart. They invited the dynamic Catholic nun for lunch and the trio quickly developed the idea of organizing a large interreligious, interracial, interethnic gathering in the Windy City that would launch a strong national movement on behalf of Soviet Jewry; one that would show America and, indeed, the world, that support for Soviet Jews was a universal human rights cause that transcended all borders and boundaries.

Such a meeting required extensive preparatory work by AJC staff members including DuBow and Graubart in Chicago along with David Geller, Jerry Goodman, Gerald Strober, and me in New York City. On March 19, 1972, the first sessions of the two-day assembly took place on the campus of the University of Chicago. On the following night, seven hundred attendees in the Holy Name Cathedral heard powerful speeches by Archbishop Fulton J. Sheen of Rochester, New York; US Congressman Robert Drinan; Mayor Charles Evers of Fayette, Mississippi; Ambassador Rita Hauser, the US Representative to the United Nations; Rabbi Marc Tanenbaum, AJC's Interreligious Affairs Director; and Dr. Cynthia Wedel, the President of the National Council of Churches.

After the extraordinary interreligious gathering, the large audience arose and adopted a "Statement of Conscience" that urged, "Mankind to make known [sic] its profound concern about the continued denial of the free exercise of religion, the violation of the right to emigrate, and other human rights of the three million Jews of the Soviet Union and of other deprived groups and nationalities."

The highly successful and well publicized meeting resulted in the creation of the National Interreligious Task Force on Soviet Jewry (NITFSJ) that would be sponsored and supported by the AJC.

Thanks to Sister Traxler's efforts, R. Sargent Shriver, President John F. Kennedy's brother-in-law and the first Peace Corps Director, became the Task Force's Honorary Chair. Later that year, Shriver was the Democratic Vice-Presidential nominee.

Marc, Chicago Theological Seminary Professor André LaCocque, the Rev. Robert Stephanopoulos of the Greek Orthodox Archdiocese of North America (his son George is a prominent TV news anchor), and, of course, Sister Traxler became the four NITFSJ National Co-Chairs. I was both pleased and excited the Task Force immediately became one of my major AJC projects, an assignment that lasted for fifteen years until the Task Force concluded its work.

As a direct follow-up to the Chicago meeting, Gerry Strober and I also secured the public support of a veritable "Who's Who" of American life of that decade. The lengthy list included Leonard Bernstein, US Senator Edward Brooke (D-Massachusetts), William Buckley, Aretha Franklin, US Senator Fred Harris (D-Oklahoma), Rabbi Abraham Joshua Heschel, Greek Orthodox Archbishop Iakovos, Tom Landry, Willie Mays, US Senator Charles Percy (R-Illinois), Jackie Robinson, and Ed Sullivan. Their names and many others appeared on the Task Force's stationery and immediately commanded public attention.

But even with our celebrity list and Sargent Shriver as the Task Force's Honorary Chair, the entire project was a high-stakes gambit because the primary target of our work was the powerful Soviet Union. Many skeptics believed the USSR was too strong and not susceptible to outside pressure. And indeed, the Communist regime constantly claimed the status of Soviet Jews was an "internal matter," and not subject to outside "interference."

To direct the newly created Task Force, Sister Traxler suggested that fifty-four-year-old Sister Ann Gillen, her personal friend and a Houston, Texas interreligious leader, become the Task Force's Director. Sister Ann of the Sacred Heart of the Child Jesus (SHCJ) order had strong academic and community organizing credentials. After meeting with Rabbi Tanenbaum and other leaders, in October 1972 she moved to Chicago to assume her new duties. Sister Ann, the Task Force's only Director, remained on the job until 1987.

During those fifteen years, she visited and spoke in hundreds of churches, synagogues, schools, colleges, and universities throughout the United States. She and another colleague, Sister Gloria Coleman (SHCJ) of Philadelphia, made several trips to the USSR where they met with Jewish dissidents, "refuseniks" (people denied permission to emigrate), as well as persecuted Roman Catholics, Adventists, and Baptists.

Not surprisingly, on her visits to the USSR, Soviet authorities followed Sister Ann's every move and interrogated and threatened her. But the diminutive Texas-born nun, only five feet, two inches in height, was not intimidated or frightened into submission.

In 1976, an international conference on Soviet Jewry took place in Brussels that drew hundreds of activists from many countries including the United States, Israel, and European Union nations. Sister Ann led a prominent group of American Christians to the conference. While in Brussels, the NITFSJ delegation met Israel's Prime Minister Golda Meir, who also attended the conference.

It was a unique moment. The Prime Minister presented a special medal to each member of the Task Force delegation. Then the two women embraced, and the Catholic sister told the Israeli leader:

> *You have won respect, admiration, and affection ... all over the world by your heroic leadership ... We pledge our commitment to this human rights cause, and as a sign of this commitment ... I present ... a copy of this 'Call to Conscience' ... We look forward to continued cooperation in the whole area of civil, religious, and human rights.*

Prime Minister Meir responded:

> *I am anxious for the sake of our Jewish children to see that our often very cruel and dangerous dialogue with the non-Jewish world shall not be the only dialogue ... I know you are preoccupied with this problem (Soviet Jewry) because you have made it yours. I praise God ... that we are not left alone. Just as we are found together today, so also somewhere, someplace may we meet again, when we have won.*

Sister Ann considered that exchange and warm embrace one of the highlights of her life. Alas, the two extraordinary women never met again.

It is impossible to count the number of hours and days I spent "on the road" with the indefatigable Catholic nun. Many mornings I would wake, sometimes before dawn, and travel to LaGuardia airport in New York City to board an early flight to Washington National Airport where I would meet Sister Ann who arrived from Chicago.

We then traveled to Capitol Hill where we would see sometimes ten members of the Senate and House of Representatives, always pressing them to support the cause of Soviet Jewry. I cannot estimate the total number of miles I walked with her, always two steps behind, on the Capitol's hard marble floors and in Congressional office buildings. Our constant ally was

Father Drinan, the US Representative from Massachusetts, who literally and figuratively opened numerous governmental doors for Ann and me.

On many days in Washington, we grabbed food when we were able because late in the afternoon or early evening there was always another local church, synagogue, or school to visit where we, a Sister and a Rabbi, would make a joint appeal for the cause. I would always catch the last shuttle flight back to New York City, and Ann returned to Chicago late at night.

On April 1, 1975, President Gerald Ford traveled to Finland where he, Soviet leader Leonid Brezhnev, and thirty-four other national leaders signed an important international document known as the Helsinki Accords. Although it lacked the binding authority of a treaty, the Accords' aim carried weight in the global public opinion arena.

Its goal was to increase détente and stability in all parts of Europe by confirming the various post-World War II national borders on the continent. Initially, Brezhnev saw this as a great victory for the USSR because it validated the Soviet Union's 1940 annexation of the three Baltic nations of Latvia, Estonia, and Lithuania. Of course, those nations regained their independence with the collapse of the Soviet Union that began in 1989.

The Helsinki Accords' second section dealt with economic and cultural cooperation and the fourth with compliance and enforcement.

But it was the document's third section—the so-called "Third Basket"—that specifically called for family reunification, religious and cultural rights, and other human rights issues that captured the world's attention. The "Third Basket" became an integral component of the Soviet Jewry advocacy movement.

In fact, the Task Force constantly emphasized the Helsinki Accords in its newsletter "The Task." Sister Ann and I constantly spoke of "Basket Three" in all our meetings with political, religious, cultural, labor, academic, and economic leaders. It was a very effective component and had real "currency" in our work.

The Task Force also strongly supported the Jackson-Vanik Amendment that denied the Soviet Union their most desired goal: The Most Favored Nation (MFN) status that would provide enormous aid to the USSR's weak economy. First introduced and debated in 1972, the Amendment to the US Trade legislation was finally adopted by Congress in 1975, despite the opposition of the Nixon Administration that believed diplomacy would change Moscow's emigration policy.

Sister Ann thought otherwise. She used her voice and pen to press for its adoption by Congress. The fact that Christians, as well as Jews, supported the Jackson-Vanik Amendment made a strong impact upon many wavering Senators and Representatives.

The Helsinki Accords established the Commission for Security and Cooperation in Europe (CSCE). The Commission convened a large meeting in November 1977 in Belgrade, Yugoslavia, to assess and evaluate the implementation of the various "Baskets." President Jimmy Carter appointed former US Supreme Court Justice Arthur J. Goldberg to lead the American delegation in Belgrade.

Sister Ann and I were the co-leaders of the National Interreligious Task Force delegation to Yugoslavia. Members of our team included Thomas Bird, Professor of Russian and Yiddish at Queens College and an expert on the Soviet Union. Joining the group was Judge Charles Z. Smith from Seattle who was the president of the American Baptist Convention; Lutheran pastor John Steinbruck of Washington, DC; the Rev. William Philippi, executive director of the Presbyterian Synod of Piedmont; Father John Radano, a professor at Seton Hall University, and Task Force Co-Chair André LaCocque.

But before our delegation arrived in Belgrade, we experienced a twenty-four-hour period of being political pawns in the Cold War tensions of that era: the clash between the United States and its allies and the bloc of Eastern European nations dominated by the Soviet Union.

Because of poor weather conditions in Belgrade, our Pan American Airlines flight was diverted to the Romanian capital of Bucharest. In 1977, that nation was under the dictatorship of Nicolae Ceausescu, a hardline Communist ruler who was later overthrown.

Pan Am provided its upset passengers with hotel lodgings for the night and we were assured our flight would depart the following morning for Belgrade. Bucharest had been hit hard by an earthquake earlier that year and parts of the city still showed some of the quake's destruction. The hotel staff viewed us with suspicion; I was even told by a waiter in the hotel dining room that we were being closely watched by the secret police (as if we didn't know).

When our NITFSJ group and the other passengers reassembled the following morning at the airport for the unanticipated last leg of our flight, we were all quick to notice the Pan Am jet was surrounded by uniformed armed men in military half-tracks, and we were informed passengers had to go through a final passport control checkpoint before we could board the plane.

The checkpoint, like the aircraft and runway, was guarded by heavily armed troops, each one of whom carried an automatic weapon, many of them aimed directly at us.

When I presented my US passport, a grim-faced uniformed border control official slowly looked through every page of my well-used passport book. When he finished his initial scan, he said—in quite understandable English—that I was eligible to be drafted into the Romanian army because I was born in Transylvania, the long-disputed region between Romania and Hungary and the fictional home of the infamous Count Dracula.

My many international travels had long ago taught me to remain calm at hostile check points. This included refraining from laughter, jesting, or exhibiting even a touch of impatience, condescension, or anger.

Once the passport officer repeated his false claim that I was a potential draftee in Ceausescu's military, I quietly replied that my passport showed I was born in "Pennsylvania, USA" and not Transylvania. Once again, he eyed me with suspicion, glanced down, and mumbled something in his native language. Then he looked directly at me with hostility as he stamped my travel document with carefully calibrated slowness.

Once I cleared the passport check point, I quickly rejoined Sister Ann and the other delegation members, and together we rode the short distance from the terminal building to our plane in a battered bus with an armed guard positioned at both exit doors. When I relayed my confrontation to our group, Sister Ann, who rarely expressed a sense of humor, said: "Well, Jim, I had it easier than you with the same official. I guess that's because I was born in Texas and not Pennsylvania."

As official conference observers, we had a private meeting with Justice Goldberg in Belgrade who reaffirmed America's commitment to human rights, including emigration and freedom of religion, for both Soviet Jews and Christians.

We also had a series of lengthy meetings with the Dutch, British, Spanish, and Vatican delegations. Some of the diplomats were surprised and somewhat confused because the Task Force represented BOTH Christians and Jews. They were not quite sure how to deal with American academics and religious leaders who were led by a nun and a rabbi.

While we naturally failed to obtain a requested meeting with the Soviet delegation, we did have an unexpected freewheeling closed-door session with the Hungarian representatives in Belgrade. I later described the meeting with words the State Department often employs following a tense, difficult encounter: "correct and candid."

The Hungarian Ambassador assured us that Jews in his country had full religious rights, including a functioning rabbinical seminary. But when Sister Ann and I pressed him on why Hungarians could not emigrate, especially in family reunification cases, the Ambassador, Janos Petran Kadar, was evasive and offered the usual wording when a diplomat is trapped by a difficult question: he promised to "look into the matter" when he returned to Budapest and, of course, we were all invited to Hungary "to see the good situation for ourselves."

While in Belgrade, we also met with several other members of the US delegation: Senators Robert Dole (R-Kansas), Claiborne Pell (D-Rhode Island), and Representative Millicent Fenwick (R-New Jersey).

When the CSCE conference ended, the Task Force group flew from Belgrade to Rome where we had a series of meetings with Vatican officials who stressed that the Holy See, while fully committed to the right to practice one's religion and the right to emigrate, chose, however, to pursue "quiet diplomacy" to achieve those goals. An angry Sister Ann expressed her impatience and displeasure with the Vatican responses to the Task Force.

While in Rome, our delegation participated in the international Sakharov Hearings at the Palazzo dei Congressi. The meeting's agenda focused on human rights and religious liberties. Holocaust survivor and famed Nazi hunter, Simon Wiesenthal, chaired the Hearings. Many of the delegates were intrigued and impressed by the interreligious makeup of the Task Force from the United States. They did not know what to make of such a unique group.

It was a hectic, but meaningful eight days in Belgrade and Rome. Most of us slept on the long flight back home. But not Sister Ann, who was busy composing her reports and articles. She was, as always, tireless and dedicated to her work to free Soviet Jews and Christians from Communist tyranny.

Three years later, in November 1980, the National Interreligious Task Force on Soviet Jewry again gained official observer status to attend the second CSCE conference, this time in Madrid. President Carter appointed attorney Max Kampelman to head the US delegation. Months earlier, I had attempted to have Sister Ann appointed as a member of the American delegation, but my efforts were unsuccessful.

Judge Smith, Pastors Philippi and Steinbruck, and Father Radano returned as members of the Task Force delegation. Also joining Sister Ann and me in Madrid were Sister Ann Marie Erst (SHCJ) and Dr. Thomas

Melady, the president of Sacred Heart University in Connecticut who years later became the US Ambassador to the Vatican.

Our group secured meetings with representatives from West Germany, Denmark, and Sweden. We also engaged in numerous off-the-record conversations with many delegates, often at meals or in the hallways of the conference center. We provided the Swedes with Task Force information about the heroic diplomat, Raoul Wallenberg, who saved many Jewish lives in Hungary during the Holocaust, and who was arrested by the Soviet Union in 1945 on the purported charge he was a Western spy.

Unlike Belgrade three years earlier, there was a distinct feeling in Madrid that the USSR and its satellite nations in Eastern Europe were no longer as tightly regulated and regimented as in the past. The Old Guard of Soviet leaders was passing from the scene and hopes were growing that Soviet Jews and Christians might finally gain their freedom.

Of course, we did not know that the USSR would collapse just nine years later, including the fall of the ugly Berlin Wall. Nor did we know that Mikhail Gorbachev would become the Soviet leader in 1985 and preside over the end of the USSR.

The culmination of the Soviet Jewry advocacy movement came on December 6, 1987, in Washington, DC, when 250,000 people gathered the day before President Ronald Reagan was to meet with Chairman Gorbachev for a summit meeting at the White House.

The giant rally brought together Americans of every religion, creed, race, ethnicity, and political position. Vice President George H.W. Bush and Nobel Prize winner, Holocaust survivor, and author Elie Wiesel were among the many featured speakers. Coretta Scott King was unable to personally attend, but her message was read by Representative John Lewis (D-Georgia), and it resonated with the crowd: "...You were with us in Selma, you were with us on the Mall with Martin Luther King Jr., and we are proud to be with you today for the fight for freedom for Soviet Jewry."

Sister Ann and I arranged for the Rev. Dr. Arie Brouwer, the General Secretary of the National Council of Churches, and Roman Catholic Archbishop William Keeler of Baltimore, to be featured speakers representing the Task Force. Ann herself did not address the rally that Sunday afternoon, but the quarter-million people were physical and visible proof of her message that American support for Soviet Jews and Christians was broad-based and fervent.

I was especially pleased with Brouwer's presence at what turned out to be a truly historic event. He said: "I believe American Christians are duty-bound to join with American Jews in demanding religious freedom in the Soviet Union." His words represented a significant shift from earlier NCC actions and policies.

Three years earlier, I had been highly critical of the NCC and its delegation that visited the Soviet Union in 1984. I was furious with their public statements when the group returned to the United States and I went public in the New York Times and other media:

"I think you all missed a rare opportunity to be prophetic witnesses ... I was also stunned to hear you did not visit one unregistered church...I find it unacceptable that people of goodwill (The NCC delegation to the USSR) did not make a prophetic witness for Soviet Jews...the NCC has not been vigorous enough in pressing for human and religious rights."

At the 1987 rally, Keeler—he became a Cardinal in 1994—declared:

>"'Let My People Go!' ... whether we speak of Jew or Baptist or Roman Catholic ... in the Soviet Union ... our hearts must ache, our voices must rise, because they are our brothers and sisters and because they suffer."

The 1987 Washington rally for Soviet Jewry was the defining moment, the high-water mark for the entire movement because not only did it bring together that enormous crowd of at least a quarter-million people, but it also had a lasting impact upon the world stage.

The driving force and the person most responsible for making that extraordinary event a reality was David Harris, my AJC colleague. David's months of hard work that made his dream become a reality was obvious to me and many others. Four years after the rally, David became Executive Director of the AJC, and later the organization's CEO.

Sister Ann, after fifteen years of nonstop work on behalf of Soviet Jewry, saw that her work at the Task Force was coming to an end. In addition to energizing countless Christians to the cause of freeing Soviet Jews, she brought along much of the Jewish community, including the AJC, to also demand religious and cultural freedom for dissenting embattled "nonregistered" Christians in the USSR.

For some Jews that was not an easy connection to make, but Sr. Ann persisted and ultimately triumphed by stressing the inextricable universal connection between Jews and Christians, not only in lands of freedom, but also between the two suffering communities in the Soviet Union.

Her battle is an eternal one. Does passionate support for one persecuted group preclude support for other persecuted groups as well? When pressed by the "particularists" who wanted the Task Force to focus solely on the plight of Soviet Jews, she always quoted Rabbi Hillel's ancient teaching: "If I am not for myself, who will be for me? And being only for myself, what am I? And if not now, when?" And she would then follow up by saying: "Political freedom, religious liberty, freedom of conscience—they are universal and indivisible."

Three years after the 1987 Reagan-Gorbachev summit in Washington, the USSR was no more and during the 1990s, nearly one million Jews emigrated to Israel permanently, enlarging Israel's Jewish population and enriching its society.

Sadly, Sister Ann contracted cancer in the early 1990s. She underwent surgery, but died on January 14, 1995, in Rosemont, Pennsylvania, surrounded by the sisters of her order. She was seventy-six.

I was both humbled and honored to be asked to deliver the eulogy at her funeral Mass. Never have I worked so hard on a public address as I did on that sad occasion. These are some of the heartfelt words I spoke at that poignant moment:

> *Sister Ann Gillen brought the Christian community into what appeared to be solely a Jewish struggle. She also brought a deep spiritual commitment to the cause of Soviet Jewry. For her it was not just a political or immigration issue, but a religious issue.*
>
> *She gave it a spiritual dimension...Each time she talked with a friend or an adversary, Sister Ann would conclude the conversation with the biblical words, "Let My People Go!" ...many considered her naïve, even foolish. She was neither. She brought the message of Soviet Jewry to tens of thousands in churches and synagogues ... She stalked the halls of the United Nations, the White House, the State Department, and the United States Congress to gain support for Soviet Jews ... She picketed Soviet embassies everywhere, prodded political leaders and diplomats at conferences in Brussels, Jerusalem, Belgrade, Madrid, and personally visited her "Jewish family" in the USSR ...*
>
> *She remained absolutely convinced that Soviet Jewry would eventually be freed. She was never overawed by the vaunted power and prestige of the Soviet Union. She taught me and everyone she met that every person was potentially redeemable, a great religious teaching.*

Everyone in the Soviet Jewry movement knew and respected Ann's indomitable spirit. She displayed enormous physical, emotional, and spiritual strength in her meetings with Presidents, Senators, and Representatives, Vatican and Soviet authorities, and members of the clergy and the media.

Our beloved Sister Ann Gillen is now with the God of freedom Who endowed her with extraordinary power and strength. Rest well, my dear, dear friend. Your achievements and memory will forever be an inspiration.

May the life and memory of Ann Gillen always be for a blessing.

Sister Ann, who was a cherished member of the order of the Society of the Holy Child Jesus, was buried wearing two necklaces: a Cross and a Star of David.

CHAPTER 19

The Future of Christian-Jewish Relations

FOUR MAJOR REALITIES will define and shape the future of Christian-Jewish relations throughout the world in the years ahead.

Those issues, albeit predictable, will remain important whenever Christians and Jews meet seriously and systematically. I refer to the impact of the *Shoah* on Christian-Jewish relations and religious thought; the persistence of anti-Judaism and antisemitism; the meaning of modern Israel for both communities; the need for historians to jointly study the appropriate Vatican archival documents and analyze the record of Pope Pius XII vis-a-vis Jews and Judaism during his nineteen-year pontificate; the prickly nexus of mission, witness, conversion, and *teshuva*; the issues of human rights, religious liberty, and freedom of conscience; the relationship between religion and state; the impact of liberation theology on our encounter; developing purposeful moral guidelines for the galloping advances in bioethics; and examining the teachings and images of the "Other" in the Christian and Jewish traditions.

In addition, much greater attention must be paid to our inadequate record of involving women, young people, and people of color in the central decision-making process of Christian-Jewish relations. We also require an effective answer to the oft-heard charge that we are merely engaging in a delicate but superficial minuet of "ecclesiastical diplomacy." I have no doubt these themes and others equally familiar will remain with us in the years ahead. They will not soon disappear; nor should they.

Four overarching realities transcend our well-defined and sometimes repetitive agenda. Four towering existential realities will shape our future together.

I place the first two realities together because they are interrelated: they are demography and geography.

The rapid and continuing global population growth has had major consequences for Christians and Jews. Since the fifth century, Europe and, more recently, North America have been the key centers of Christian population, clerical leadership, religious thought, and theology. However, today most of the world's Christians reside in South America, Africa, and Asia; it is a demographic trend that is accelerating even as the number of Christians is either barely holding steady or declining in Europe and North America.

Christian and Jewish communities on those two continents are older in age and fewer in number than their co-religionists in the rest of the world, especially when compared to residents of the Third World.

This shift in population centers will influence both Christianity and Judaism in the twenty-first century and especially interreligious relations. Some recent figures reported in the Vatican's Statistical Yearbook of the Church make the point.

Between 2000 and 2008, the Catholic population in Asia grew by 33 percent, by 15.6 percent in Africa, in Oceania by 11 percent, and in the Americas by 10.9 percent; most of the latter growth took place in Central and South America. The increase in the European Catholic population during those same eight years was only one percent. One of every five Catholic priests today is from either Asia or Africa, and European priests make up only 47 percent of the world's Catholic clergy, a drop of four percent in less than a decade.

Could Europe and North America, the longtime spiritual, intellectual, and population cores of Christianity and Judaism, be losing their dominance and influence? We do not know the answer to that question because human history is always more than a series of demographic statistics and geographical trends. However, several examples are perhaps indicative of things to come. Interestingly, the experience of one major faith community is illustrative.

The Anglican Church was established by English King Henry VIII in the sixteenth century; the break with the Holy See in Rome came in 1534. As the British Empire expanded throughout the world, Anglicans left Britain and established "mission churches" in colonial possessions in Africa, Asia, Oceania, the Caribbean, and South America. It was a classic example of faith following flag; in this case, the flag was the Union Jack.

Today the Anglican Church in the United Kingdom and its American counterpart, the Episcopal Church, are suffering losses in membership, but the younger Anglican "mission churches" are increasing in size and are politically and theologically more conservative than their ecclesiastical mentors. It is an old story: the child has grown up and broken from the inherited views, opinions, and beliefs of its parent.

Pope Emeritus Benedict XVI has repeatedly expressed his concern about the shrinking number of active Catholics on the European continent. The causes for the Pope's concern are many, including the clergy sexual abuse scandals, the secularization of the First World, and the decreasing Catholic birth rate in North America and Europe. These factors have created a growing shortage of priests and sisters on both sides of the North Atlantic. It is a trend likely to continue.

Christians in general and clergy in particular from Africa, Asia, and much of Central and South America often have had minimal contact with large viable Jewish communities. As a result, there is frequently a gap in Christian knowledge of and personal experience with Jews and Judaism. Similarly, Jews, except for those living in certain regions of Central and South America, have had limited contact with Christian clergy and laity from the three Third World continents.

But the future may be surprisingly different because in an ironic twist of history, some painful past events may offer unanticipated and unexpected opportunities to build positive Christian-Jewish relations. While some see a large breach, even an abyss, between Hispanic Christians and Jews, the fissure may not be as wide as it may first appear.

I am indebted to Professor Jacqueline M. Hidalgo of Williams College in the United States for alerting me to this unique possibility in interreligious relations. Her essay on Hispanics and Jews appears in the volume of essays dedicated to the memory of the late Rabbi León Klenicki. Dr. Celia Deutsch, a Sister of Zion, was the editor in chief, and Dr. Eugene Fisher and I were the coeditors.

Professor Hidalgo recounts that a sizeable number of the early European settlers in Latin and South America were *conversos* or crypto ("secret") Jews who fled the Iberian Peninsula because of the Inquisition and the Expulsions from Spain and Portugal. Such refugees who fled to the Americas and the Caribbean islands came into direct contact with the indigenous natives, the "Indians" of the region, who, Hidalgo documents, were also victims of Spanish/European religious and political prejudice and persecution.

Hidalgo shows how *conversos*, crypto-Jews, and the native tribes were often united in their hatred of the European colonialists. Incredibly, today that long-ago shared history between Jews and Native Americans is increasingly coming to light as the descendants of both groups are rediscovering their family roots. Modern descendants of "secret Jews" are in contact with their Hispanic Jewish past even as Roman Catholic Indians are rediscovering their own family tribal histories that predate conversions to Catholicism.

While Hidalgo's research in this area is a pioneering effort, it does offer a fascinating and hopeful glimpse into the possibilities of developing a new set of relationships, an additional and unexpected bridge of human solidarity between Judaism and Christianity. It merits our collective future attention.

Following the horrific expulsions of Sephardic Jews from Spain and Portugal in the late fifteenth and early sixteenth centuries, the religious influence of that once-influential group was diminished and frequently overshadowed by Jews of Central and Eastern Europe (the Ashkenazim). That history is well known since most American Jews trace their family roots to Europe.

Poland, Germany, Austria, France, former Czechoslovakia, Lithuania, Hungary, Ukraine, Romania, Belarus, Russia, and other European countries became important centers of Jewish life. When the antisemitic persecutions intensified in that part of the world, especially in the nineteenth and twentieth centuries, new Ashkenazi centers grew in size and influence in modern Israel and the United States.

But one result of Israel's creation in 1948 was the arrival of 900,000 non-Ashkenazim Jews from Arab and/or Muslim countries in Africa and Asia. Some members of that group were descendants of the expelled Spanish and Portuguese Jews, but most stemmed from ancient Jewish communities in Iraq, Iran, Egypt, Libya, Tunisia, Morocco, Yemen, and Ethiopia that had existed for over a thousand years. Not surprisingly because of their critical population mass, they are challenging and changing the dominant Ashkenazi image and reality of modern Israel.

For two thousand years, the overwhelming majority of Jews lived in the Diaspora outside of Israel, their biblical homeland. However, a major population change is currently underway, and soon, if not already, more than half the world's Jews will live in Israel, a nation that many people forget is located not in Europe or North America, but southwest Asia.

But Israel also has a growing Christian population, the only nation in the region to show such growth. Phillippe Fargues, Director of the Euro-Mediterranean Consortium for Applied Research on International Migration, reports that in 1914, Christians constituted 26.4 percent of the total population in what is today Israel, the Palestinian areas, Jordan, Lebanon, and Syria, but that percentage has rapidly declined.

In another twist of history, the land in Asia that both faiths call holy is likely to be a future major arena for Christian-Jewish relations; a land where Jews, unlike the sites of other encounters, are the majority and Christians the minority.

The third reality after geography and demography that will influence future Christian-Jewish relations is chronology, the relentless "march of time." The Second Vatican Council and the *Nostra Aetate* Declaration took place in 1965. That means two generations of Christians and Jews throughout the world have been born since then, and many of them are often unfamiliar with, at best, or unaware of, at worst, the recent advances in Christian-Jewish relations the Council set in motion.

Chronology also means the eyewitnesses to the best and worst in our shared history—victory in World War II, the *Shoah*, the creation of the State of Israel, the Second Vatican Council, and the remarkable actions of several Popes and Jewish leaders—will become fewer and fewer with each passing year.

I speak often to college, university, and seminary students, and I have discovered that the mists of legend and forgetfulness often obscure much of the remarkable achievements in Christian-Jewish relations. This reality demands that we redouble our educational efforts to make the record of the past decades permanent and meaningful, especially for younger Christians and Jews.

It was the sociologist Max Weber who raised the issue of whether and how religious charisma can be transmitted and "routinized" from one generation to another. Christians and Jews have, by Weber's standard, done a good job in "routinizing" Christianity and Judaism for thousands of years and successfully transmitted our charisma, teachings, and traditions from generation to generation.

But are we doing as well in transmitting the charisma of positive and constructive Christian-Jewish relations? Or will our efforts be at first minimized, then marginalized, and finally, God forbid, trivialized as future generations of Christians and Jews, of priests, pastors, nuns, and rabbis engage in more "important" work than interreligious projects and programs?

To paraphrase Heraclitus: "No person ever steps into the same river twice, because it's not the same river and it is not the same person." Chronology may not entirely shape our future but is an irreversible reality of Christian-Jewish relations.

The fourth and final reality that will influence our future relations is technology. In 1965, there were no fax machines, no email, no Internet, no Skype, no Zoom, no iPads, no Kindles, and few if any conference calls. There were no online academic courses, no "virtual" colleges, universities, and seminaries that exist today only in cyberspace.

In 1965, there were no e-books, e-magazines, and "texting" back then referred to biblical studies and not to instant communication between people. There were no online Internet partnerships among libraries, including the connection between libraries in Berlin and Israel.

There were no social networks like Facebook and Twitter, no personal blogs, mobile cell phones were a rarity—a luxury—and the personal computer we take so much for granted today was in its early development stage. Today's laptop, I am told by experts in the field, has more power than the computers of the 1969 spacecraft that first brought humans to the moon.

Like the other three realities mentioned above, technology will dramatically shape our future relations with one another. Let me count the ways.

Jews and Christians today can now easily communicate with one another outside the once-formal boundaries of Church and Synagogue. It is not simply that Christians and Jews often share the same workplace or workspace. Rather the technology that is so easily available allows them to "go global" and encourages people to discuss any issue at any time and from any place.

They can do this with a series of contacts in all parts of the world. They no longer require the leadership of clergy, the physical setting of a college or university campus, or reading actual books in libraries; none of that is needed to establish, develop, or strengthen Christian-Jewish cyberspace encounters. Naturally such Christian-Jewish encounters are frequently independent of academic or clerical guidance and leadership. A papal declaration, a rabbinical statement, and a personal blog all look the same on a computer screen.

In addition, technology now provides what some have termed "webinars" as opposed to traditional "seminars." Webinars allow teachers to reach in one morning more students around the globe than they could ever reach in person during their entire academic careers.

For centuries, Jews and Christians conducted worship services as faithful "Peoples of God" in stationary physical buildings: churches and synagogues. One biblical commandment in Exodus commands us: "Build Me a sanctuary that I may dwell among you." [Exodus 25:8]. The text does not say that God dwells in the sanctuary, but rather God dwells within the people assembled inside the sanctuary. As an Internet devotee, I interpret this verse to mean that God also dwells among those connected to one another via the computer.

We are also seeing the proliferation of "couch churches" or "sofa synagogues." That is, the creation of decentralized gatherings of Jews and Christians who study, pray, and "share" meals together in a nonstructured form often without clergy leadership.

My point is a simple one. Advocates of Christian-Jewish relations must learn to utilize the new communications and information technology that is exploding throughout the globe. The horrific COVID-19 pandemic has driven home the fact that millions and tens of millions of people can communicate, analyze, and organize their political, economic, cultural, social, and religious lives in a single instant, a single click of the computer.

Christian and Jewish interreligious leaders need to recall that in the past, control of land routes and river and sea lanes was vital to gain influence and shape history. Today, control of cyberspace and social networking is paramount.

I am aware there is no substitute for "up close and personal" interreligious encounters. We are all the beneficiaries of such encounters, but I am also keenly aware that many leaders of Christian-Jewish relations often operate as if it were still 1965 or even earlier, as if the world and the people they are supposed to be leading are somehow waiting to be taught or motivated. Not at all. Technology has empowered them to create their own interreligious realities. We must do the same.

Those engaged in the Christian-Jewish encounter might recall Bette Davis' famous line in the American 1950 award-winning film, *All About Eve*: "Fasten your seat belts. It's going to be a bumpy night."

But Hollywood must not have the last pessimistic word regarding our future relations. I conclude with the biblical prophet who spoke of "prisoners of hope." [Zach. 9:12]. And that is who we must always be in the future.

CHAPTER 20

Ten Personal Interreligious Commandments

DEVELOPING CONSTRUCTIVE RELATIONS between Christians and Jews is not the sole domain of rabbis, Christian clergy, or academics. Indeed, the strength of those relations ultimately depends upon the efforts of laymen and women who actively seek to change the troubled history of the past. The following suggestions and guidelines are the result of decades of interreligious programming and have been kitchen tested for their effectiveness in achieving positive results.

Lay people often approach interreligious encounters with anxiety, even fear. They do not want to be embarrassed by either their faith commitments or their lack of knowledge about their own religion or the religion of the "Other." It is necessary to stress that dialogue is a conversation, not a test or exam, nor is it a device to seek openly or covertly religious conversions.

Based on my experience, here are "Ten Commandments" for successful Christian-Jewish dialogues:

1. Be there. Show up. As that great American philosopher Woody Allen once said: "Showing up is 80 percent of life."

2. Don't try to defend the indefensible regarding one's faith. Dialogue participants frequently become sidetracked and backed into a corner. It is important to acknowledge errors and mistakes that members and leaders of your faith community have made. Then move on. Keep the discussion focused on subjects that can be supported and defended.

3. Listen. Frequently, dialogue participants are poor listeners. It is important to hear what those of another religion are saying. It is counterproductive to interrupt someone to challenge a specific remark. Do not talk over each

other—it's rude. Sometimes waiting until the end of a presentation will allow you to pick and choose the points to which you'll respond.

4. Focus. You can't cover everything in Christian-Jewish relations. Focus on two or three points and develop them firmly. Don't spread yourself all over the interreligious map.

5. Avoid simply preaching Bible texts, history, dogma, and law. Don't concentrate solely on historical, scriptural, and legal perspectives or rationales, because if you do, audiences' eyes will glaze over as you speak. Provide authentic information, but remember that theology is not counting "angels on the head of a pin." It is autobiographical.

6. The person with the most words usually loses. You are not participating in a word contest or a court case. In short, less is often more.

7. Know your dialogue audience. Are they academics? Attorneys? Businesspeople? Politicians? Homemakers? Religious leaders? Elderly? Educators? A particular presentation of one's religious tradition may be inappropriate for one audience, but "on the mark" for another.

8. Journalists may sometimes be inadequately informed, but they are usually interested in religious matters. Journalists cover many different subjects on deadlines or short notice. Often, they don't know what to ask when covering an interreligious encounter. Try to get them to focus on a few points and emphasize context, context, context.

9. Seek areas of solidarity and mutual respect. Emphasize the "values we share," and not merely "what you have done to us."

10. Don't try to change people's minds; concentrate on enlightenment, explanation, and clarification. A Christian-Jewish dialogue is not a contest with winners or losers.

Organizing Interreligious Programs

All programs should be respectful, reciprocal, and constructive in both substance and tone. Participants need to be reminded that true dialogue is a lifelong process, not a "quick fix." Pope John Paul II accurately described Christian-Jewish relations as a "culture of dialogue ... a harmony of differences."

How should an interreligious program be organized?

1. Interreligious engagement should lead to mutual respect and understanding between religious groups. It is also possible for the dialogue process to produce joint action on specific problems or themes, including public statements, educational materials, the interpretation of key issues for public officials, and/or domestic and overseas study missions. In all cases, there must be no hidden agendas on the part of the participating individuals or groups.

2. There should be adequate joint planning by both the Jewish and Christian participants in any interreligious engagement. This planning includes not only the various logistical details of a program but the specific themes and topics as well. The planning process is an integral part of the total dialogue experience and should not be minimized. A bad or inadequate planning process can doom the entire program.

3. Appropriate co-sponsorship from both faith communities is required. The co-sponsor(s) can be a local house of worship, a clergy/rabbinic association, seminary, religious or community organization, college/university, or institute.

4. The precise number of sessions should be announced at the beginning of the program so participants will know exactly how much time they are expected to give to the undertaking. An open-ended program is a recipe for failure. For example, if the Christian and Jewish participants agreed on six sessions, it will require proper scheduling so that each session be structured to cover specific topics or themes.

5. If possible, there should be an equal number of participants from each community, and women and young people from the involved religious communities must be adequately represented.

6. An appropriate balance is needed between clergy and laypeople among the participants. Obviously, this does not apply if the program is for clergy only or laypeople only. It is always important to ensure that clergy members do not dominate an interreligious encounter when laypeople are

present. While the clergy are professionally involved with their religion and may be "experts," the laity constitutes the membership of every religious community.

7. While some programs may take place in a home setting, it is better to house an interreligious dialogue in a synagogue, church, school, or similar public location. The programs can be rotated from one location to another.

8. Two discussion leaders should be selected in advance, one from each community. These leaders should meet before the formal program so they can jointly develop the project and decide on ground rules, themes, reading assignments, etc.

9. Ideally, basic reading materials and/or audiovisual materials from both communities should be sent to all participants in advance of the program. Experience has shown, however, that participants frequently do not read articles and papers before dialogue sessions. Only once the dialogue is underway do participants often turn in great interest to the printed or visual materials they have received. All participants should receive the same materials to ensure a successful program.

10. Once a dialogue project has started and matured, it may be useful to feature guest speakers or specialists who can focus on a specific issue or theme. However, this should not take place until the participants themselves have had an opportunity to bond and to establish their own identities in the dialogue process.

11. Caution should be exercised regarding "interreligious services," to ensure that the character and sensitivities of each religion is respected. The danger in interreligious services is that no matter how well intentioned, they can result in reducing the particular faith commitments of the participants to the lowest common denominator. Preferably, each religious community should be encouraged to conduct its own authentic service.

    Christian participants should be invited to attend a Jewish service and vice versa as a way of developing mutual understanding and respect. Let each group do what it does best: genuine authentic worship services. Artificially created services frequently satisfy no one.

12. The presence of "Hebrew Christians" in interreligious activities may skew the dialogue and create unnecessary dissonance and polarization.

13. Once the specific programs are formally concluded, contact should be maintained with the participants by the sponsoring groups. Such alumni are useful in developing future programs, relating to the general and religious media in a community, and encouraging friends, associates, and family members to become involved in Christian-Jewish relations.

14. A final word of caution: Christian-Jewish programs must not be used as either individual or group therapy sessions to center on such topics as intermarriage, intra-family conflicts, anger directed at various clergy, etc.

Christian and Jewish participants in the dialogue process, especially laypeople, can undertake joint "doable" projects that will strengthen relationships. As always, careful planning is necessary to ensure success. Some projects might include:

1. Joint visits to local churches and synagogues to attend religious services or to tour the facilities with an emphasis on learning about the sacred objects found in the various houses of worship.

2. Researching one's family tree with special attention paid to the religious identities, practices, and beliefs of previous generations. Building religious oral histories of families is easy to assemble and distribute thanks to the many technological tools currently available.

3. Joint visits to a local Holocaust Museum or, if possible, visits to the United States Holocaust Memorial Museum in Washington, DC. A shared study mission to both Israel and the Vatican has proven to be "life changing" for both Catholics and Jews. Trips could also include educational visits to the areas in Germany that were central to the rise of the Protestant Reformation culminating with a study mission to Israel.

4. Contributing appropriate books, periodicals, CDs, DVDs, and other educational material to local public libraries or schools.

5. Writing op-ed articles and/or letters to the editor for the general and religious press. Especially helpful is when a Christian composes a piece for a

Jewish newspaper and vice versa. Such articles can also be useful to condemn racist, antisemitic, and anti-Christian articles if they appear in a local community or region.

6. Swift and strong joint denunciation for any hate crime, cemetery desecration, or vandalization of houses of worship. These responses to bigotry should appear in print, electronic, and Internet media.

7. Development of community-wide services to commemorate both the *Kristallnacht pogrom* of 1938 and *Yom HaShoah*. Many churches and dioceses already conduct such annual remembrances in various houses of worship.

8. Organize a four-person lay panel—two members from each faith community—that can address local service club meetings (Rotary, Kiwanis, Lions, Elks, B'nai Brith, Knights of Columbus, etc.) to highlight Christian-Jewish relations and to enlist new participants.

9. Useful interreligious community social action projects may include regional and local issues (religious/racial profiling, discrimination in employment, education, housing, etc.). A strong Christian-Jewish voice frequently carries more weight than a single religious community's action.

10. Publicly acknowledge the men and women who make significant contributions to authentic dialogue. Such recognition can be annual awards that honor leaders in building interreligious relations.

CHAPTER 21

Some Basic Questions that Will Never Appear on *"Jeopardy!"*

THIS DISCUSSION GUIDE focuses on the major issues in Christian-Jewish relations within three broad historical eras: the biblical period and the early years of Rabbinic Judaism and Christianity, the medieval/pre-modern time span, and the contemporary period.

Each study session should have a fixed time frame, and the discussion leader must make sure there are no lengthy speeches or time-consuming two-person debates that do not involve the entire group. Participants in an interreligious study group should receive the questions and issues to be discussed in advance of the actual sessions.

Ideally, Christians might analyze a specific Jewish theme, and similarly, Jewish participants might study a specific Christian theme. This "crossover" procedure is an excellent method for enhancing Christian-Jewish discussion. In addition, shared visits to churches and synagogues along with explanations of various sacred objects and religious holidays strengthen interreligious encounters.

The questions for study listed below are intended to inaugurate a fruitful conversation and dialogue. If these questions are used in a more formal educational setting, it is important that teachers, especially clergy, do not dominate the conversation because of their expertise or knowledge of the subject matter.

Often the most dynamic and fruitful discussion sessions occur when participants speak in autobiographical terms and use questions as a "launching pad" for fruitful dialogue.

The Biblical Period

1. Why did the early Christians call themselves the "New Israel" even though the majority of church membership just a few decades after Jesus's death was Gentile and not Jewish? What implications did the Gentile church have for future relations between the two faith communities?

2. Why do you think Paul was so adamant for followers of Jesus to abandon Jewish dietary laws and ritual circumcision? Why did the leaders of the Jerusalem church retain them as religious obligations?

3. Why did the Church make the *Tanakh* a.k.a. The Old Testament, a part of its sacred canon?

4. Compare and contrast the Jewish and Christian views of the Messiah.

5. If the early Christians were part of the Jewish people, what caused the parting of ways?

6. Why do some scholars believe that without the Maccabean victory in 165 BCE (the *Hanukkah* story), there might not have been either Judaism or Christianity?

7. If you were a Jew living in ancient Israel during the Roman occupation, would you have identified with the Sadducees, Pharisees, Essenes, or Zealots?

8. Can a Christian passion play be free of anti-Jewish themes and images, especially the deicide charge? Discuss the roles of Pontius Pilate and Joseph Caiaphas in the death of Jesus.

9. How has biblical typology affected Christian-Jewish relations?

The Medieval/Pre-modern Period

1. Describe the intellectual cross-fertilization between major Jewish and Christian philosophers during the medieval period. How was Aristotle a bridge between the two religious communities? How did Moses Maimonides influence the teachings of Thomas Aquinas?

2. How did the Crusades significantly change relations between Christians and Jews?

3. What role, if any, do the seven Noahide Laws play in interreligious relations?

4. Is there a difference between what has been called the Jewish Jesus and the Christian Christ? Is there a difference between anti-Judaism and antisemitism?

5. Why did many church leaders attack the *Talmud* while revering the *Tanakh*?

6. What caused the rabbis to discourage messianic speculation among Jews as well as turning inward during the medieval period? How did the Protestant Reformation affect Christian-Jewish relations?

7. Why was the conversion of the Jews so important to church leadership?

8. Describe the status of Jews living in Muslim Spain during the eleventh century and those who lived in Christian France or Germany at the same time.

9. Professor Salo Baron of Columbia University has written that "suffering is part of the destiny of the Jews, but so is repeated joy as well as ultimate redemption." Do you agree with his rejection of what he has called the "lachrymose" concept of Jewish history?

The Contemporary Period

1. How did the Age of Enlightenment impact Christians and Jews?

2. Do Jews and Christians have different expectations about dialogues with one another?

3. What should be the relationship between religion and state in the United States?

4. Some Christian leaders make a direct connection between the church's "teaching of contempt" and the Holocaust. Others disagree and believe the

Shoah was an expression of paganism, not Christianity. What is your opinion on the origins of the Holocaust?

5. Define "religious pluralism."

6. How has the creation of modern Israel in 1948 affected Christian-Jewish relations? What has been the influence of the Second Vatican Council, which concluded in 1965?

7. What is your opinion of joint Christian-Jewish worship services?

8. Are Christian-Jewish-Muslim "trialogues" valid interreligious programs?

9. How are the two patriarchal traditions of Christianity and Judaism dealing with the role of women in their respective faith communities?

CHAPTER 22

The Unfinished Journey: To Infinity and Beyond

WHEN GEORGE ALLEN was the head coach of the Washington professional football team in the 1970s, a reporter asked if he was planning to build up his team slowly in the next few years. An annoyed Allen answered: "The future is now!"

He didn't want to wait for future draft selections, and the coach was not interested in assembling a group of talented rookies who perhaps might win a championship in three or four years once they matured as a team. George Allen wanted to move forward and win now.

While he didn't invent the term—there was a long-forgotten 1955 movie with the same title—the National Football League coach's pithy phrase rapidly became a permanent part of the American lexicon. And those four words describe my own feelings about my work and, indeed, all interreligious efforts.

One area where "The Future Is Now" surely applies is in developing constructive relations with the Muslim community. In 2000 when I retired from active duty with the AJC, Islamic-Jewish relations in the United States were in their infancy. In the 1990s, I developed the first-ever pair of national conferences with the Muslim community; both took place at the University of Denver and its Institute for Islamic-Jewish Studies.

The first meeting in 1993 was entitled: "Muslims and Jews in North America: Past, Present and Future." Academics and experts from major universities, including Princeton, Howard, Colorado, Syracuse, as well as Tel Aviv University, gathered for a series of groundbreaking discussions that covered many issues and themes.

At that conference, I declared: "It is time for Muslims and Jews alike to speak out boldly and honestly to each other, to come to know and understand each other as people and not as spiritual abstractions."

A year later in 1994, we held a second conference to foster understanding between Muslims and Jews. Its title was "Women, Families, and Children in Islamic and Judaic Traditions." The conference focused on issues of commonality between the two religions and cultures.

In a memorable phrase, a Muslim conference participant told the group he was concerned, like Jews, about the strong American forces of cultural assimilation. I will always remember his comment:

"I am not worried my children will not know who Mickey Mouse is, but I am fearful they will not know who Muhammad was."

In addition to the two conferences, during the 1990s there were Muslim-Jewish dialogue groups in New York City and in other locations that involved AJC lay leaders.

Back then, especially before the 9/11 terrorist attacks on the United States, many of the Muslim participants were "non-Arabs," mostly men and women from the Indian subcontinent and other areas of southeast Asia, African American Muslims, and some conference participants from Egypt and Jordan, the two nations that had peace treaties with Israel at that time.

During the same years, I reached out to followers of the Nation of Islam (NOI) leader Elijah Muhammad and his son Warith Deen (Wallace) Muhammed, and I met several times with the group's top leaders in cities across the US. The most famous converts to the NOI community were the world champion boxer Cassius Clay a.k.a. Muhammad Ali and basketball All-Star Lew Alcindor a.k.a. Kareem Abdul-Jabbar.

After Elijah Muhammad's death in 1975, the NOI splintered, and Louis Farrakhan emerged victorious over Warith Deen Muhammed in the organization's bitter power struggle and the community broke apart.

Farrakhan has long preached antisemitic sermons and long delivered a constant stream of vile anti-Jewish speeches, including calling Judaism a "gutter religion." As a result, relations currently remain shattered between the Jewish community and the NOI leader.

Tragically, it required the 9/11 terrorist attacks on the United States to hasten the need for Jews and Muslims to begin a serious and systematic process of engaging one another in dialogue in a much broader context.

As those relationships move forward, it is important to remember the acknowledged success of the Christian-Jewish encounter since World War II is not a useful or appropriate template to employ for an Islamic-Jewish project. Christian encounters with Jews have their own unique dynamic that focuses heavily on theological and biblical concerns and historical issues.

But a different set of relationships has made it imperative that authentic Muslim-Jewish programs must include a series of political concerns as well as discussions about the Hebrew Bible and the Qur'an, the Prophet Muhammad's relations with the Jewish communities of his day, the long and often painful history of Jewish minority communities in Muslim-majority countries, and, of course, the current Arab-Israeli conflict.

Finally, I am opposed to so-called "trialogues" that involve Jews, Christians, and Muslims. The cliché "two's company, three's a crowd" aptly describes such projects. Just as Muslims and Jews have a huge number of bilateral issues to work through, so, too, do Christians and Muslims when they engage in dialogic conversations and programs.

I am especially pleased that the AJC has recently established a senior staff position to advance positive relations with the Islamic world. That office is headed by Dr. Ari Gordon, a specialist in Islamic Studies.

Since 1945, many Christian church bodies throughout the world have issued declarations, statements, resolutions, guidelines, proclamations, pastoral letters, teachings, and decrees about the imperative for churches and individual Christians to repent for their anti-Judaism and antisemitism of the past. and There are numerous calls for Christians to move forward toward reconciliation with the kinsfolk of Jesus: the Jewish people.

In addition to the 2000 *Dabru Emet* statement discussed in an earlier chapter, in 2015 a group of prominent Orthodox/traditional Jewish scholars and rabbis from the United States, Israel, South America, and Europe issued an irenic statement called: "To Do the Will of Our Father in Heaven: Toward a Partnership between Jews and Christians."

I salute their effort to move toward a positive relationship with Christians and Christianity. It has not always been easy for Jews to overcome centuries of suspicion, but there is a growing recognition that not all, but many church bodies and their leaders are permanently committed to the delicate but necessary process of achieving mutual understanding and respect.

I have long asserted we no longer require many additional Christian statements. Fortunately, we have them in abundance, and they are easily available on the Internet. But "The Future is Now" maxim demands we move from what I term the wholesale emphasis on Christian-Jewish relations to the retail arena, a purposeful shift from a constant stream of high-level religious gatherings, denominational assemblies, and meetings, and instead press forward with a continuing series of local, parish congregational-centered programs that include an exploration of current Christian liturgy, rituals, teaching, preaching, education, music, hymnology, and all other features of church life that relate to Jews and Judaism.

As some political leaders like to say: "We need to think big."

How Christian-Jewish relations play out on Main Street America is now more decisive and important than ever.

I am encouraged my AJC successors and friends—Rabbi David Rosen in Israel, Rabbi Noam Marans, and Emily Soloff in the US—are continuing the organization's long-standing interreligious mandate to engage other religious communities. Their vital work comes during a difficult time when political extremism and religious polarization are increasing along with a disturbing rise in vicious acts of antisemitism in many parts of the world as well as the rise of the BDS (Boycott, Divest, Sanctions) movement that is aimed only at the State of Israel.

Historians of the future will judge us harshly if we now rest on our hard-earned interreligious laurels. While we have all come a long way since the end of the horrific Holocaust that took place in the heart of Christian Europe and from the heady days of 1965 when the world's Roman Catholic Church, under Popes John XXIII and Paul VI, promulgated the *Nostra Aetate* Declaration, much remains to be done.

An ancient rabbi who lived between 70 and 135 CE stated our current condition even better than Coach Allen's dictum. Rabbi Tarfon taught: "It is not for us to finish the task that faces us, but neither are we free to desist from it."

But perhaps the words that best sum up my optimism for building and strengthening positive relations among the billions of people who profess a myriad of religious beliefs goes to the beloved Hollywood animated character Buzz Lightyear, who appears in the wondrous *Toy Story* films.

Buzz said: "To infinity and beyond…!"

Afterword I

"There can be no peace among the nations without peace among the religions," the Swiss Catholic theologian and prolific author Hans Küng asserted in his 1991 book, *Walls to Bridges*. "There can be no peace among the religions," he continued, "without dialogue between the religions."

But dialogue among the religions doesn't just happen. It requires knowledgeable and skillful leadership and dedication.

Rabbi James Rudin's book is a testimony to the effort and commitment involved in fostering interreligious understanding. It bears witness to intense work—holy labor, but labor, nonetheless. His extensive international travel may sound glamorous, but 42 round trip trans-Atlantic flights in coach class attest to more quotidian realities.

Five trips to Auschwitz-Birkenau and three to the Oberammergau Passion Play came with an emotional cost. Rudin recounts many official meetings with eminent ecclesiastical and political leaders; he also notes only in passing the many "off-the-record heated meetings, closed-door angry encounters, and stormy confrontations." Ameliorating difference requires tact and perseverance. Conflict is not magically erased.

Born in Pittsburgh, Pennsylvania, and raised in Alexandria, Virginia, Rabbi Rudin grew up in Southern Baptist territory and interacted primarily with Protestant classmates. Involved with synagogue life, first in Pittsburgh's Temple Rodef Sholom and then in Alexandria's Beth-El Hebrew Congregation, two rabbis served as powerful mentors for him. After his own rabbinic ordination at New York City's Temple Emanu-El in June 1960, Rabbi Rudin served as an Air Force chaplain at Itazuke Air Base, about six-hundred miles southwest of Tokyo, while making monthly visits to Osan Air Base near Seoul, Korea.

Chaplaincy was deeply formative for the young rabbi. He witnessed how the military had worked out policies and procedures that allowed each religious tradition to be practiced. Respect for the religious Other was evident. Especially significant were friendships with other chaplains who taught him about Christianity and its various denominations.

In turn, Rudin engaged in long conversations with them about Jewish life. In many respects, his experience as chaplain set the stage for his career in interreligious relations at the American Jewish Committee. It also opened his eyes to anti-Asian bias from Air Force personnel.

Another involvement with the U.S. government about thirty years later offered a less salutary experience of interreligious understanding. Appointed to the Camp David Chapel Committee in 1989, Rudin and his fourteen Christian colleagues were entrusted with raising private funds for the construction of an interfaith chapel at the presidential retreat in the mountains of Maryland. In that task, they were successful.

A second task, however, proved far more contentious: approving the architectural plans and artistic design of the stained-glass windows. Some committee members seemed to assume that while the chapel was to be interfaith in name, in practice it would be primarily Christian. The initial design for the eight stained-glass windows included six windows bearing denominational logos of Christian churches, a seventh with a cross, and the eighth with symbols of Judaism, Islam, and Buddhism.

Hearing no objections from fellow committee members, Rudin spoke up, arguing that having seven of the eight windows representing Christian denominations dishonored American jurisprudence and traditions. Rather, the Camp David chapel should contain no permanent representation of a particular faith; instead, religious symbols should be introduced as necessary for a worship service, as was the practice of the military. The debate became intense and lengthy: the "Battle of Camp David."

At stake was whether the United States is a Christian nation or a religiously diverse one that has no established faith. The issue was resolved in favor of diversity and inclusion when it opened with an interfaith service in 1991. Rabbi Rudin wonders whether that resolution would be the same today, given the prominence of the Religious Right and their insistence on the superiority of Christianity.

Rudin terms the "Battle of Camp David" a high point of his career. By the time of that controversy, he had already spent twenty-one years working in interreligious affairs for the American Jewish Committee. His extensive involvement with Christian clergy and institutions and experience of military chaplaincy had shaped his appreciation for American religious freedom and pluralism.

It is instructive to read his chapters on engagement with "mainline" Protestants, the Black Church, and Evangelicals. He knows American Protestants in ways very few people do, and the various projects and conferences with which he was involved reveal the importance of building networks. His chapter on the Black Church includes his work for civil rights and the chapter on Evangelical-Jewish relations shows his nuanced understanding of the complexity of the Evangelical "tent."

Similarly, Rabbi Rudin has an insider's perspective on Catholicism, both on the American scene and internationally. He writes of his close relationship with the late Cardinal John O'Connor and the ultimately successful efforts to achieve diplomatic relations between the Vatican and Israel in 1994. He may have spent more time at the Vatican and met with more Popes and high-ranking officials than any Jew in history—and certainly to greater effect than any of his rabbinic predecessors, thanks in large part to the church's changed posture toward Jews.

Rabbi Rudin knows well Catholicism's shadow side as manifested in the ugly controversy in the mid-1980s over the presence of a Carmelite convent in the Auschwitz building where the Nazis had stored the Zyklon B gas used to slaughter Jews. As he documents, it was a complicated crisis, resolved only by the direct intervention of Pope John Paul II in 1993. Rudin also analyzes the insights and flaws in the Vatican's 1998 document on the "We Remember: A Reflection on the *Shoah*," and of a Jewish group's 2000 statement, "Dabru Emet."

While reading the chapters on his experiences with Catholicism, I was struck with the bitter realization that at the official level, relations with Jews are dominated entirely by male clerics. This was not news to me, but Rudin's narrative unintentionally brought the patriarchal control into high relief. I suspect that a woman rabbi of equal knowledge and achievement would not have enjoyed the access and influence of Rabbi Rudin. Even when his wife Marcia accompanies him to a 1998 conference at the Vatican, her presence at the Domus Sanctae Marthae (along with that of Julia Walsh, spouse of Dr. Philip Cunningham), is treated suspiciously, eliciting my exasperation and embarrassment in equal measures.

Rudin speaks with deep affection and respect for the leadership of Sisters Ann Gillen and Margaret Ellen Traxler in the campaign to free Soviet Jews. Their leadership, however, flourishes only outside official church structures. In his chapter on "The Future of Christian-Jewish Relations," Rudin writes "much greater attention must be paid to our inadequate record in involving women, young people, and people of color in the central decision-making process of Christian-Jewish relations." An understatement!

Rabbi Rudin is mindful that Christian-Jewish relations are affected by four key developments. Demographics and geography mean that the Christian population now lies principally in the global South and that secularism has increased significantly in the West. Chronologically, Vatican II and the ecumenical and interreligious initiatives it unleashed now lie nearly sixty years in the past. Each year means that fewer survivors of the *Shoah* are alive to bear witness to their experience. Technology has enhanced communication in ways unimaginable even a decade ago; social media, however, spread hate speech and conspiracy theories with devastating effects.

I've known Jim Rudin for over 30 years through my work in Christian-Jewish relations, albeit principally through my teaching at Boston College and Union Theological Seminary. His book documents the significant advances on the interreligious front through the eyes of one whose vision is steady and perceptive. Readers may deduce that his personal qualities enhanced his professional qualifications.

Jim clearly has a strong work ethic. He is curious, in the best sense of that term, about the religious beliefs and practices of others and he enjoys friendships across the religious spectrum. He is entirely at home in Judaism and carries his rabbinic title without pretense.

The "romantic miracle" he experienced on New York's East 56th Street lives on in his devotion to his wonderful spouse of more than 50 years, Marcia. A few other qualities readers might not take notice of: Jim is very good company. He is lively, engaging, and genuine. He is also generous, a very proud father of his two daughters, and an avid cyclist. He and Marcia are very gracious hosts and terrific human beings.

The late Rabbi Jonathan Sacks—and British Lord—wrote in his 2002 *The Dignity of Difference* that the "test of faith is whether I can make a space for difference." Rabbi Jim Rudin spent a lifetime making such a space—and what a marvelous difference he has made!

Mary C. Boys, ThD
Union Theological Seminary in the City of New York
Skinner and McAlpin Professor of Practical Theology
and a vowed member of the
Sisters of the Holy Names of Jesus and Mary

Afterword II

Three important dates in history—1945, 1965, and 2023—are defining keys to understanding the future course of global Christian-Jewish relations. The year 1945 brought the unconditional surrender of Nazi Germany and the suicide of its Jew-hating leader, Adolf Hitler. The year also marked the end of the Holocaust, when more than six million Jews were killed by the Nazis and their murderous collaborators—all taking place in the very heart of what Pope John Paul II called "Christian Europe."

In 1965, the world's Roman Catholic bishops, in an overwhelming vote (2,221–88), adopted Nostra Aetate, calling for the end of nearly 2,000 years of Catholic hostility and contempt toward both the Jewish people and Judaism. The declaration, only 624 words in the English version, also condemned antisemitism and called for the building of mutual respect, knowledge, and understanding between the two ancient faith communities. Nostra Aetate has permanently transformed interreligious relations.

The year 2023 brought Hamas's brutal assault on the Jewish state of Israel. The ensuing Israel-Hamas war in Gaza severely damaged Christian-Jewish relations, and the conflict triggered a sharp increase in violent, sometimes deadly, antisemitic acts throughout the world. Without taking into account and processing the momentous events of those three years, there can be no productive relationships between Christians and Jews. The years 1945, 1965, and now 2023 will shape the future; they comprise a complex legacy—one filled with both confident hope and horrific pain.

For me, World War II and the Holocaust are inextricably linked, not only in time but also because of their lasting effect upon me. In the early chapters of this book, I describe my childhood in Alexandria, Virginia, near Washington, D.C., during "the War"—a term that can only mean the cataclysmic conflict that took place between 1939 and 1945. One special note: my father, a WWII U.S. Army lieutenant colonel, and my mother are buried in Arlington National Cemetery overlooking the Pentagon. Their eternal resting place—section 65, grave 1299—are precious numbers deposited in my personal memory bank.

Twenty years later, in 1965, I had completed an active tour of duty as a United States Air Force chaplain stationed in Japan and South Korea. My multiple responsibilities included working closely with many Christian chaplains of various theological and ethnic backgrounds. That experience created within me a strong interest in improving relations between Christians and Jews. In 1965, I was a busy congregational rabbi in Champaign, Illinois, but I made time to closely follow the historic deliberations of the Second Vatican Council then taking place in Rome. Three years later, I joined the American Jewish Committee's interreligious affairs department, and its headquarters in New York City became my professional home for the next 32 years until my retirement.

The 2023 Hamas assault on Israel took place well into my retirement years, and it quickly shattered what some observers had termed a Christian-Jewish "Golden Age" in the United States. This book describes that era of shared optimism when it seemed ancient hostility, misinformation, bigotry, prejudice, and religious stereotypes were being purged from general society. Positive Christian-Jewish relations that were never before achieved in world history seemed a permanent reality—a true spiritual revolution … or so we believed.

In the eighty years following the end of WWII, many church leaders in Europe and North America were driven by the soul-shattering remembrance of Christian culpability for the Holocaust. That constant memory was a significant factor in the extraordinary joint efforts to improve Christian-Jewish relations. But even before the Hamas attack on October 7, warning signs appeared that knowledge and awareness of the Holocaust—widely thought to be a constant guardrail against antisemitism—were diminishing, despite the extraordinary attention given to the painful topic in secular and religious education, media programming, interreligious missions to Holocaust sites in Europe, and pilgrimage-like visits to museums and memorials.

More than three generations of Christians of all religious beliefs have been born since 1945. That irreversible chronological fact—the passage of time—is clearly manifest whenever I speak publicly about the horrors of the Holocaust to young people in churches, high schools, colleges, universities, and Christian seminaries. For them, the eighty-year time gap has made the mass murder of Jews an increasingly remote historical event—not unlike the eight decades of remoteness between General William Sherman's fiery destruction of Atlanta in 1864 during the Civil War and my fifth-grade history assignment in 1944, which I describe in this book.

Villanova University Professor Massimo Faggioli, writing in the book Stress Test: The Israel-Hamas War and Christian-Jewish Relations, notes the rapid Christian population growth in South America, Africa, Asia, and Oceania and the declining Christian demographics in Europe and North America. The implications of these facts are obvious. One example of what lies ahead is the 2025 election of Pope Leo XIV. Although born in the United States, his long-time primary and formative ministry was in Peru. And Leo, born in 1955, represents a new generation of Christian leaders who did not live during the Holocaust and who were young children during the three years of the Second Vatican Council.

It is clear that the current leaders of Christian-Jewish relations must expand their geographical scope and move beyond themselves and other European/North American-based interreligious participants. New ethnic, religious, and racial groups from Asia, South America, Africa, and Oceania must be brought into the Christian-Jewish conversation. Involving younger, more geographically diverse communities of Christians and Jews in this vital effort should not be difficult. Just as there has been an extraordinary spike in the Christian population outside Europe and North America, a similar spike has occurred within the global Jewish community.

These trends exist because the world's largest and youngest Jewish population is today located in southwestern Asia—within the State of Israel—and that often-overlooked fact will increasingly shape future Jewish interaction with the rapidly growing youthful Christian communities also outside Europe and North America. Without the inclusion of young Christians and Jews, the extraordinary dynamism of past generations will atrophy and become a relic of the fading post—World War II/Holocaust era.

Heraclitus, the sixth-century BCE Greek philosopher, wrote, "No man ever steps into the same river twice, for it's not the same river and he's not the same man." A philosopher of our own time echoed Heraclitus' belief when Bob Dylan composed these lyrics:

Come gather 'round, people, wherever you roam
And admit that the waters around you have grown
And accept it that soon you'll be drenched to the bone
If your time to you is worth saving

And you better start swimmin' or you'll sink like a stone
For the times, they are a-changin'[1]

Interreligious leaders of today's global Christian-Jewish relations must heed both teachings if they intend for their hard-won enterprise to succeed in the future. The stakes are high as we enter a new and different era from the past. And as I heard so often while serving in the Air Force: "Failure is not an option."

Rabbi James Rudin
2025

---

1. Bob Dylan, "The Times They Are a-Changin'," *The Times They Are a-Changin'* (Columbia Records, 1964), vinyl LP.

Suggestions for Further Reading

There are thousands of books dealing with Christians and Jews and their relations with one another. For that reason the listing below hardly exhausts the vast subject. I extend special thanks to Mary C. Boys and Marvin R. Wilson for their invaluable assistance in assembling this bibliography.

Ariel, Yaakov. *An Unusual Relationship: Evangelical Christians and Jews.* New York University Press, 2013.

Baeck, Leo. *Judaism and Christianity.* Jewish Publication Society. 1958.

Banki, Judith H., and John T. Pawlikowski. *Ethics in the Shadow of the Holocaust: Christian and Jewish Perspectives.* Sheed and Ward, 2001.

Berger, Alan L., and David Patterson, eds. *Jewish-Christian Dialogue: Drawing Honey from the Rock.* Paragon House, 2008.

Berger, David. *Persecution, Polemic, and Dialogue: Essays in Jewish-Christian Relations.* Academic Studies Press, 2010.

Boys, Mary C. *Redeeming Our Sacred Story: The Death of Jesus and Relations Between Jews and Christians.* Paulist Press, 2013.

Carroll, James. *Constantine's Sword: The Church and the Jews.* Houghton Mifflin, 2001.

Connelly, John. *From Enemy to Brother: The Revolution in Catholic Teaching on the Jews 1933–1965.* Harvard University Press, 2012.

Cunningham, Philip. *Education for Shalom: Religion Textbooks and the Enhancement of the Catholic and Jewish Relationship.* CLiturgical Press, 1995.

Cunningham, Philip, ed. *Pondering the Passion: What's at Stake for Christians and Jews*. Rowman and Littlefield, 2005.

D'Costa, Gavin. *Catholic Doctrines on Jews after Vatican II*. Oxford University Press, 2019.

Deutsch, Celia, Eugene J. Fisher, and James Rudin, eds. *Toward the Future: Essays on Catholic-Jewish Relations in Memory of Rabbi Leon Klenicki*. Paulist Press, 2013.

Diprose, Ronald E. *Israel and the Church: The Origin and Effects of Replacement Theology*. Authentic Media, 2000.

Evans, Craig A., and David Mishkin, eds. *A Handbook on the Jewish Roots of the Christian Faith*. Hendrickson, 2019.

Federow, Stuart. *Judaism and Christianity: A Contrast*. iUniverse, 2012.

Fisher, Eugene J., and Eric J. Greenberg, eds. *The Saint for Shalom: How Pope John Paul II Transformed Catholic-Jewish Relations*. Crossroads, 2011.

Flusser, David. *Judaism and the Origins of Christianity*. Magnes Press, 1998.

Fredriksen, Paula. *When Christians Were Jews: The First Generation*. Yale University Press, 2018.

Garr, John D. *The Church Dynamic: Hebraic Foundations for Christian Community*. Golden Key, 2019.

Goldman, Shalom. *Zeal for Zion: Christians, Jews, and the Idea of the Promised Land*. University of North Carolina Press, 2009.

Greenberg, Irving. *For the Sake of Heaven and Earth: The New Encounter Between Judaism and Christianity*. Jewish Publication Society, 2004.

Heschel, Abraham Joshua. *Israel: An Echo of Eternity*. Farrar, Straus & Giroux, 1969.

Heschel, Susannah. *The Aryan Jesus: Christian Theologians and the Bible in Nazi Germany*. Princeton University Press, 2008.

Hummel, Daniel G. *Covenant Brothers: Evangelicals, Jews, and U.S.-Israeli Relations*. University of Pennsylvania Press, 2019.

Isaac, Jules. *The Teaching of Contempt: Christian Roots of Anti-Semitism*. Holt, Rinehart & Winston, 1964.

Jennings, Willie James. *The Christian Imagination: Theology & the Origins of Race.* Yale University Press, 2010.

Jenson, Robert W., and Eugene B. Korn. eds. *Covenant and Hope: Christian and Jewish Reflections.* Eerdmans, 2012.

Jodock, Darrell. *Covenantal Conversations: Christians in Dialogue with Jews and Judaism.* Fortress Press, 2008.

Kessler, Edward. *An Introduction to Jewish-Christian Relations.* Cambridge University Press, 2010.

Klenicki, Leon. ed. Toward a Theological Encounter: Jewish Understandings of Christianity. Paulist Press, 1991.

Kogan, Michael S. *Opening the Covenant: A Jewish Theology of Christianity.* Oxford University Press, 2008.

Larson, Marion H., and Sara L. H. Shady. *From Bubble to Bridge: Educating Christians for a Multifaith World.* IVP Academic, 2016.

Lazin, Fred A. *American Christians and the National Interreligious Task Force on Soviet Jewry: A Call to Conscience.* Lexington Books, 2019.

Le Donne, Anthony, and Larry Behrendt. *Sacred Dissonance: The Blessing of Difference in Jewish-Christian Dialogue.* Hendrickson, 2017.

Levine, Amy-Jill. *The Misunderstood Jew: The Church and the Scandal of the Jewish Jesus.* HarperCollins, 2006.

Levine, Amy-Jill, and Marc Zvi Brettler, eds. *The Jewish Annotated New Testament,* 2nd. ed. Oxford University Press, 2017.

Marty, Martin E. *Pilgrims in Their Own Land: 500 Years of Religion in America.* Little, Brown, 1984.

Lipstadt, Deborah E. *Antisemitism: Here and Now.* Schocken Books, 2019.

McDermott, Gerald R. *Israel Matters: Why Christians Must Think Differently about the People and the Land.* Brazos, 2017.

McDermott, Gerald R. *Understanding the Jewish Roots of Christianity: Biblical, Theological and Historical Essays on the Relationship.* Lexham Press, 2021.

Parkes, James W. *End of an Exile: Israel, the Jews, and the Gentile World.* Micah, 2005.

Phelan, John E., Jr. *Separated Siblings: An Evangelical Understanding of Jews and Judaism.* Eerdmans, 2020.

Rittner, Carol, Stephen D. Smith, and Irena Steinfeldt, eds. *The Holocaust and the Christian World: Reflections on the Past, Challenges for the Future.* Continuum, 2000.

Rosen, David and R.T. Kendall. *The Christian and the Pharisee.* Hodder and Stoughton, 2006.

Rosenthal, Gilbert S., ed. *A Jubilee for All Time: The Copernican Revolution in Jewish-Christian Relations.* Pickwick, 2014.

Rudin, A. James. *Christians & Jews Faith to Faith: Tragic History, Promising Present, Fragile Future.* Jewish Lights, 2011.

Rudin, A. James. *Cushing, Spellman, O'Connor: The Surprising Story of How Three American Cardinals Transformed Catholic-Jewish Relations.* Eerdmans, 2011.

Sandgren, Leo Dupree. *Vines Intertwined: A History of Jews and Christians.* Hendrickson, 2010.

Sarna, Jonathan D. *American Judaism: A History.* Yale University Press, 2004.

Schafer, Peter. *The Jewish Jesus: How Judaism and Christianity Shaped Each Other.* Princeton University Press, 2014.

Sherman, Franklin. *Luther and the Jews: A Fateful Legacy.* Institute of Christian-Jewish Studies, 1995.

Signer, Michael A. ed. *Memory and History in Christianity and Judaism.* University of Notre Dame, 2001.

Spangler, Ann, and Lois Tverberg. *Sitting at the Feet of Rabbi Jesus.* Zondervan, 2009.

Stendahl, Krister. *Paul Among Jews and Gentiles.* Fortress Press, 1976.

Swidler, Leonard. *Yeshua: Jesus the Jew A Model for Everyone.* iPub Cloud International, 2020.

Swidler, Leonard, Rueven Firestone, Khalid Duran. *The Power of Dialogue.* iPub Cloud International, 2018.

Tanenbaum Marc H., Marvin R. Wilson, and A. James Rudin. *Evangelicals and Jews in Conversation.* Baker Book House, 1978.

Williams, Reggie. *Bonhoeffer's Black Jesus: Harlem Renaissance and an Ethic of Resistance.* Baylor University. Press, 2014.

Wilson, Marvin R. *Exploring Our Hebraic Heritage: A Christian Theology of Roots and Renewal.* Eerdmans, 2014.

Wilson, Marvin R. *Our Father Abraham: Jewish Roots of the Christian Faith.* 2nd. ed. Eerdmans, 2021.

Wyschogrod, Michael. *Abraham's Promise: Judaism and Jewish-Christian Relations.* Edited and introduction by R. Kendall Soulen. Eerdmans, 2004.

Index

A

Abdul-Jabbar, Kareem, 187
African American churches, 86, 87
Alcindor, Lew, 187
Alexandria, Virginia, 4, 5, 10, 21, 66, 75, 99, 138, 190
Ali, Muhammad, 187
Allen, George, 186
Allen, Richard (Rev.), 88
Allen, Woody, 176
Alperin, Mimi, 127
Ambassador to Christians, xxiii
American Academy of Religion, 137
American Jewish Committee, v, vi, xi, xvi, xvii, xxi, xxii, xxiii, 2, 3, 5, 22, 31, 32, 33, 36, 41, 42, 44, 45, 53, 55, 58, 62, 68, 74, 76, 77, 78, 79, 80, 82, 83, 84, 85, 89, 91, 92, 93, 94, 96, 97, 99, 103, 106, 107, 108, 121, 124, 126, 127, 129, 130, 134, 135, 136, 140, 142, 143, 149, 156, 158, 159, 166, 186, 187, 188, 189, 191
Anglican Church, 170
Anglo-Saxon Protestantism, 74, 76
antisemitism, xiv, xvii, 1, 2, 3, 4, 6, 26, 32, 34, 35, 39, 41, 52, 55, 65, 68, 69, 77, 79, 86, 98, 103, 104, 109, 110, 111, 112, 126, 128, 136, 137, 138, 140, 141, 142, 155, 169, 184, 188, 189, 200

apartheid, 3, 77, 86
Aquinas, Thomas, 183
Arab-Israeli conflict, 188
Arafat, Yasser, 81
Archdiocese of Los Angeles, 42
A Reflection on the Shoah, 40, 192
Arfa, Cyrus (Rabbi), 31, 37
Auschwitz-Birkenau, xv, xxii, 40, 61, 62, 63, 64, 65, 66, 67, 72, 151, 190, 192
Axelrod, David (Dr.), 147, 148

B

Bahat, Shulamith, v, 44
Balfour Declaration, 30
Banki, Judith H., 91
Banki, Judith Hershcopf, 33
Battle of Camp David, 114, 116, 117, 119, 121, 122, 191
Beall, J. Glenn (US Senator), 115
Beersheba, Kansas, 139
Begin, Menachem, 119
Beta Theta Pi, 12
Biafra, 149, 150, 151
Biblical Period, 183
Bird, Thomas (Dr.), 43, 162
Birkenau, 61, 62, 63, 64, 66, 190
Bir Zeit University, 79
Black Churches, 85

Black Revolution, 90
Blake, Eugene Carson (Dr.), 87
Bonhoeffer, Dietrich (Rev.), 72
Boys, Mary C. (Dr.), v, 43
Brezhnev, Leonid, 161
Buber, Martin, 21, 80
Buchanan, James (Rev.), 43
Bush, Barbara (First Lady), 122
Butterfield, Victor (Dr.), 11

C

Caiaphas, 125, 130, 183
Camp David, 114, 115, 116, 117, 118, 119, 120, 121, 122, 123, 191
Carroll, James, 66
Cassidy, Edward (Cardinal), 41
Catholic Church, xii, xxi, 1, 33, 38, 40, 41, 59, 67, 69, 87, 103, 132, 189
Catholicism, xvi, 8, 22, 38, 39, 40, 41, 42, 46, 49, 52, 55, 57, 63, 64, 69, 70, 71, 75, 84, 95, 99, 102, 118, 129, 136, 159, 171, 180
Center for Catholic-Jewish Studies', 43
Chaney, James, 28
Chaplain Earl Minor, 99
Charlottesville, 3, 6, 7
Christian supersessionism, xvii
Christ killer, 102, 153, 154
church-state separation, 8, 19, 103, 104, 112, 120
Clay, Cassius, 187
Cohen, Jody (Rabbi), 44, 96
Coleman, Gloria (Sister), 43, 139
Congregation Beth Israel, 97
Congregation Gates of Prayer, 97
Connell, Joan, v
Connolly, Fidelis, 23
Contemporary Period, 184

convent crisis, 62, 65, 66, 67
Cooke, Terence (Cardinal), 50, 53
Cook, Michael (Dr.), 18
Costen, James (Dr.), 91, 92
Council in Rome, 1, 34, 39
COVID-19, 148, 175
Cummings, Elijah, 86
Cunningham, Julia Walsh, 45, 46
Cunningham, Philip (Dr.), 43, 44, 45, 126, 133, 192
Cuomo, Mario (Governor), 53, 145, 149

D

Dabru Emet, 67, 71, 72, 73, 188, 192
Dalai Lama, 5
Davis, Bette, 175
Deutsch, Celia (Dr.), 171
Dillard University, 97
Dingman, Maurice (Bishop), 142
Divine Principle, 136, 137
Dole, Robert (US Senator), 164
Douglass, Frederick, 88
Dreyfuss, Richard, 151

E

Eastman, Theodore (Bishop), 115
Eckstrom, Kevin, v
Eternal Light Award, 43
Euro-Mediterranean Consortium for Applied Research on International Migration, 172
Evangelical-Jewish relations, xviii, 102, 110, 192
Evers, Charles (Mayor), 158

F

Farrakhan, Louis, 187
Feldstein, Donald, v

Fenwick, Millicent (U S Representative), 164
Fenwick, Millicent (US Representative), 164
Films
    All About Eve, 175
    Braveheart, 132
    Gone with the Wind, 96
    His Land, 106
    Inherit the Wind, 101
    The Passion of the Christ, 131, 132, 133
    Toy Story, 189
First Amendment, 8, 116, 119
Fisher, Eugene (Dr.), 68, 126, 171
Fisk University, 89
Flake, Floyd, 86
Flannery, Edward H. (Rev.), 40, 43
Fleischner, Eva (Dr.), 44, 126
Forman, Lori (Rabbi), 44
Forsyth, Georgia, 93, 94
Fox, George, 17
Freehof, Solomon B. (Rabbi), 10, 11
Frizzel, Lawrence (Dr.) (Rev.), 44
Fruitland, Tennessee, 84

G

Gayle-Almelah, Benita, 44
Geller, David, 158
Gibel, Inge Lederer, 44
Gibson, Mel, 131
Gillen, Ann (Sister), 43, 155, 159, 160, 161, 162, 163, 164, 165, 166, 167, 168, 192
Glemp (Cardinal), 64
Goldberg, Arthur J. (Justice), 162
Gold, Bert, v
Goldman, Ari L., 92
Goldwater, Barry (US Senator), 29
Good Friday, xxiii, 133, 152, 153, 154
Goodman, Andrew, 28
Goodman, Jerry, 158
Gorbachev, Mikhail, 165
Gordis, David, v
Gordis, David M. (Dr.), 140
Gordon, Ari (Dr.), 188
Gore, Al (Vice President), xxii, 84
Gorsuch, John (Bishop), 12
Gorsuch, Neil (Justice), 12
Gospel of John, 34, 152
Graubart, Judah, 158
Great Synagogue in Rome, 40
Greenberg, Eric (Rabbi), 130, 199
Greenberg, Irving (Rabbi), 43
Greenebaum, Gary (Rabbi), 130

H

Hamas, 194, 195
Harrell, Lynn, 151
Harris, David, v, 84, 96, 97, 166
Harter, William H. (Dr.), 127
Hart, Gary (Senator), 94
Hattiesburg, 27, 28, 77, 85, 94, 102
Hauser, Rita (Ambassador), 158
Hebrew Bible, 11, 34, 87, 97, 103, 111, 122, 188
Hebrew Union College - Jewish Institute of Religion, 12, 13, 15, 16, 18, 20, 31
Helsinki Accords, 161, 162
Hepner, Thomas (Rev.), 20, 22, 23
Heraclitus, 173
Hidalgo, Jacqueline (Dr.), 171, 172
Hiroshima, 20, 27
Hirt-Manheimer, Aron, v
Hitler, Adolf, xiv, 4, 9, 27, 126, 194
Hodgeman County, Kansas, 139

Holocaust, xiv, xv, xvii, xxiii, xxiv, 2, 9, 12, 21, 26, 30, 34, 40, 42, 43, 52, 53, 54, 55, 60, 61, 63, 65, 67, 68, 71, 72, 73, 83, 92, 93, 94, 96, 97, 98, 103, 112, 126, 127, 149, 151, 152, 155, 157, 164, 165, 180, 184, 189, 194, 195, 198, 201
Hooks, Benjamin, 86
Horsham-Brathwaite, Barbara, 95
Huber, Otto, 130
Huston, Robert (Dr.), 82

I
Ingber, Abie (Rabbi), 43
Interdenominational Group of Catholics and Protestants, 71
International Cult Educational Program, 137
International Cultic Studies Association, 137
International Jewish Committee for Interreligious Consultations, xi
Interreligious Affairs Director, 31, 34, 44, 53, 127, 158
Ioudaioi, 153
Israel-Arab Six-Day War, 29
Israel Defense Forces, 96
Israel-Hamas war, 194, 196
Itazuke Air Base, 20, 21, 22, 23, 24, 190

J
Jackson, Henry (US Senator), 157
Jackson, Jesse (Rev.), 85, 86
Jackson-Vanik Amendment, 161, 162
Jesus, xvii, xxiii, 1, 6, 7, 21, 34, 35, 63, 66, 69, 95, 100, 102, 104, 108, 111, 123, 124, 125, 126, 127, 128, 129, 130, 131, 132, 133, 136, 152, 153, 154, 159, 168, 183, 184, 188, 193, 198, 199, 200, 201, 202
Jewish-Christian relations, xi, 93
Jewish Frontier, 28
Jewish Theological Seminary of America, 33
Jones, William A. (Rev.) (Dr.), 89
Judith Hershcopf Banki, 33

K
Kadar, Janos Petran, 164
Kansas Bureau of Investigation, 142
Kaplan, Marcia, 36
Kaplan, Max (Dr.), 37
Karski, Jan, 43
Kelly, Thomas, 142
Kelman, Kurt, 127
Kennedy, Robert F. (USAG), 33
kibbutz, 81, 95
Kindertotenlieder, 151
King, Coretta Scott (Mrs.), 93, 165
King, Martin Luther Jr. (Dr.), 27, 158
Kingsley, Ralph P. (Rabbi), 20
Kirk, Arthur F., Jr. (Dr.), 42, 43
Kishinev, 32
KKK, 93, 94
Klenicki, León (Rabbi), 171
Kristallnacht, 11, 57, 181
Küng, Hans, 190
Kyushu Island, 20, 24

L
LaCocque, André (Dr.), 159
Landon, Alfred (Governor), 27
Langer, Ruth (Dr.), 43
Lara-Braud, Jorge (Dr.), 136
LaSor, William S. (Dr.), 105
Law, Bernard (Cardinal), 64
Lazin, Fred A. (Dr.), 155

Leningrad Airplane Hijacking, 156
Let My People Go, 157, 166, 167
Levine, Gilbert, 151, 152
Levine, Irving, 127
Lewis, John (US Representative), 86, 165
Lincoln, C. Eric (Dr.), 90
Lipstadt, Deborah (Dr.), 43
Lux, Richard (Dr.), 44
Lynch, Robert (Bishop), 42

M

Macharski, Frantiszek (Cardinal), 63, 65
Madges, William (Rev.), 43
Maimonides, Moses, 183
Manworren, Donald (Rev.), 142
Marans, Noam (Rabbi), 130, 189
Mario, Cuomo (Governor), 53, 145, 149
Marty, Martin E. (Dr.), 101
Mathews, James (Bishop), 114, 115, 116
May, Fenton (Bishop), 115
McManus, Dennis (Rev.), 43
Medieval/Pre-modern Period, 183
Meir, Golda (PM Israel), 156, 160
Minor, Earl (Rev.), 21, 23, 99
mishpacha, 153
Mittleman, Alan (Dr.) (Rabbi), 44
Moon, Sun Myung, 135
Most Favored Nation, 161
Muhammad, Elijah, 187
Muslims and Jews in North America, 186
Muszynski, Henryk (Archbishop), 41

N

Nagasaki, 20, 24, 27

National Baptist Convention, 89
National Catholic Conference on Interracial Justice, 158
National Conference of Catholic Bishops, 38, 83, 126
National Council of Churches, xxiii, 44, 74, 75, 76, 77, 78, 79, 80, 81, 82, 83, 84, 87, 96, 99, 101, 107, 136, 158, 165, 166
National Interreligious Task Force on Soviet Jewry, 44, 155, 158, 159, 160, 162, 164, 200
Nation of Islam, 187
Nazism, xv, 2, 57, 72
Neo-Nazis, 3
Nevins, John (Bishop), 43
Nevison, Howard (Cantor), 151
New Orleans, Louisiana, 97
New Testament, 8, 18, 21, 100, 105, 123, 125, 128, 152, 200
New York State Task Force, 144, 145
Night of the Murdered Poets, 156
Nostra Aetate, xvi, xvii, 1, 22, 33, 39, 40, 41, 44, 51, 55, 57, 71, 126, 154, 173, 189, 194
Novak, David (Rabbi), 43

O

Oberammergau Passion Play, xxiii, 124, 125, 126, 127, 129, 130, 133, 134, 190
O'Connor, John (Cardinal), xxii, 44, 46, 51, 64, 192
O'Donnell, Paul, v
Organizing Interreligious Programs, 177
Orlinsky, Harry M. (Dr.), 18
Oswiecim, 63

P

Passion plays, 124
Pawlikowski, John T. (Rev.), 43, 130, 198
Pell, Claiborne (US Senator), 164
Penn, William, 17, 51
Personal Interreligious Commandments, 176
Pew Research Center, 75
Philippi, William (Rev.), 162, 164
Pilate, Pontius, 124, 128, 130, 183
Pondering the Passion, 133, 199
Pope
    Benedict XVI, xxii, 38, 131, 171
    Francis, 48, 61, 71, 131
    John Paul II, xxi, xxii, 35, 38, 40, 44, 45, 46, 49, 50, 51, 54, 55, 56, 57, 59, 60, 63, 65, 68, 73, 131, 133, 151, 152, 177, 192, 194, 199
    John XXIII, 33, 131, 189
    Leo XIV, 196
    Paul VI, xvi, 33, 131, 151, 189
    Pius XII, 70, 71, 169
Posse Comitatus, 142
Poulenc, Francis, 61
Prinz, Joachim (Rabbi), 27
prisoners of hope, xv, 175
Prison or Paradise
    The New Religious Cults, 137
Procario-Foley, Eleana (Dr.), 44

R

Radano, John (Rev.), 162, 164
Reagan-Gorbachev summit, 167
Reform Jewish Movement, 15, 37, 139
Religion on the Line, 89, 135
Religious Right, 104, 107, 108, 109, 111, 112, 123, 191
Rittner, Carol (Sister), 44
Riva, Daniel (Colonel), 24, 25
Romney, Mitt, 76
Rosenbaum, Amy (Dr.), 44
Rosenbloom, Louis, 4
Rosen, David (Rabbi), v, xii, 2, 189
Ryan, Paul, 76

S

Sadat, Anwar, 119
Saint Leo University, v, xvi, 42, 44
Sandmel, Samuel (Dr.), 18
Sandons (Mr. and Mrs.), 117, 118, 119, 120, 121
Saperstein, Sanford (Rabbi), 43
Scalfaro, Oscar Luigi (Italian President), 152
Schechter, Philip E. (Rabbi), 20
Schwerner, Michael, 28
Second Vatican Council, xvi, 1, 22, 33, 39, 40, 41, 51, 57, 77, 103, 131, 153, 173, 185
September 11 attacks, 114, 187
Shabbat dinner, 16
Sharpton, Al (Rev.), 86
Sheen, Fulton J. (Archbishop), 158
Sherman, Franklin (Dr.), 127
Shoah, xiv, 34, 40, 60, 67, 68, 69, 70, 71, 72, 151, 169, 173, 185, 192, 193
Shriver, Robert Sargent Jr., 158, 159
Silverman, Ira, v
Silverman, William B. (Rabbi), 26
Sinai Temple, 28, 29, 30, 31
Sirat, Rene-Samuel (Rabbi), 63
Skorka, Abraham (Rabbi), 43
Smith, Charles Z. (Judge), 162, 164
Socolovsky, Jerome, v

Soloff, Emily, 189
Soloman, Haym, 51
SONY, 23
Southern Baptist Convention, 1, 21, 100, 106
Soviet Jewry, xi, xxiii, 44, 52, 53, 106, 110, 155, 156, 157, 158, 160, 161, 164, 165, 166, 167, 168, 200
Soviet Jewry advocacy movement, 155, 156, 161, 165
Spellman, Francis (Cardinal), 48
State Department, 150, 163, 167
State of Israel, xv, 3, 15, 21, 26, 32, 34, 41, 52, 57, 59, 103, 106, 107, 110, 173, 189
Steinbruck, John (Rev.), 162, 164
Stephanopoulos, Robert (Rev.), 159
Stiffman, Jeffrey (Dr.), 81
St. Martha's Residence, 44, 45, 46
St. Peter's Square, xxi
Strober, Gerald, 78, 89, 105, 158
Stückl, Christian, 130
Sugarman, Alvin (Rabbi), 94
Swidler, Leonard (Dr.), v, 44, 127

T

Tanenbaum, Marc H. (Rabbi), v, 31, 33, 83, 89, 105, 126, 149, 158
Tapie, Matthew (Dr.), 42, 44
Temple B'nai Jehudah, 26
Temple Emanu-El, 18, 55, 190
Temple Rodef Sholom, 10, 190
Temple Zion, 16
Terry, Dixon, 142, 144
The African Methodist Episcopal Church, 88
The Challenge of Peace, 50
The Christian Methodist Episcopal Church, 88
The Dialogue of the Carmelites, 61
The High Holydays, 36
The National Association for the Advancement of Colored People, 85
The Rural Crisis, 143
The Vortex of Evil, xxii
Toyota, 36
Traxler, Margaret Ellen (Sister), 157, 192
Treaty of Versailles, 30
Trifa, Valerian (Archbishop), 82, 83
Trosten, William, v
Tubman, Harriet, 88
Tuggle, Reginald (Rev.), 95

U

Unification Church, 135, 136, 137
United Methodist Church, 1, 72, 82, 100, 114, 117
United Nations, xv, 49, 55, 81, 156, 158, 167
United States Catholic Conference, 38
US Presidents
    Biden, Joseph R., 39
    Bush, George W., 109, 122
    Carter, Jimmy, xxii, 101, 108, 162
    Clinton, Bill, xxii, 84
    Eisenhower, Dwight David, 76, 115
    Ford, Gerald, 161
    Jefferson, Thomas, 6, 8, 116
    Johnson, Lyndon Baines, 29
    Kennedy, John F., 39, 158
    Reagan, Ronald, xxii, 108, 165
    Trump, Donald, 110
    Wilson, Woodrow, 31

V

VanderWerf, Nathan (Rev.), 81
Vanik, Charles (U S Representative), 157
Vanik, Charles (US Representative), 157, 161, 162
Varick, James, 88
Vatican, xvi, xxi, xxii, xxiii, xxiv, 1, 2, 22, 33, 38, 39, 40, 41, 44, 45, 46, 47, 51, 55, 56, 57, 58, 59, 60, 65, 67, 68, 69, 70, 71, 76, 103, 110, 126, 128, 131, 133, 151, 152, 153, 157, 163, 164, 165, 168, 169, 170, 173, 180, 185, 192, 193, 199

W

Waldheim, Kurt, 55, 56, 68
Wallenberg, Raoul, 165
Ware, Ann Patrick (Sister), 44
Warnock, Raphael, 86
Weber, Max, 173
Wedel, Cynthia (Dr.), 158
Weiss, Avraham "Avi" (Rabbi), 64, 65
We Remember, 40, 67, 68, 69, 70, 71, 192
We Shall Overcome, 94
white supremacists, 3
Wiesel, Elie, 73, 165
Wiesenthal, Simon, 164
William B. Silverman, 26
William Paterson College, 36, 137
Williams, Avon, 91
Wilmore, Gayraud (Dr.), 92
Wise, Isaac Mayer (Rabbi), 15
Witter, David (Dr.), 138
Wolff, Bob, 13

Y

Yad Vashem, 94, 96, 97

Young, Andrew, 86

Z

Zionist state, 93

About iPub Cloud International

iPub Cloud International is a 501(c)(3) nonprofit publishing house dedicated to elevating the voices of the disenfranchised, marginalized, and those unable to afford the high costs of traditional publishing. As a women-owned and women-led organization, we also take immense pride in having individuals with disabilities in senior leadership roles, reflecting our mission of inclusivity and empowerment.

We are not just a publisher; we are a champion for change, seeking to amplify stories that matter. By fostering a culture of enlightenment and progress, we empower voices that inspire action, provoke thought, and pave the way for a more compassionate and understanding world. Our work touches lives—not only through the authors, contributors, and team members who make it possible but also through the readers and communities who engage with the transformative ideas we bring to light. At iPub Cloud International, every book, story, and idea we publish is a step toward building a brighter, more inclusive future.

iPub Cloud International
Poughkeepsie, NY 12603
Visit our website to stay up to date on your favorite writers and subscribe for news on new releases, events, and promotions:
www.iPubCloud.org
Join the conversation at iPubForum.com

www.ingramcontent.com/pod-product-compliance
Lightning Source LLC
Chambersburg PA
CBHW050900160426
43194CB00011B/2234